THE SPANISH
CONNECTION

THE SPANISH CONNECTION

JOHN LIGHTFOOT

**His explosive account of how infiltrating
the drug barons for HM Customs made him
an international fugitive**

BLAKE

Published by Blake Publishing Ltd,
3 Bramber Court, 2 Bramber Road,
London W14 9PB, England

First published in 1999

ISBN 1 85782 328 1

British Library Cataloguing-in-Publication Data:
A catalogue record for this book is available
from the British Library.

Typeset by BCP

Printed in Great Britain by
Creative Print and Design (Wales), Ebbw Vale, Gwent

1 3 5 7 9 10 8 6 4 2

For Kath, Mum and Dad

With acknowledgement to the people who assisted me when I needed help. They are too many to mention individually, but they know who they are. Thanks to Christian and Sylvie Traineau. Also to Sentley Wilson, my lawyer, who continues my campaign for justice.

Especial thanks are due to all my family, without whose unflagging support and belief this book would not have been possible.

Contents

Dear Reader

Welcome to the fourth title in Blake's True Crime Library — the best true crime for under a fiver!

Every day our newspapers are crammed with disheartening stories of the misery inflicted on our streets by the peddling of illegal drugs. Yet the shadowy underworld of the illicit cartels that bring these narcotics into our country is murkier and more cut-throat than you might imagine.

In the midst of this terrible trade are heroes like John Lightfoot. Bravely and fearlessly, Lightfoot single-handedly took on these cartels in a selfless attempt to make our streets safer for all of us.

His story almost defies belief as it takes him across Europe, living like a real-life James Bond, taking on some of the most dangerous men in the world with scarcely a thought for his own safety. Read on if you want to find out how these cartels operate — and just what it takes to outmanoeuvre them ...

Adam Parfitt
Editor
Blake's True Crime Library

1

A Day in the Life

It was hot, with an early afternoon temperature in the upper 90s. The sun was streaming in mercilessly, accompanied by a hot onshore breeze, the north African wind coming over the Mediterranean bringing no relief from the stupefying heat. Wearing summer bikers' gear of shorts, white tee shirt, desert boots, mirror sunglasses and an open-faced Chips-style helmet I was sitting astride my candy-apple red Goldwing motorcycle listening for the 'Go' message on the built-in CB. I could feel the tops of my legs burning even though they had been weathered against the tropical summer heat of Spain's Costa del Sol.

I was waiting on a small spur alongside the busy, dusty dual carriageway between Fuengirola and Marbella, near to the Banana Beach turn-off, about a mile from the Marbella Clinic. I was hot and sweaty, and with the passage of time I was becoming increasingly pissed off. Something had gone wrong again. I had been here for more than an hour and felt as obvious as a pimple on a page-three model's bum.

Two police jeeps went cruising past. Their occupants, the Guardia Civil, remote and blank faced behind their dark sunglasses, had already given me a good visual checking out. Those guys weren't regular traffic cops, they were multitasked specialists with on-board radio equipment that would enable them to check a British registration plate in seconds by cooperation with NCIS, the National Crime Intelligence Service, based in Croydon, England.

High tech was at last being used by the Spanish authorities to crack down on the ever growing illegal narcotics trade from north Africa to Europe, which, despite the efforts of European-wide policing and enforcement agencies, was still growing at a rate of 15 per cent per year. The available profit to successful smugglers was so high that wannabes were flocking to the Spanish coastline like lemmings.

A piercing scream brought me back to the present. I peered across the road into the sun over the flat, blue Mediterranean. Yep, another crazy tourist, egged on by mates and a few bottles of San Miguel beer, had decided to make the death-defying bungee jump on Banana Beach. Customers drinking at the round, thatched tables screamed their delight and waved bottle-clasping hands towards him as he bounced up and down at the end of the elastic rope. I noticed he wasn't screaming back his delight at them.

My shirt was sticking to my back, and I was quickly developing a stress headache. I wiped the sweat from my face with the back of my leather glove and climbed off the bike. Rummaging around inside the top box I found a couple of dodgy-looking Brufen tablets, which I quickly swallowed with a drink of tepid mineral water from a plastic bottle.

Just as I closed the box lid my mobile twittered. I snatched it from the Velcro holding straps. 'Hello,' I answered testily as I climbed back aboard, careful not to touch the hot metal parts with my bare legs.

'John, it's Rog,' a breathless voice said. 'Have you seen them yet?'

'No sign of them. Don't tell me they've got lost again. They must know the route by now,' I answered. Something's going wrong here, I thought, as Rog pondered on this latest setback.

'They better not be pissed again. You stay cool and wait for them,' he instructed and hung up before I could respond.

Great, I thought, I get to sit here melting in the sun, while he's playing Mr Organization, sitting in his air-conditioned pad drinking cold beer and telling me to stay cool. Suddenly I heard the faint sound of helicopter rotors beating the thin air. Squinting up into the sky I could see a chopper coming along the coast over Marbella. If it landed at the Marbella Clinic it would be OK, just an air ambulance ferrying another car crash victim. If it carried on towards Fuengirola it could be a Guardia Civil or Aduana (Customs) chopper, and that could spell trouble for us.

It didn't land at the clinic. As it came closer I could make out the definitive black and white markings on the fuselage and see the Nightsun spotlight hanging below its belly. It was a police chopper, and I watched as it steadily beat its way up the coast roads towards Fuengirola and Torremolinos, watching the traffic and the deserted areas of coastline for unusual road-traffic or maritime activity. I knew they were in contact with the ground forces.

Those choppers were state of the art, utilizing digitally encrypted voice communications and containing look-down radar and thermal-imaging camera equipment slaved to video cameras. I knew they could downlink real-time imagery direct to police control vans during pursuits and infrared images in darkness. The first convictions had recently been secured against smugglers where the use of video imagery had been a key piece of the prosecution evidence. The odds were slowly but surely mounting against the smugglers.

The CB crackled to life, and Phil's excited voice came over the air.

'John, we're coming through the town now, is it clear?' I could hear the car stereo playing, and someone talking excitedly in the background. Dickheads, I thought. Probably high on speed, they had thrown their own plan out of the window again.

I pressed the talk button and said, 'Go.' Just the one word said everything I had to impart. It was a waste of time trying to explain the problems to the idiots now. That could wait until later, if there was a later. I turned on the ignition and pressed the start button, the alloy six-cylinder engine purred comfortingly into life. I settled my sunglasses more comfortably, smoothed the thin leather gloves and kicked up the side stand, feeling the centre of gravity change between my thighs as the bike balanced upright. Checking the mirror I waited for a gap in the traffic and pulled quickly on to the road. Easing into the fast lane I kept to a steady 50 mph, our previously agreed speed.

A massive tour coach with dark-tinted windows started pushing me from behind, but I had no room to move in. He edged closer and flashed his lights. The driver was probably feeling a bit jealous, wishing he could change places with me rather than driving his big bus load of cackling tourists. I think all Spanish drivers secretly covet the opportunity to drive speed bikes rather than any other more mundane form of transport.

I flicked him the finger over my shoulder and dabbed the brakes to slow him. These drivers were lethal, and unperturbed by my flashing brake lights he didn't back off. My rear view was cut off by the coach, so, desperate to see behind and catch sight of the car I was supposed to be baby-sitting, I slowed quickly, indicated and cut in front of a Seat Uno dawdling in the slow lane. The bus roared past with a blast from its roof-mounted air horns. I felt the sting of grit flung from his wheels on to my bare legs as he passed. The tourists in the Uno were gawking and pointing at the bike as I pulled back into the fast lane.

I flicked on the stereo and listened for a moment to 100 watts of Meatloaf pounding 'Bat out of Hell' through the speakers. I grinned to myself. This was the life. Momentarily thoughts of the operation drifted away as I felt the blast of powering up the road. I waved at the tourists in the Uno who seemed to be trying to climb through the windows to get a better view. Clicking the handgrip-mounted PA button I spoke over the helmet mike: 'Hi, guys, having a good holiday?' My voice boomed from the four speakers and the PA system over the intervening roadway.

An American-built fully dressed bike with a 1500cc engine, the Goldwing is the biggest production bike in the world, and, as the ultimate touring machine, it's a showstopper, much admired by bikers and non-bikers the world over. Other road users were always completely knocked out when I talked to them from the bike on the road. It sounded as clear as if I were sat in their car. The waving increased frenetically, and the driver pipped the horn. I let go with my air horns and nodded back at them. Posing, I grinned and waved at them and thought how it always impressed them, even the staid blue-rinse brigade smiled and waved back at me.

My reverie was interrupted as suddenly the stereo stopped and Phil's voice cut in on the CB, 'John, I can see you, move over I'm coming through.'

I looked in the rear-view mirror. Sure enough there was Phil in the Mondeo coming up fast in the outside lane. I pressed the CB switch. 'Slow down, let me lead,' I said. Too late, he covered the few hundred yards in no time, and as I pulled in he flashed past me doing a good 80 mph.

Dropping a gear I pulled out again and accelerated easily up behind him. I flashed the lights at him, while Mike in the back seat waved, grinning like an idiot. Phil pulled over a few feet, and I edged past with a gap of less than four feet between me and the central concrete divide barrier.

According to the plan I had to maintain a minimum one-mile gap between us so I could warn them of any police activity ahead. I gunned the bike to more than 100 mph and quickly left them behind. Within seconds I was back up behind the tourist coach, which was still hogging the fast lane.

Without slowing I switched the headlights on main beam and went through on the inside lane. The driver hadn't seen me come up behind him and must have had a coronary when I screamed past his inside, bursting into view of his windscreen at 100 mph plus. He blasted the horn again. Too late, mate.

Luxuriating in the moment I deliberately turned three-quarters way round in the seat, smiled and gave him a good slow V-sign.

Hammering up the hot tarmac for a quarter of an hour I left Marbella way behind as I passed through wooded areas concealing camp sites on both sides of the road in the largely undeveloped coastal area of Los Pinellas. I could smell the clean, evocative scent of the pine trees coming from the hundreds of acres of virgin land nearby. I motored on until I saw a Repsol filling station a few hundred yards ahead, a usual police parking spot. I quickly scanned for police, and sure enough there was a jeep parked just off the road in front of a couple of cheap-looking truckers' bars.

Slowing rapidly I saw them staring at me. No problem, I thought, they're just watching the bike. Nevertheless I radioed back. 'Phil, there's a jeep parked in front of the garage before Calahonda. Take it easy.' This shouldn't have been a surprise to him. We had recced the route several times, and I had pointed out several likely hiding spots for police and radar cars.

I slowed way down and pulled off at the next exit to watch. From the top of the slip road I had a bird's-eye view. Ignoring my warning the Mondeo came tearing down the hill towards the police jeep. He braked more or less in front of it and then was past, still doing 70 mph. I saw the red and blue light bar flicker on, and the police jeep immediately jumped forward to give chase.

'Go! They're after you, dickheads. I told you not to go too fast,' I shouted into the CB.

The operation was starting to go to ratshit. I went across the exit ramp and joined the opposite slip road. The Mondeo shot past me at high speed. The problem now wasn't so much the Nissan patrol police jeep behind them as their colleagues they would call in by radio. I shot on to the main road and gave chase.

Flying along I went past Calahonda at a ripping pace and saw another police jeep coming to join the chase. I was in the clear. They couldn't catch me in a speed chase, and they didn't usually bother about bikes unless you were speeding in the town streets. In any case my papers were in order, and I wasn't carrying.

On the other hand the Mondeo was a stolen car and had two gun-packing crazies on board delivering 50 kg of cannabis resin into Fuengirola, part of a shipment that had arrived the night before from Morocco. Now having abandoned the prepared plan and tearing along the main Marbella highway they were in the shit. Spanish police always loved a good chase, which I suspect increased their sense of machismo. If they felt they were losing the speeding car they would call in for help.

Obviously the Mondeo would now have to be dumped. It had only been used on this trip and had cost Rog more than £2000 with a set of false papers. He wouldn't be very happy. Such thoughts were academic, because first they had to escape from their pursuers. Their only chance really was to get into the town and off the main road.

Because I was travelling at speed I didn't hear the helicopter return, but I did see it. It must have heard the call for assistance from the first police jeep. Rounding a bend giving on to a beautiful view over the ocean, I came face to face with the chopper, hovering a few hundred feet in the air, just off the side of the road, the pilot and passenger clearly visible as they watched the traffic below them. I waved at them, just a happy tourist, and shouted into the mike. 'There's a police chopper just before the Fuengirola camp site near the bends, slow down and drive normally for Christ's sake,' I urged.

'Too late, mate, they're up my arse,' Phil screamed back, while in the background I could hear Mike shouting, 'Go, Go, Go' from the back seat.

I carried on the mile or so past Fuengirola castle on my right and took the Fuengirola exit. They needed to get into the underground car park just off the avenida Don Juan near to the vegetable market, where they could dump the car and escape by one of the many exits. Maybe if the police lost them for a few seconds, and they turned off the road without being spotted, then the car could be collected later from the parking garage, although volunteers for that collection job would be thin on the ground.

The timing was all wrong, and the initial delay in Marbella meant that now the roads were jammed with workers returning to their shops and offices after the siesta. That extra volume of traffic coupled with the mix of tourists crawling along looking for nonexistent parking spaces and getting lost made for traffic chaos in the streets. I knew it would clear in an hour, but these boys didn't even have five minutes to spare. I took the white-line route up between the traffic keeping an eye out for roaming kids whilst I watched for any police activity. Sure enough two jeeps screamed around the red traffic lights up ahead, lights flashing and sirens blaring.

'Take the back road,' I spoke into the mike. No answer. One of them had the transmit button still pressed or had inadvertently changed CB channels. Out of contact with the car I was now redundant, so I slowed way down and watched the events unfold.

Two minutes later the Mondeo came into the town engine and tyres screaming as Phil slowed to accommodate the slow-moving traffic. The car noise was accompanied by the deeper sound of the police chopper as, now in full pursuit, it had to rise to clear the tower blocks. Helicopters were no good following cars in built-up town centres. Phil drove like a madman up the centre of the road scattering cars and pedestrians alike, but he saw the temporary roadblock too late. The pursuit jeep appeared behind him off the main road, so there was no return that way. Phil veered sharply across the road and, tyres screaming, disappeared up a narrow cobbled side street. In his panic he misjudged the turn and clipped a table at a corner sidewalk bar. The lightweight aluminium and plastic chairs went skipping and tumbling across the pavement in a crescendo of noise.

The helicopter presence, the sound of breaking glass and the screams of passers-by seemed to alert everyone that a chase was taking place in the vicinity. Chaos erupted as cars turned away from the noise or stopped dead in the road. People rushed out of nearby shops and bars for a better look, and foolhardy teenagers gave chase on their go-faster striped mopeds. This confusion worked in the Mondeo's favour as the police pursuers were momentarily stalled.

By now I had stopped at the roadside, and turning off the engine I unclipped the comms lead and removed my helmet. I climbed off the bike and locked the helmet on the rack. I took my mobile from the top box and smoothed my hair down. Watching with the crowd I awaited the final outcome. To evade pursuit in a busy town you have to blend in and disappear into the crowd. Tearing around side streets in a stolen car followed by a flock of mopeds is not the way to do it. The Mondeo was standing out like a pair of tits on a bull and was about to pay the price of not sticking to the prepared plan.

I walked to a nearby bar and ordered a San Miguel from the London-accented owner. Already lost in an alcoholic haze despite the mid-afternoon hour, he seemed oblivious to the screams, sirens and chaos just outside his door. 'Having a good time then, mate?' he enquired. Amazed at his ability to be so completely out of touch with reality I nodded at him, paid a tourist price for the beer and sauntered back outside.

The show was more or less over. People were dispersing, going back to their own activities, the police were sorting out the traffic chaos, and small groups of old Spanish women were babbling away in doorways. An older man wearing Afrika Korps-style desert shorts and a hideous Hawaiian shirt was walking towards me, his brown leather open sandals and grey socks marked him down as a British expat.

'What was all that about then?' I asked.

'Oh, just some fellas in a stolen car,' he replied. 'The silly bastards crashed it in the underground car park, seems they tried to go the wrong way and drove into the front of a car coming out.'

Shit. 'Did they catch them?' I asked casually.

'The driver is still trapped in the car,' he answered, then, offering a gratuitous opinion, he added, 'They should shoot these car thieves when they catch them.'

'Yeah, they probably do here, I reckon,' I said. He nodded absently and walked on, mumbling to himself.

Feeling drained by the comedown following the adrenaline rush I walked up the road and cut across a

the spanish connection

back street towards the underground car park. There were crowds of rubberneckers in the vicinity, pointing and talking together. Police cars and bikes were scattered haphazardly across the road, and there seemed to be hundreds of policemen strutting officiously about the scene.

I pushed towards the front of the crowd just in time to see a handcuffed Phil with a bloody towel wrapped around his head being pushed none too gently at gun point into a police jeep. He looked dazed and dejected. No wonder, he knew the police would find the 50 kg of cannabis hidden behind the back seat. There was no way it would remain undiscovered. Once they found the guns it would trigger a thorough search of the car. Cannabis resin, handguns and a stolen car, it was Goodbye, Phil, I thought.

I found a payphone and called Rog, on a landline.

'Don't plan on having a drink with Mike and Phil tonight,' I said. 'They've had a crash in town, and Phil's on his way to the clinic with a police guard, I think Mike's done a runner.'

'Oh, my God,' he wailed, 'there was 50 kg in that fucking car! What's Chris going to say?' It was a rhetorical question. There was no answer required of me. Anyway Rog had bigger troubles than losing 50 kilos, but he just didn't know it yet.

'See you tomorrow at Patsy's for breakfast,' I said and hung up. I decided to phone home for a chat, and then it would be time for a shower and tea.

At 10 am the next morning I was sitting outside Patsy's Bar on the front in Fuengirola, across from the marina

6

and small fishing-boat dock. The screaming gulls swooping around two blue-painted boats indicated they were awaiting their departure so they could feast on the gutted fish and debris floating in the dock waters. Meanwhile the tourists were up and about, the newcomers standing out like barbers' poles with their white and red striped skin. Reading yesterday's *Sun* and sipping the first of the day's many *cervezas* they waited docilely for their fried bacon and egg English breakfast special.

Patsy's Bar is typical of the thousands of small family-owned and run British bars that infest the Mediterranean coastal resorts from Portugal along the whole of Spain's coastline and islands and up as far as Greece. They are easily spotted with their amateurish hand-painted signs announcing English pub names and often sporting crude Union Jacks or British bulldogs. Too many small tables are crammed into the seating area and overflow on to the pavement, jockeying for space with tables set out by the neighbouring bar.

At this hour tables were all set for breakfast with white paper tablecloths pegged at the corners against the stiff breeze. Laid with cheap cutlery and the ubiquitous tomato and brown sauce bottles, Heinz ketchup and OK Fruity they provide a feeling of British normality for homesick tourists. Many of the bars serve breakfast specials — a glass of orange, cup of tea or instant coffee, fried bacon rashers and egg, beans and tomatoes with a couple of rounds of toast all for less than 250 pesetas, or just over £1.00. I didn't see how they could make a profit, and there again most of them don't. It is a constant round of new faces serving at the bar and tables year in and year out. Only the estate agents make money from the bars and cafes. You can spot them circling like carrion around a dying animal, awaiting the next inevitable round of bankruptcies.

I ordered a coffee and toast and awaited my contact. He soon swung purposefully around the corner and plonked himself down across the table from me. Slim, despite a hard-drinking lifestyle, sun-tanned and dressed in smart shorts and a Ralph Lauren tee shirt, he was carrying the handbag-size leather wallet *de rigueur* for the entrepreneurial set in this part of Europe. With his gold Rolex Oyster on his wrist he looked every inch the successful businessman, which I suppose he was in his world. Rog was a middle-ranking player in the Costa drug-smuggling fraternity.

I smiled at him. 'Morning, Rog,' I said as he signalled into the gloomy depths of the bar for a coffee. And so the game continued. I was acting my role as freelance organizer and driver ready to undertake any dodgy job for cash, and now I sat there and listened as Rog bemoaned the loss of 50 kg of gear. It was his own fault, and he knew it. A relatively straightforward transport job had been blown because he had used a few local drug-happy dickheads.

A friendly enough man with expensive tastes that were amply funded by his forays into the smuggling of illegal drugs I knew that Rog would have me killed instantly, without any hesitation, if he ever learnt that I was an undercover agent working with handlers in the Manchester office of the Drug Investigation Unit of Her Majesty's Customs & Excise. It was a bizarre experience, sitting in the hot sunshine surrounded by families of tourists with nothing more on their minds than which part of the beach to lie on or where to eat their next

meal, whilst we were discussing the intricacies of delivering illegal narcotics from the Costa del Sol up to the
north of England.

Anyone who has been in similar situations knows the
buzz of adrenaline that comes from constantly living on
the edge, mixing with vicious criminals who all share a
visceral hatred of informers and nodding along with
them before sneaking off to a quiet phone cabin and
placing a call back to your UK-based Customs handlers.
Like drugs the buzz is addictive and despite half-hearted
warnings from handlers you chase the buzz like a junkie
screaming for another fix; finding yourself constantly
taking more and more risks and risking exposure just to
beat the odds again.

Having won again the resultant high borders on the
orgasmic. The sweating palms, pounding heart and gut-
twisting cramps that hit at the time of maximum risk are
the ignored indicators that signal the damage you are
inflicting on your mind and body. You can carry on
wheeling and dealing, but at the back of your mind you
know the piper will have to be paid eventually.

Right now I had to convince Rog that the previous
day's *débâcle* was caused by his driver's speeding, in
both meanings of the word, and dumb bad luck.

'OK, so what went wrong yesterday?' he asked.

I told him what I knew, and then I said, 'I'm afraid
you can kiss the gear goodbye.'

Taking a sip of coffee Rog looked at me carefully.
'Yeah, we saw them tow the car away last night,' he
said, 'so the gear's gone. One bit of a result was that
Mike turned up later at Frankie's Bar, when we went
along late on for a chat. The twat was pissed as a fart.

'It seems they decided to call in at a mate's for some

whizz. These young punks have no idea of security, only thinking of fucking birds and getting out of their heads,' he moaned. 'Anyway Mike won't be bothering with the birds for a bit. Chris was a bit pissed off at his attitude and the stupid loss of 15-grand worth of gear and the car, so he glassed him pretty good. Then he dragged him outside and worked a hammer over his wrists, fucked his hands big time.'

As he delivered this chilling tale of pain and future disablement I felt my guts quiver with fear. I lit a cigarette and was pleased to note that my hands weren't shaking.

'Serves him right,' was the best response I could come with, injecting just sufficient indifference into my voice that my lack of commitment went unquestioned.

Rog's problem now was that he had through his own stupidity lost a load of gear destined for a British buyer, who would still want either his 50 kg of cannabis or else his money back with a healthy profit on top. If he didn't deliver then Rog would soon find someone taking him outside to rearrange his skeletal structure. I thought he looked remarkably calm for someone under such a cloud.

Then Rog hit me with a big juicy one.

'It's not that important because we've just ripped off a Paddy in Torremolinos who wanted to buy 20 kg for Northern Ireland, so I can trade that. And I've already made an arrangement to buy another 50 kg off Juan tonight and ship it up to the north of England this weekend. Problem solved.'

I nodded coolly, although I could feel the first internal tremors that signalled another buzz was coming up.

'Why don't you come over tonight? We'll have a barbecue and talk. Discuss arrangements and so on. There'll be a couple of grand in it for you when the stuff gets to the UK,' he smiled.

'No way,' I said, 'I'm not having my wages depend on your wrapping skills. I'll pitch in with you, but I want paying when the gear is safely on a ferry and leaves for the UK. You can't blame me if it gets lost after that.'

He looked at me appraisingly for a long moment, 'OK,' he nodded at me and then stood up, indicating the meeting was over. Without looking backward he walked out of the seating area and disappeared around the corner. Arrogant bastard.

The young waitress from Birmingham swooped in and started to clear the table. I noticed that Rog had left me with the bill again. Cheapskate, I thought, the guy's a millionaire, and he always leaves me with the bill. Still I couldn't complain, a quick phone call, and I would put another nail in the bastard's coffin. I stretched and smiled at the waitress, saying, 'Have a nice day now.' I winked and flicked her a 2000 peseta note and left the patio, giving her probably the biggest tip she would make that day.

Shortly after lunch I walked up to the main post office, and after a swift look around I entered the telephone cabin farthest from the door. I quickly dialled the Manchester number from memory and when the operator answered asked to speak with Rob Williams.

'Hi, Rob.' After I'd introduced myself I said, 'There was a bit of bother here last night. The local police picked up a young Scottish lad called Phil in a stolen car in the centre of Fuengirola, with 50 kg of cannabis stuffed in the boot. The gear was owned by our friend

Rog and was for shipment to Salford. I don't know who the buyer is yet, but Rog's off organizing another load at the moment. I'll try and find out later.'

'Good work, mate,' said Rob. 'Find out when it's coming over and who's picking it up if you can.'

'Oh, by the way, another lad, Mike, got a working over last night. He's probably in a bad way,' I told him.

'Yeah,' he replied, disinterested, 'that's the price of messing with the big boys.'

'See you later,' I said and hung up, wondering what Rob would comment if I received a similar treatment from unhappy drug dealers in the future. On that disquieting note I headed back into town and decided to have a drink before meeting Rog later.

2

Me and My Family

Born in 1956 and brought up in north Manchester I attended the Norman House preparatory school in New Moston followed by the Hulme Grammar School for Boys in Oldham. School was all right, but I couldn't conform to the string of petty and, to me, meaningless regulations. Having made a mess of most of my O levels I was slated to take the re-sits in the winter. Unhappy and suffering from a virulent form of adolescent rebellion I upped sticks and left school without any warning.

I also chose that inauspicious moment to leave home, and without any indication of my plans I left Failsworth and my long-suffering parents in the dark and caught a train to Truro in Cornwall, where I had holidayed two summers running on school surfing breaks. Looking back it is a surprise to me that at 16 I managed to survive for so long on my own. But survive I did, and I was feeling pretty good. I had a job in Truro in a hardware store and lived in a holiday cottage in St Agnes, which a friendly owner let me rent cheaply in the closed season.

For a while it was great. I learnt to smoke, beginning with Park Drive, and I discovered scrumpy, a particularly vicious type of cider. I quickly caught on to the benefits of a couple of aspirin and a greasy bacon and egg sandwich for quelling hangovers. I will also remember St Agnes as the place where I lost my virginity, or more accurately where I spent weeks desperately trying to throw it away. Finally I succeeded, with a rather well-built local lass, Sue, who seemed to think that a couple or three afternoon romps on the clifftops amongst the heather and the screaming seagulls meant we were going to get married.

Nothing was further from my mind, and an invitation from my father to join him at work in Manchester seemed like a godsend. I quickly packed my meagre belongings and hightailed back to Failsworth to venture into the dirt and grime of an engineering apprenticeship. Luckily for me my dad had convinced his rather naïve boss that having benefited from a private education I was an ideal candidate as a trainee combustion engineer. Thus I was spared the indignities forced upon many of my mates during their first year of apprenticeship.

So I entered the employ of Associated Heat Services, a company part-owned by the National Coal Board and specializing in operating district heating schemes. These were large, usually coalfired boilers located in central boiler-rooms and providing heating and hot water to massive council-home estates by a complex web of underground water mains. My dad was the manager for the Lancashire region of Associated Heat Services, which meant I could move around the county at will. Wielding my dad's name and vicariously imbued with his power I thought I would be impervious to threats and be able to dodge anything that smacked of real work.

The first thing I had to do was to learn to drive and pass a driving test. Unfortunately my dad had accurately sized up my intentions with regard to work and killed two birds with one stone by placing me into the care of Joe Philbin, an ex-miner of small stature. Recruited by my dad as a general factotum, he had free reign on all the company sites and was a well-respected 'hard man', guaranteed to enforce the company's will. What he may have lacked in physical size he made up for in brute strength. Not many people crossed Joe.

Driving an old ice-cream van he was always threatening to convert into a camper van, Joe spoke in a broad Lancashire dialect that I could scarcely understand as English. Especially when he lost his temper, and his mouth started running away with him. He was the original motormouth. Quick to anger and always ready to cuff me playfully if I answered back, he was also quick to smile, displaying startlingly white teeth in a broad grin. He always reminded me of a grown-up street urchin.

Joe was pleased with his new role of baby-sitter cum driving instructor, mainly because my dad provided him with an old company Morris 1000 van. The vehicle was knackered and should have been traded in years ago. But it had been retained as a site runabout. Joe set me to cleaning out years of accumulated filth from the van, and then sporting a new set of L-plates we were off. The insignificant fact that I had never before driven a vehicle on a road didn't deter Joe in the slightest.

He threw me the ignition keys and said, 'Don't go on them motorways yet, but drive me up to Oldham St

Mary's.' Having been brought up near to an M62 motorway access link all journeys of any length had involved a motorway trip. Other than an occasional bus ride into Manchester city centre I hadn't got a clue how to navigate around Manchester or the city. But I became a quick learner, encouraged by Joe leaning back in the passenger seat and commenting on girl pedestrians and drivers, wolf-whistling and generally pratting about, seemingly uncaring about the ominous grinding noises emanating from the gearbox and engine.

Joe showed me the techniques necessary to drive a van with its own idiosyncrasies. I quickly mastered the rudiments of double de-clutching, signalling, overtaking women drivers, flicking a V to other drivers and the like, continually coached by an ever observant Joe who would cuff me if I made the same mistake more than twice.

We must have looked a sight in a rusty white van lurching and kangarooing around the city with me trying to read street signs and Joe turning the air blue with his choicest pit language. It is a testament to him that I passed my driving test on the first attempt, soon after my 17th birthday.

Under Joe's guiding hand I learnt about the dark mysteries of boiler engineering and soon discovered I had a natural bent for things mechanical. Drilling, burning, welding, turning and milling all revealed their secrets to me, and I became proficient in reading technical drawings, repairing conveyors, scapers, drive shafts and the myriad devices that comprise a modern industrial plant. Bonuses were paid by way of attendance at manufacturers' technical courses, and slowly but surely I became a proper trainee combustion engineer. I was well on the way to being self-sufficient in the complex world of boilers, burners, steam pipes and controls that supply the motive power for most industrial processes.

I revelled in the order and logic apparent everywhere in engineering; at last things around me seemed to make sense. Problems could be solved by application of practical learning, which to me was streets ahead of the abstract world of learning at school. I thrived and prospered, eventually taking the plunge and attending Openshaw Technical College, where I mastered the mix of technical training and practical skills. I never could handle technical drawing, the shapes and patterns of my doggy-looking papers were far away from the pristine accurate drawings of my classmates. Still, I never said I was perfect.

After a couple of years my father left his secure job and started his own engineering firm. Perhaps unsurprisingly Associated Heat Services decided shortly thereafter they no longer needed my services, and I was invited to leave, with a three-month payment in lieu of notice. It took me all of one minute to consider their proposal. The next week I started working for my dad. The formal training schedule was binned, and I was straight on to the tools; it was great.

After a couple of months we were making some money, and in 1974 my dad ordered a brand new minivan for me from the local Austin Rover dealership. I loved it; I fixed a massive pair of spotlights on the front bumper and installed a below dash Motorola stereo of dubious former ownership that I bought for a few quid in a local pub. A big whip antenna sprouting from the roof completed the picture.

At the time I had a girlfriend called Gill, a blonde Irish girl who lived in Birkdale near Southport, about 40 miles away from our house. I couldn't wait to show her the new van, which I did, nearly every night. We cruised forever up and down Lord Street in Southport, posing outside the Wimpy bar and the amusement arcades on Bath Street. I consoled my faintly troubled conscience by convincing myself I was running the van in nicely and steadily by the motorway driving between Manchester and Southport.

Of course, it all went wrong when I fell asleep at the wheel about four o'clock in the morning on the M63 motorway, following a late-night tryst on a Southport beach. Entirely unaided I managed to drive up an embankment, tumble back down and roll backwards into the central reservation.

Strike one minivan. It was just three weeks old and had covered more than 1000 miles a week. I was picked up by a police Range Rover, and after a Breathalyzer test and a lecture from a stern-faced sergeant in Eccles police station I was released into the cold, uncompromising dawn light, to explain to my mum and dad how it had happened. I treated the replacement van with a good deal more respect.

The small foundling business prospered by dint of hard work, long hours and some well overdue good luck. More contracts came in, and the scope of our work increased month by month. I discovered that in addition to understanding things mechanical I could cope fairly easily with business correspondence, preparation of estimates, quotations, reports and the like.

This was a great boon for my dad who hadn't had a

formal education. He was drafted into the coal mines as a Bevin Boy during the Second World War, where he served his time as a mechanical fitter. He lifted himself out of a rough working-class start by attending night school and passing some City and Guilds exams. Having learnt the theoretical side of engineering his career blossomed, and he climbed the ladder of success. But he never did relish report writing and was more than happy to leave it to me.

Gradually I spent less time on the tools and more and more time in the office, where I found the commercial side of a business needs the same steady hand as the turner on the lathe or milling machine. As the business progressed the family wealth steadily mounted. When I was 20 I bought a 3-litre Capri complete with a first-generation carphone, whilst my dad had a new Granada Ghia. We thought we were the bollocks. With plenty of cash swishing around life was good. We held large parties, inviting friends and works' associates from miles around.

As I turned 21 I moved into my own place. Dolled up in my mohair suit and black James Bond polo-neck I drove around town on a weekend in my new Capri. I was sure I cut a dash, especially in the local pubs. Probably I looked a pretentious little pillock.

A good engineer friend of mine introduced me to his wife's girlfriend Kath, a local midwife. She had blonde hair, a petite frame and a charming smile. Older than me, she seemed very sophisticated. I was smitten from our first meeting. The fact that she was recently separated with three young sons all under six didn't bother me at all. Needless to say the family weren't too happy with this turn of events. They had me slated for more suitable suitors.

I chased Kath for ages, always rebuffed as being a toy boy. My charm was wasted; she looked through me as if I wasn't there. Of course the truth of the matter is that chat-up lines that work the oracle on teenage girls fall completely flat on a married woman with three kids. One night I met her and her friends having a few drinks out. She wasn't too well, and I offered to drive her home. As we sat outside her small semi-detached in Failsworth, she gave me her phone number. That was it, I had to get to know her better. I plagued her for weeks, phoning at all hours, dreaming up the wildest excuses to convince her that she should go out with me. I didn't know it at the time but she was depressed by the sudden departure of her husband, and she didn't need some young jerk mooning about and trying to get into her knickers.

Eventually she relented and invited me round to hers for some cheese and wine, provided that I supplied the wine. I whizzed into the local off-licence and bought a selection of the most expensive wines in the shop, as well as nuts, crisps of every flavour and the world's supply of cigarettes. We had some good laughs that night as she admitted she had asked me over because she was fed up with me mithering her and because she thought my persistence deserved some recognition. Personally I think she was just a lonely and isolated young lady, up to her ears in debt with a full-time job as a community midwife, an old banger of a car and three bread snatchers who were driving her insane.

The next morning I awoke with a mother of a hangover and noticed a pair of round eyes peering at me. Focusing hard I realized that the eyes belonged to a little kid, a sector of society I had always been nicely distanced from since I was at prep school. Oh, boy, was I about to have another education.

I soon left my own house empty and moved in with Kath, much to the disgust of her neighbours and work colleagues. Neither of our families was ecstatic at the match. Still we were in heaven on earth, at least for the first few months until the grim reality of bringing up kids set in.

Things were progressing nicely at work and a large industrial manufacturing group made an irresistible offer to buy us out. My dad hadn't been too well of late, and it seemed like the ideal time to get out and reap a good profit.

We sold out to the Hargreaves Group from Wetherby in 1983, and both my mum and dad retired on the proceeds of their shares sale. Meanwhile I was contracted to work as a manager for the new owners. It was goodbye to the Capri and hello to a Cortina Crusader, and the writing was there on the wall from the outset, but I just didn't see it. After a few months I knew it wouldn't work out. Work had become a ghastly re-run of life at school, where petty rules and regulations were the order of the day again. Every day there seemed to be another meeting, with bods appearing from head office to tell us how to run a business that had worked perfectly well before they got involved. Pettifogging accountants, planners, safety officers, union negotiators, we had the lot; the place was drowning in paperwork and procedures.

Of course the extra administrative load meant that more staff had to be recruited, and the additional overheads meant more sales had to be achieved. We were caught in the spiralling budget trap, and some of the staff were too busy fiddling expenses to have much company loyalty and involvement. Sales dropped because overheads increased our quotation prices, and everybody lacked commitment. It was a downhill race to oblivion. I jumped off before I was swallowed up whole and disappeared down the plughole with the rest of the business.

By this time Kath and I had married and set up home in Saddleworth, a stockbroker belt north of Manchester, a picturesque rural community nestling in the foothills of the Pennine Range. On the days when it didn't rain and the ever present mist cleared momentarily it was beautiful. The trouble was that the sky didn't clear for long; I think Saddleworth has a shorter summer than Reykjavik.

We lived in a large stone house set in a couple of acres of rough meadow. Though we were both still working full time we found time to raise pigs, cows, goats, chickens and a family of ducklings. In between fighting rising damp and galloping dry rot in our old house we recklessly decided to breed from our Great Dane bitch. A few weeks later a local farmer friend sat in the kitchen drinking tea and surrounded by barking and yelping puppies. He looked around in amazement and pithily remarked, 'Definitely a fuck too far, John.' He was right, but still it was fun.

Faced with the demise of the old family firm and disillusioned by the machinations of big business we decided to get out of the rat race and sample the Good Life. We made seemingly endless trips to Wales and

Scotland to inspect farms and smallholdings. That period has left me with a lifelong mistrust of anything spewing forth from an estate agent's brochure. We drove hundred of miles to visit 'an idyllic retreat set in five acres with its own fresh water', where the reality we often found was a tumbledown cottage, surrounded by near vertically inclined hills and an access road that demanded a Land Rover or army half-track.

Eventually we decided to try abroad. We had holidayed in Spain, which at the time was all the rage amongst those British who wanted an alternative lifestyle. After further inspection visits we made our minds up; Spain it was to be. We sold everything and in 1984 set off in our Toyota Carina estate car – me, Kath, three boys and a great Dane – for the trip of a lifetime to Benidorm.

Passport and immigration control in the northern Spanish port of Santander were a riot. We didn't speak a word of Spanish, and the guards reciprocated by not speaking any English. We looked like the Beverly Hillbillies; all we were missing was a shotgun-toting grandma sat in a rocking chair on the car roof. All our papers were carefully scrutinized; the dog and her papers subjected to a separate scrutiny by a pompous little vet. Customs officers made ready to examine the car, but when they opened the doors and looked inside, the smell and detritus of the imprisoned kids and dog wafted out over them. Reeling back they nodded and decided we were safe enough to enter the country, and so we were in. We left the port and started the long road journey, for which we didn't even have an up-to-date roadmap.

A nightmare journey to Benidorm ensued, which

involved a three-hour circular tour of Madrid's motorway ring road and a near miss with a suicidal horse-pulled cart in Burgos. We arrived in Benidorm in the early morning before dawn broke. Tired to death we crawled up to our apartment, and only realized after a sleep that we had left all the suitcases on top of the car. We could have saved ourselves the wasted energy in rushing down the seven flights of stairs because the suitcases and all our newly bought clothes were long gone. Another of life's little knocks. Hello, Spain.

We bought a small cocktail bar, complete with bronze wall-to-wall mirrors, a massive bar, seductive lighting and ceiling fans. It was in the old town area of Benidorm, a rabbit warren of narrow, sometimes cobbled streets leading down to a small cove, where old-fashioned fishing boats were still pulled on to the beach by hand each day. It seemed a different world to the concrete jungle, high-rise infested new Benidorm on the far side of the headland.

The bar was situated in a long narrow street, the Calle de Palmas. Proud of our new purchase we couldn't understand why the locals were cynical and embittered. We soon learnt why. Unaccustomed to the mind-slowing heat, bureaucratic officials endlessly demanding money in return for stamped scraps of paper, a lack of tourists and almost permanently pissed neighbours our enthusiasm evaporated like spit on a hot stove.

We should have sat down and analysed our position, abandoned the bar and the car and caught the next flight home to civilization. Instead we decided to stick at it, a decision that still ranks as one of the worst moves I have made since my birth. The bar was like a bottomless pit, and our not insubstantial savings haemorrhaged into the pit within months. Everything was either unavailable or expensive, except for the beer, which we, like other hapless and desperate bar owners, were selling at cost price just to attract trade.

At the time there were only two available brands of beer, Mahou and San Miguel. The two beer sales reps provided a constant source of light relief, attacking each other as they rode their little mopeds down the streets, legs flying, wielding clipboards and biros like bizarre modern-day chariot racers doing battle, all to secure the next meagre order from a bar owner who probably couldn't afford to pay them.

We stuck it for about a year before we returned home broken spiritually, mentally and financially. Meanwhile, just after we'd taken over the bar, my parents had bought a villa in a beautiful location overlooking the town. At night Benidorm was lit up and looked just like a fairytale, the distance hiding the grim reality within.

Having escaped back to England and Oldham Kath quickly secured her old job as a midwife, delivering babies in the largely Asian community, centred around the now declining cotton industry. I replied to every advert in the *Daily Telegraph* that remotely called for my skills. I secured an interview in Bletchley with Energy Equipment, a subsidiary of the Brussels-based giant oil company, Petrofina.

I travelled down by train and was interviewed by a retired naval officer who seemed suitably impressed with my schooling and ability to talk technically about the merits of modern boilers. I got a job as a self-employed technical writer, paid at the dizzy rate of £8 per hour. I quickly found digs in a local pub and set to work with a will, writing technical manuals, travelling home just for weekends.

Over the next year life improved, and we had the satisfaction of watching our bank balance grow again. I was promoted several times and eventually ended up with a roving commission troubleshooting and managing sites ready for handover to clients.

In 1987 I was seconded into another Petrofina subsidiary, which manufactured prison security systems and did high-tech security work at military establishments around Britain. I soon became familiar with the inside of various prisons: Full Sutton, Winson Green, Guernsey, Dumfries and the like. Petrofina had the same problem with its subsidiary that we had suffered with our Spanish bar: it was costing too much to operate and was losing money hand over fist. The business was discreetly offered for sale, but because most businessmen had at least a modicum of common sense no buyers came forward.

By this time the business was being managed by a golden-boy accountant from head office. Driving a new Golf GTi and sporting a chalk-stripe three-piece over his corpulent frame he dearly wanted to be seen as a corporate hit man, a saviour who rescued the company from its failing subsidiary. He was an ideal vehicle for my ambitions.

Over a few beers in a local pub in Olney, Buckinghamshire, I put a proposal to him that was calculated to make his career, he thought. I would buy the business contracts for a nominal sum if I could have the benefits left in the contracts and the payments currently due from the contractors. I offered him a lifeline, which he accepted with all the business flair and panache of a baby grabbing a biscuit. A month later, in September 1988, I bought the business from Petrofina.

I immediately called in all the debts and stopped any further work on the sites. All the staff had previously been absorbed into Petrofina, so contract engineers were laid off, and the company ceased working. This was a complicated form of asset-stripping or corporate piracy, and a very profitable operation it was too, although it took me two years to finalize.

In the meantime, in February 1987, Kath gave birth to her fourth child and first daughter whom we named Natalie Kate. A beautiful little girl sound, as they say, in wind and limb. This was a milestone event in my life, and overnight changed my outlook, giving me an unhitherto profound sense of responsibility.

By now we had moved to another small rural community in Humberside, to a locally famous village where they still practised farming in the medieval style. Now we had a farmhouse, a few more acres of land and felt we were finally getting closer to our goal of financial security, contentment and peace and quiet.

Using and developing my business contacts I opened a specialist employment agency. From a small start in a Scunthorpe office we developed within two years into greater things. Supplying technical staff to the petrochemical, steel and other heavy industries we had engineers placed throughout the UK and Europe, including Italy, Greece, Turkey, and Eire, as well as in

Saudi Arabia and Libya. The business was rolling along excellently, picking up momentum and surely destined for a successful and profitable future.

I was content, living in a beautiful location, where I could drive to work daily from home for the first time in seven years. My daughter was at private school and growing well; the boys were making friends and acquiring girlfriends; Kath was again developing her all embracing passion in animals and had recently taken up horse riding again, one of her childhood loves.

Then on the car radio on the way into work I heard that Saddam Hussein, the Iraqi dictator, had invaded his neighbour, the sovereign oil-rich country of Kuwait and was taking Westerners as hostages. I watched the situation develop with dismay, as each day brought worse news. Iraq was using Western hostages as a human shield, while the United Nations was going to defend and liberate Kuwait. The TV started showing footage of soldiers trooping into cargo planes carrying their kitbags, and lines of sand-coloured army vehicles could be seen waiting on docks to be loaded on to troop carriers. These scenes, evocative of the Falklands conflict, convinced me that the dispute would not be settled quickly or diplomatically.

At the office we had seen promised orders for oil personnel dry up overnight. Now British companies were pulling out their overseas-based personnel; GEC Turbines, Rolls-Royce, NEI and other core businesses were taking stock and cancelling orders. The writing was on the wall in big bloody lettering. No company supplying personnel overseas would receive any more orders until the Middle East had settled down, and with half the Western nations teetering on the brink of an all out war with the Moslem states who could say when that would be.

At work the situation was becoming drastic. Money was being paid out, and we were no longer earning anything. I moved quickly to stop the rot. After a week of heavy sessions with lawyers, accountants and bankers I decided the only way forward was to wind up the company. With a heavy heart I phoned a liquidator and arranged a meeting. Within a month the company was gone, closed down and in voluntary liquidation; it would take more than twelve months for its affairs to be completely finalized.

Caught up in world events completely outside our control we had seen a good viable business go down the tubes and sink without trace because some raghead megalomaniac had let his ego and greed get out of control. I was sorry when after invading Iraq Stormin' Norman's boys stopped on the main highway and didn't go all the way to Baghdad and shoot the bastard.

So now there I was skilled in business management but out of a job and disillusioned. Fortunately we had a reasonable amount of money tucked away. I cut down our expenses, sold off the horses, sent back my BMW to the dealers and prepared for the leaner times ahead. Compared with some we were lucky: we still had our family close by, our health and some of our wealth intact. We'd taken another knock, but we were still in the ring and raring to go.

After hours and hours talking and looking at other business prospects we decided to give it a try overseas again. There followed some months of planning, after which I finally left the UK in an elderly Mercedes van in 1993. I headed for the south of Spain, this time intending to set up a business in the tourist area of the Costa del Sol.

After their seven-year idyllic sojourn there my parents had now returned to the UK from Spain following my father's second heart attack. They were comfortably ensconced in a bungalow we had built for them in the grounds of the farm. I departed for Spain alone, leaving the family together as best I could to offer each other mutual support while I investigated the opportunities available. I had ideas about the form a business could take, but I just needed to check it out for myself before committing the family again. My first trip to the Costa del Sol was made with just that intention in mind.

3

Costa del Crime

My second drive into Spain was more auspicious than the first journey in 1984 had been when we drove for a new life in Benidorm. This time I elected to take the Portsmouth to St Malo car ferry, drive through France and enter Spain via the Hendaye border crossing. I would continue along the Bilbao coastal road and then cut inland over the mountains into Burgos. From there the route was straightforward enough: Burgos to Madrid and then south past Toledo until I hit Granada. It was then a relative skip and jump to the Costa del Sol coastal road. I didn't have a firm destination in mind at that time, but I wanted to arrive on the Costa del Sol within the week.

We knew from our experiences in Spain that domestic electrical products were very expensive, especially when compared with UK second-hand prices. I had reasoned that it would be worth purchasing bulk loads of electrical equipment and retailing them with warranties in Spain. I spent a week buying up goods, intending to sell them as a pilot scheme to dealers and domestic buyers alike to test out the market and my theory. So after tearful farewells from the family I set off on the long journey loaded up with domestic white goods, second-hand microwaves, Baby Belling cookers, Burco boilers and small freezers.

The journey through France was uneventful, except that my failure to master French at school was revealed as a mistake: I couldn't even order a sandwich and coffee in a roadside cafe without looking a complete moron. The first night near Bordeaux was a disaster, but after much finger-wagging and hand-waving I somehow secured the bridal suite in a hotel. Why they thought I wanted a bridal suite I never did discover, but the coffee and croissants for breakfast were heavenly.

By the second evening I was near to the Franco-Spanish border, and I knew that barring any accidents I should be in Spain before the day was out. I decided to make a small detour to travel through Biarritz, a beautiful picture postcard town, quaint, clean and expensive, and one of France's treasures hidden away from most foreign tourists. Late that night I arrived at the border and was surprised to find it unmanned on the French side. I cruised slowly past the closed guard kiosks and the open barriers towards Spain. Crossing the Spanish border I saw an officious-looking guard waving at me imperiously from a floodlit area ahead.

I pulled over and wound down the window.

'Buenas noches, señor,' he greeted me. I responded in kind and thereby used up nearly half my Spanish vocabulary. Unfortunately my ready and correctly delivered response made him think I was conversant in his tongue, and he launched into a barrage of rapid-fire Spanish.

I was flustered and said in my best British Raj voice, 'I'm sorry, I do not understand you, señor.' The guard was a little taken aback, and I could see he was thinking I was taking the piss.

Not to be outdone he waved at me saying, 'Papers, por favor.' I scrambled to the passenger side and collected all the paperwork: passport, driving licence, insurance papers and green card for European travel. He carefully perused them under the glare of the lights and then motioned me out of the van. One of his moustachioed mates joined us.

It was then I realized these weren't border guards but Guardia Civil. With their peculiar little pillbox-style hats the Civil Guard was formed by the dictator Franco as a paramilitary force to administer the country. They are definitely high up on the list of people with whom not to tangle. This one wasn't amused and pointed to the rear doors in the universal symbol of 'Open up'.

I did just that, and he stared impassively at an interior full of kitchen appliances, topped off with clothes, personal gear and a sleeping bag. A quick jabber between the two of them, and again he demanded 'Papers'. I understood immediately that he wanted to see the invoices for the goods, and I was prepared for this eventuality. Within a couple of minutes I had handed over a sheaf of invoices relating to all the goods in the van, but he obviously hadn't got a clue what they were. Nevertheless he scrutinized them carefully, and after tut-tutting a couple of times he handed them back to me. With a minuscule nod thrown over his shoulder he marched away into the darkness, and I took this as a sign that my entrance into Spain had been sanctioned. I slammed shut the van doors and quickly jumped in and set off before he changed his mind and asked me to empty out all the goods and carry out an inventory. We would have been there all night.

As I drove along in the darkness I decided I could understand them searching vehicles leaving Spain, but what on earth would anybody smuggle into Spain? Try as I might I could only think of pirated video tapes and some decent reading material. I hadn't got a clue that such searches and the reasons for them would be a major part of my life in the next few months.

Other than a tyre blow-out on the Madrid ring road, which gave me an interesting insight into Spanish driving habits, the rest of the journey passed relatively peacefully. Two days later I followed the route over the mountains and through the two vast tunnels that drop the road on to the Costa del Sol, where I arrived hot, dusty and tired in the well-known concrete jungle of Torremolinos.

Lingering long enough for a quick drink and to buy a local large-scale road map I headed down the infamous coastal road, passing above Benalmadena. I knew the highway was nicknamed the street of death because of the inordinately high number of fatal accidents that occur on it during each of the summer tourist-infested months. I drove south towards Marbella, in search of accommodation in one of the smaller towns just off the coastal highway.

Approaching Fuengirola I marvelled at the majestic sweep of this multilaned super highway, paid for with European Community money. Obviously no expense had been spared in creating this monument to tourism. Bridges are made of beautifully sculpted concrete sections, footbridge ironwork is ornate rather than workman-like, and the tarmac contrasts blindingly with the white concrete rain guttering that shimmers in the bright Mediterranean sun.

Things move a little down-market when passing through the urban sprawl of Fuengirola town. There low-rise painted buildings, scrapyards and the debris of car crashes that litter the hard shoulder combine to give a feeling that you're driving in downtown Mexico. Rounding the long right-hander out and away from Fuengirola, however, there is a panoramic view of the sea that knocks the breath out of you. Passing the old castle ruins on the crest of a small hill overlooking the sea and the camp site on the inland side of the road, things start to improve again.

Suddenly the scent of pine trees wafts through the open windows, and the crisp clean aroma drives away any lingering sewer-like smell emanating from the back streets of Fuengirola. This is a reminder of Spain as it must have been before the tourist boom gave rise to the proliferation of tacky 'urbanizations' of identical white-stucco walled villas clamouring for space on the rise of every little crest.

When granting planning consent for the myriad of exotically named estates the urban planners obviously hadn't heard of visual pollution. A helicopter ride shows how the rash of creeping development has spread up and down the coast over the past decade. Now, years later, the developments are filled with expatriates suffering from the crippling water shortages caused partly by ever increasing domestic demands and the construction of massive world-class golf courses. The housing estates and the golf courses all feed from a system of natural underground wells. The problems are exacerbated by the fact that water is being withdrawn faster than mother nature can replenish stocks; the inevitable result is an ever worsening water supply with no solution in sight.

Pondering on the uncertain future of one of Europe's natural beauty spots I pulled off the road into a small beach area on the southern outskirts of Fuengirola in search of accommodation. This I soon found in a small family-run pension, which was clean, comfortable and modestly priced. The Spanish proprietor was not in evidence so I had the pleas-ure of dealing with Carmen, his wife. She was a beautiful, doelike creature with jet-black shiny hair held in place by a white hair band, a drop-dead gorgeous face and a beautifully turned and trim body. She looked stunning in a cropped white tee shirt and pink shorts. Definitely a woman to lust after. Carlos the boss was a lucky man.

Following the wondrous globes wobbling provocatively in Carmen's shorts I limped along the corridor to a well-proportioned room complete with a *cama matrimonial* and an en suite bathroom.

'Very nice, I'll take it,' I assured her. Carmen smiled. She instinctively knew what I was thinking. Though she may not have understood what a double entendre was, she certainly got my meaning. I paid a week's rent in cash and watched her as she waltzed out of the room and went back to sunning herself on the porch.

I caught sight of myself in the wall mirror and took a good look at my reflection. Pale skinned with white legs poking out below my shorts, a slight paunch and tired bags under my eyes, at 39 years old who was I kidding? Carmen and her ilk were only a watching activity for me and thousands of other middle-aged

Romeos. I was quickly skidding towards being a dirty old man. So what? I could always join the club of the loose-change jiggling bar-goers, but I didn't intend to buy a gold chain in an effort to become the oldest swinger in town.

I unpacked and showered, feeling sorry for myself. Later I headed back into Fuengirola town and had a walk around the promenade whilst deciding in which café to eat. It wasn't an easy choice for there are hundreds of eating houses there displaying tempting cuisine from virtually every corner of the world.

Over the next few weeks I was kept busy making the first moves to get a business off the ground. First I needed an office with typing and fax services, a Post Office box number, a bank account, mobile phone and all the other trappings of modern commerce. Having established all that I retained a firm of lawyers and another of accountants, and finally placed adverts in the local English-language newspapers.

Business was brisk, and all the electrical goods I had brought from the UK sold in double-quick time, leaving the interior of the van as clean as whistle with not a microwave in sight. Encouraged by the successful start I put phase two of the business plan into gear. Scouring antique shops for suitable bargains I came across a giant-size Castilian-style reproduction sideboard. After a mammoth bargaining session I bought the piece of furniture from a 90-year-old gimlet-eyed geezer whose tongue had been honed on thousands of bargain-hunting tourists.

With the sideboard loaded into the van and

protected by old blankets I set out again for home.
Everything went smoothly until I reached Hendaye. At
the border this time French Customs had a proper go at
me. Whilst one official checked my passport details,
another examined all the van documents and my
driving licence; a third poked around under the van
with a probe and a mirror. I noticed they paid special
attention to the diesel tank and spare wheel. In a final
flurry of determined bad will they brought in a dog and
encouraged it to jump all over the interior of the van,
sniffing, I supposed, for concealed drugs. Apart from
wagging its tail and trying to piss up one corner of the
sideboard it did nothing productive. With apparent
regret the French Customs guys returned my documents
and signalled that I was free to continue my journey.

Including the border inspection I was stopped by
French police four times during that journey from the
Spanish border up to the Channel port of Cherbourg.
Then, to add insult to injury, the police there carefully
examined everything again before letting me board
the ferry.

By now I was becoming something of an expert in
searches and the techniques thereof. Strange, I thought,
how these guys always seemed to stop single male
drivers. This only shows my naivety at that time. What
I didn't understand was that I was driving up the Hash
Highway, the most notorious trade route for the
shipment of illegal drugs from Spain into northern
Europe.

Safely back in the UK the sideboard was entered into
a local fine-arts auction and later realized a 100 per
cent profit. I was pleased that I had proved to myself, if
not to the rest of the family, that white kitchen goods

could be exported to Spain. Return loads with carefully chosen pieces of furniture for the UK market completed the picture and reduced the travelling expenses to virtually nothing. I could look forward to the hard but enjoyable work of building up a business from scratch, a job that was right up my street.

On my next journey to Spain a few weeks later I took Nick along with me. He is the youngest of Kath's sons and at that time was 18 years old. Never a scholarly type he was good with his hands and a hard worker but was struggling to get a decent start in the rural area where we lived. He was unemployed for the moment and fancied the idea of a complete change of scene. Personally I liked the idea of some company and of somebody else to do the lifting and carrying instead of me.

During the next two months things progressed pretty well. We soon discovered which goods sold and which didn't. Second-hand microwaves, table-top washers, fridges and freezers are sought-after commodities in southern Spain. Back in the UK the English will apparently buy anything that has an old-fashioned Spanish look about it, and in my experience the darker the wood the easier it will sell.

For entertainment I was having fun watching Nick's antics with the local girls. An attractively lithe lad with a pleasant personality he seemed to have an almost magnetic attraction for females of all ages. As the youngest boy he had always been fussed over by neighbours and relatives. Now he was being fussed over by women who had more basic designs on him, and he was loving every minute of it.

Most nights after work we would shower and set off

into town to eat and grab a beer. As the winter gave way to spring tourists started to arrive in ever greater numbers, like blossom appearing on a tree. This was manna from heaven for Nick; it was as if he had access to his own private harem. He would swagger around posing, brazenly going from table to table and bar to bar chatting up girls indiscriminately. Clearly I was out of touch with how the scene works because as obvious as he was he inevitably stayed behind when I returned at night to the pension. I could sometimes hear him creeping in as dawn was breaking.

Carmen realized what he was up to, but this didn't make her impervious to his cheeky charms. It's never been confirmed, but a couple of times I noticed that particular eye contact and knowing looks passing between them that always signals carnal knowledge. The dirty, lucky bastard.

Being in a place like Fuengirola ensures it isn't long before you come face to face with drugs and the drug scene. Pushers are easy to spot, and we often used to sit outside bars watching their activities as they plied their trade more or less openly outside the discos and nightclubs.

They would target small groups of teenage tourists, approach them and engage them in short, whispered conversations, usually followed by head shaking or a surreptitious handover. Ecstasy, speed and hash were sold relatively freely on the street. Coke was not popular with tourists because they couldn't afford it, and it wasn't a drug with which they were familiar on the UK nightclub scene.

The results of the trade could be viewed from about midnight onwards. Couples or groups would wander into the road, falling over, staggering or skipping like children in a park, completely oblivious to traffic, the stares of passers-by or the presence of the police. If you have ever sat outside a disco in southern Spain and watched the young revellers then you certainly understand the terms 'off your face' and 'out of your head'. When on a high or tripping they have no sense of danger or responsibility to themselves or anyone else, and it is surprising to me that so few of these people are killed or injured.

I've seen scantily clad girls jump in the sea still drinking or smoking, with their shoes on and their handbags swinging from their shoulders. I've witnessed teenage lads running at full pelt down the middle of the road screaming blood-curdling threats and insults to passing cars and taxis, contemptuous of the dangers of moving vehicles only inches away from them. Voyeurs can have the time of their life wandering the beach in the early-morning hours. Frenetic fumbling and humping seems to be everywhere, with occasional muffled screams as yet another holiday-maker seals the romance of the day. A late-night walk on the beach is instructive and provides an insight into the permissive society of today. Forget the swinging 60s. It's all happening on Spanish beaches with the 90s' nightly love-ins.

During the wee small hours is when the dealers appear in their shiny BMW cabriolets or astride chromed Harley Davidson motorcycles. Cruising the streets with their sycophants, stereos blasting reggae beats, they smoke and chat with their pavement-treading minions as they crawl along, ignored by the police in their dark-blue Seat patrol cars.

The police just seem to sit like neutral observers in their cars parked on street corners. Windows open, they smoke and watch the activities going on before them. An occasional burst of car horns or a prolonged scream will draw their attention momentarily. They might look in the direction of the noise, but after a couple of seconds unconcernedly turn back round, laugh and continue smoking. Sometimes they climb from their cars, stretch and walk over to a bar, where they chew the fat with the owner or a waiter and drink a coffee or a *cerveza* before wandering back to the car, the epitome of boredom.

From time to time they rush off down the road, lights blazing and tyres squealing in response to a radio call. Considering the number of arrestable offences being enacted in front of them I always wondered what type of major event must be in progress to require such a display of energy. Later I would find out for myself.

The police on the Costa del Sol have a declared softly-softly policy towards tourists. This is understandable, because it is ultimately holiday-makers who keep the whole community ticking over. Remove them, and the whole economy would collapse within a year. Unfortunately by not policing firmly the authorities are perhaps seen to condone open drug abuse.

Belatedly the police have begun to realize the problems they have created, as family groups now tend to avoid the older Spanish resorts. These are increasingly populated only by property-owning expatriate pensioners who share the bars with beer-swilling lager louts of both sexes desperately seeking a couple of weeks' sun, booze and sex. It's like dying and going to heaven for the pissheads and druggies.

Further evidence of the drug trade can be found in the darkened corners of back alleys. There teenagers of both sexes who have followed the lure of a good time and travelled to Spain for work can often be found selling their bodies for a few hundred pesetas a time.

The summer travellers seeking work find a job in a bar, cafe or disco. But then they need visas or work permits, which they can't easily obtain, and so they jump from bar to bar in an effort to stay one step ahead of the local police. The downside of this existence is that the bar owners know their plight and some pay pitifully inadequate wages. There are many casual workers who work a 12-hour day for 2000 pesetas, about £10.00. They work in the kitchens in unbearable temperatures or end up serving tables, constantly with a weather eye out for the police.

Still in search of a dream these youngsters visit the discos after work, but they haven't the money to buy drinks at the exorbitant prices charged in the clubs. So they buy an ecstasy tablet for a few hundred pesetas, believing the effects are the same. Get out of your head, forget your problems for a few hours, that's the Costa philosophy in a nutshell.

Many don't realize they are on the slippery down slope until it's too late. Spending their money on drugs and fags they party all night. When they then can't perform well at work, or they start to look pasty, ill nourished and used up, the charitable bar owners kick them out and offer their job to the next appealing bright young thing to appear on the doorstep.

Some of this black-market abused labour is processed further and appears on street corners selling time shares or working as 'proppers'. Everyone who has been on holiday to Spain has at some time been approached by a bright youngster bearing an armful of cheap invitation flyers. Whether a young provocatively dressed girl targeting the male punters or a tall, tanned Gladiator-type for the women pedestrians, they invite you to a club or bar and promise a wild night of enjoyment complete with a free drink on entry. They are propositioning you, hence the term 'proppers'. Successful proppers can earn good commission, depending on how many luckless punters they can entice into their employers' bar. These jobs are much sought after, and I have witnessed many a street scuffle as proppers fight to protect their turf on a busy street corner.

If they can't get a time share or propping job many disillusioned and broke youngsters drag their sorry butts home, no doubt spouting to their mates about what a great time they've had in Spain. The really unlucky ones progress further down the spiral and end up selling themselves, or, worse, acting as pushers for the more established peddlers and dealers.

Unwittingly they form the vanguard of the drug world. They are the infantry, sent out in large numbers as cannon fodder. If they succeed they sell drugs to other similar-aged tourists; if they are caught by the police they are quickly tried and summarily condemned to prison sentences of anything up to five years.

Rival pushers often fight both inside and outside clubs. The fights are short and brutal. A 20 year old from Britain is not normally mentally or physically equipped for a street brawl with another desperate youth from a *barrio* in South America. A flash of a knife or a broken glass, and it's all over; another casualty of the drug war at its lowest level will traipse home, whimpering, carrying a scar for the rest of their sorry lives as a constant reminder that the school of life can be a bastard for the unprepared.

The dealers like the generals of old stand back and watch as their infantry take the fall, either in a police raid or to a rival pusher. Each pusher only carries a small quantity of drugs at any time in an effort to reduce losses if they are nicked or mugged. This encourages the pushers in the belief that the dealer has their interests at heart. So the investment in each pusher is minimal and the risk to the dealer insignificant. If a pusher falls it's no big deal. There's always some other poor bugger desperate for a few quid who will rush to fill the shoes of a luckless predecessor.

The rewards for a successful pusher are excellent when compared with the wages paid in the bars. On a good night they can make upwards of 25,000 pesetas or £125. With no taxes and working every night, they are making reasonable money, and of course, another spin-off is that they can then buy drugs for themselves at discounted rates.

Suddenly with spare cash in their pockets they reappear on the streets wearing expensive Nike trainers and sporting clothes carrying inordinately large manufacturers' logos, thereby advertising their street credibility and selling prowess. Apparently they don't stop to think that the police can recognize all the symbols of their newly acquired wealth and thus know exactly who to target during one of their periodic purges.

I bet the drug peddlers and dealers don't tell the newly recruited pushers that the Spanish have built a new prison at the small inland town of Alhaurin el Grande. This jail has one large wing dedicated to holding only foreign prisoners, which is full to overflowing. Living in the intolerable heat and cramped conditions are many young Britons of both sexes who thought they had the system beaten.

This sad comment on modern life is not confined to the British youngsters. I have met Irish, Swedish and Dutch beauties, Germans, French and many South American cuties all swimming in the same sewer. Strangely enough most of the bigger dealers are Spanish or British, and there is a pretty large Dutch contingent on the Costa too, but other nationalities are few in number. Maybe the British are either the most gullible or the most greedy, but I don't know which is correct because I've met many of both categories.

I didn't know it at the time, but I was about to drop out of the safe, comfortable world I had always inhabited and jump headlong into this pool of amoral sharks who display all the human sensibilities of decency, honour and kindness of an Auschwitz guard.

With the onset of the full tourist season the roads were becoming busier by the day, and many of the smaller streets and back ways were blocked with hire cars. Driving the Mercedes van was thus becoming more of a problem. It was too big to be handled comfortably, and of course being a right-hand drive model I was seated on the wrong side of the road. I decided to hunt around for a more suitable left-hand-drive car or van.

Enquiries amongst the British expats whom I knew led to Colin Benson, a man who bought and sold second-hand cars. I eventually got hold of his phone number and called him. I expressed my interest in buying a car, and we arranged to meet later that week at the home of Doug, a mutual acquaintance.

Doug was from an upper-class family, and he came complete with a plummy voice and a charming air of culture despite his pathetic lifestyle. He reminded me of one of the seedy lead characters from the cult film *Withnail and I*. He was in his mid-30s, as gay as they come and with a witty and humorous camp attitude that endeared him to older women and caused him to be ridiculed by macho men. He made a basic living selling china and porcelain figurines and poor- quality prints at car boot sales. It was good fun to stand in the markets with him watching as he whistled at the shorts-clad younger male tourists and the ever present Spanish gays — although I noticed that I did develop a deeper voice when out with him.

Doug lived about 20 miles inland amongst the solitary goatherders. His family had bought him a few acres of upland scrub upon which stood a small cottage. Though prettily decorated and incorporating a beautiful Spanish tiled floor it had only three rooms. The modern necessities of running water, electricity and access roads were things non-existent, to which Doug always claimed he would attend when he had the time and the money. Sometime never, I thought, looking around. It took him all his efforts just to scrape together enough money to feed himself and his menagerie of dogs.

So I made the first move along the route to meeting Benson. The Chinese must have a meaningful phrase for such a start on a path of fate, but I don't know what it is.

Colin Benson is British born, from Lancashire, and was then in his late 40s. He is not very tall but broad and heavily built with a chest and arms that look oddly out of place on his short frame. An ex-boxer, the good life and a thirst for whisky have given him a rounded, comical appearance that belies his true nature. He looks like a butterball, but he is a hardball. The years haven't been too friendly to him, and he looks older than he is. With his well-coiffured head of thinning grey hair and affable, self-deprecating smile, his Benny Hill glasses give him a comical look. A broad Lancashire accent and a big cigar in his mouth convey a first impression of a moderately well-off semi-retired businessman, a look he cultivates with exquisite care.

Benson claims to be a dealer in second-hand cars and caravans, occasionally selling boats or other expensive, glitzy toys. Well known in the British expat community he also operates as moneylender to other expats who have need of a quick loan. He doesn't use written contracts but rather agrees a date for repayment with an arbitrary sum of interest. Defaulters have been known to suffer beatings; their cars have mysteriously vanished or been set on fire or their apartments or villas burgled.

I know many people who wouldn't argue with Colin Benson, and I recognize him now as a hardened criminal already with a long prison sentence behind him. But like most professional criminals he can wear the mask. His street cunning guides and protects him, and he can be the life and soul of a party and an affable friend when he wants. However, his disguise of geniality can drop in an instant chameleon-like to reveal the darker, truer side of his personality.

When I first met him he was, of course, Mr Affability himself. He offered me a diesel-engine Land-Rover Discovery, left-hand drive on English plates, complete with a current tax disc on the windscreen. The car was ridiculously cheap at £7000, which he justified by spinning a yarn about a bar owner in another resort whose wife had left him. The man was quickly cashing in and selling up, and he knew a 'left hooker' was not worth much in the UK.

Colin professed he was organizing the sale without profit to himself. He was merely doing a favour for a mate who was struggling. Obviously I thought, Oh, oh, a stolen car, but Benson showed me the DVLA Vehicle Registration Document for the Land-Rover. I inspected it carefully and compared it with the one belonging to the van. It was not a copy. I held the paper up to the sunlight and could clearly see it bore the same watermark and the correct typeface. Everything seemed perfectly in order.

Swayed by the price I became the proud owner of a Discovery. Benson seemed a charming guy, and I had no hesitation in accepting his invitation to a weekend barbecue at his villa. On Saturday afternoon Nick and I drove up to Cartama, the village where he lived in a beautiful villa, built on the crest of a small hill with a private drive that led to tall wrought-iron gates and the villa itself beyond. It was set in a couple of acres of land built up in a form of wide terracing. The lawned garden included a tiled swimming pool, barbecue, sweeping gravel drive and a large carport.

Brick-built kennels were ranged along the lower terrace area. They apparently also ran a hotel for dogs. It was an impressive array of about 20 large kennels divided into two blocks, each with its own private run and separated one from the other by galvanized fencing. This was no rickety, slipshod construction common to the inland villages. It had obviously been carefully designed and built and was now well tended. On the lowest terrace level, adjacent to the road frontage, was a storage and display area for caravans and the odd speedboat. Served by another set of iron gates the whole area was enclosed by quality chain-link fencing and covered by mast-set floodlights. It was a very imposing set-up.

Up the hill at the villa we were given a quick tour by Susan, introduced to me as Colin's wife. Later I discovered she was in fact his long-term, live-in girlfriend. Their home was tastefully furnished with a pine bar, an imposing local stone fireplace and marble-tile flooring. Not bad for a Lancashire lad I remember thinking as I sat down on a patio chair. The barbecue itself was well attended with neighbours and friends coming and going throughout the afternoon. We had good food, and there was beer and wine on tap. All in all it was a pleasant way to spend a Saturday afternoon.

Later when the eating was over and most of the guests had departed Colin sat down with me to share a few drinks. In expansive mood he told me how he operated as a dealer in cars, caravans and boats. He would trade locally, as in the case of my Discovery, or he would buy from the UK and sell into the ex-patriate community in Spain. He said he frequently travelled backwards and forwards to the UK tying up deals and spent a lot of time going up and down the Spanish Costas. He certainly seemed to know his way around Alicante, Benidorm and Javea on the Costa Blanca.

He expressed a deal of interest in my fledgling business, and driving back to the coast later that evening Nick and I reflected upon what a good contact we had made. Benson seemed to know everyone and certainly had fingers in a lot of different pies. Obviously life on the Costa was working well for him as his large house and apparently relaxed lifestyle bore witness.

A week or so later I was due to return to the UK to collect another load of goods. A couple of nights before we were ready to leave Colin telephoned me and asked if I could do him a favour when I was in the UK. He had sold a car to a guy on the coast near Nerja, he said. The customer was from Manchester and wanted to pay in sterling. Colin didn't want the money to go through a bank account because, as he said, the less the tax man knew the better. He said that if I could call into Manchester and collect the money, about £8000, then he would pay me for my expenses and trouble. OK, I thought, this isn't a problem. I could do him a favour and get paid for it.

So when we got back to the UK I dropped Nick off at home and phoned the number Colin had given me. I made arrangements to meet a man called Mark in Harry Ramsden's fish and chip restaurant near Granada Studios in Manchester. I duly arrived and found Mark in the reception area, who handed me a sealed padded Jiffy-bag-type envelope addressed to

Colin Benson, Malaga. Everything was very relaxed and friendly, but I declined fish and chips and left after a quick chat to return home. I thought no more of the matter until I returned to Spain.

On the business front matters were still going well, and I was negotiating to buy a container load of second-hand fridges, freezers and washers. These were trade-in appliances from various electricity-board shops around the country. The prices were ridiculously cheap per item, and each appliance was tested and came complete with an electrical test certificate. I could easily view this as the springboard we needed to really make the business take off. I decided to make enquiries about renting a warehouse with a loading dock when I returned to Spain.

Nick and I drove back to Spain again, and after our arrival I visited Colin and gave him the envelope, exactly as it was given to me. He opened it and counted out the money, apparently it was correct. I was surprised when he gave me £200 for my trouble. I thanked him, and, after making arrangements to see him later for a drink in town, I left.

One day later Nick came storming in madly waving around a 2000 peseta note. Normally equivalent to around £10, this one was in fact worth nothing. It was a forgery, and he had just tried to hand it over in a local shop, where quite rightly they had refused to accept it. We decided it must have been passed to him in his change in a bar the previous night. Upon inspection I could see it was obviously a poor-quality counterfeit. There was no watermarking, the colours were blurred, and one edge was very ragged. Nick put it back in his pocket, and after a good laugh about it I forgot about the matter.

Later that week we were having a drink with Colin in a bar in Benalmadena when Nick pulled out the note and showed it to Colin. He inspected it and laughed, telling Nick he was a dickhead for being tricked into taking such a poor forgery. Without more ado he took out his wallet and showed Nick another 2000 peseta note. 'That's the real McCoy,' he declared proudly.

On the table top we could easily distinguish the fake from the real note. Then he pulled out another note, indistinguishable from the previous one, so now there were two real notes and one fake on the table.

'Now then, lads,' he said, 'which is genuine and which is fake?' I didn't know it then, but we were about to hit a watershed in our dealings with Mr Benson. Nick and I both pointed to Nick's poor-quality forgery, but Benson only smiled and pointed instead to the original note he had placed on the table.

'That's a proper bit of hooky money,' he said, 'not that bit of old tat,' indicating Nick's fake. I stared at him, and in the words of Bertie Wooster, 'The scales had fallen from our eyes.'

Benson looked over and could see me grappling with the situation. I will always remember him relaxing in the chair and smiling smugly at my discomfiture. I should have just shot the bastard there and then, and if I had known what was to come I probably would have. But not having a crystal ball to reveal the dangers ahead, I just sat there and listened as he told us both the story of counterfeit money operations on the Costa del Sol. He did so by distancing himself and telling the story as a third party. He told us he had a mate 'up the coast' who made a living in 'hooky' money. But neither of us believed him. He knew too much about the job not to be involved himself in some way.

The way it works is this. Medium-value foreign denomination notes are produced in south London. The big operators are active in Spain, Portugal, the Greek Islands and Malta. They move from country to country dependent on the seriousness of police hassle. If a government issues a new design of note to beat the forgers, the counterfeiters move in immediately. They quickly obtain forgeries of the new notes and hit the designated country before the shop and bar merchants are themselves familiar with the new design.

At that time they were working Spain with 2000 and 5000 peseta denomination notes. These are shipped down in bulk by couriers in camper vans, touring caravans and cars. That is what the Guardia Civil guys had been looking for at the border crossing all those months before when they had wanted to check out my van contents.

In Spain the organizer rents a couple of cheap apartments in different run-down tourist areas, always paying in cash in advance. Next small-time petty thieves are recruited from the UK, usually from the foyers of magistrates' courts up and down the country. The organizers sit in court and listen to the cases until they see someone they fancy. They proposition them outside and offer them a couple of weeks in the sun, wages and an aeroplane ticket. Not surprisingly they don't have any trouble recruiting staff, especially in the deprived inner-city areas of Liverpool, Birmingham, Manchester and London.

Life has been made slightly harder for the organizers
now. In the early days anyone could obtain a 12-
month British Visitor's Passport on demand at a main
post office. Now British Visitor's Passports are obsolete,
so they have to obtain full ten-year ones. These cost
more, more stringent checks are made before their
issue, and they generally take a few weeks to obtain.

Still, having recruited a team of up to 10 or 15 staff,
they are shipped as tourists in groups of five or so
down to Spain. Briefed in their apartments they are told
they will work in units of two or three for up to eight
hours each day. One of them sits on a hired motor
scooter wearing a sports shoulder bag and the other
two work the bars, cafes, shops and kiosks up and
down the town. Markets and night-time bars are their
favourite spots.

The techniques used are easy to spot if you know
what to look for. A teenager enters a bar and asks for a
Coke or Fanta never a beer or they would be pissed as
rats after a few hours and tenders a 2000 peseta note. If
pushed he or she will frantically search through shorts
pockets and come up with loose change that is a few
coppers short.

The greedy shopkeeper won't sell a drink cheap,
so he takes the offered note and gives about 1900
pesetas change. The whole deal takes less than two
minutes. The teenager nods his thanks, sips his drink
and coolly walks out of the bar back to his mate on
the scooter just around the corner, where he collects
another note and tries his luck at the next bar. They
continue to work at that rate for a couple of hours
before having a break and switching to a different area
or town or another village.

the spanish connection

It is an easy business. If a shopkeeper spots the fake then the teenager, who is still pale and obviously a newly arrived tourist on his holidays, pleads ignorance. If the police are called he is searched, but obviously he has no other fake notes on his person. Sophisticated gangs operate by ensuring each operator has another genuine 2000 peseta note and a 5000 peseta note in his pocket, thereby indicating to a policeman that he hasn't pulled a scam on purpose and that in fact he tendered the fake by chance. At that time he starts objecting and claims that someone must have passed the fake note to him. This is usually enough to swing the argument, and the brazen operator moves off. He will be back at work a few hours later with a change of clothing in a different area.

The profits that can be obtained in a planned operation after a two-week period are astronomical. Imagine fifteen teenagers working in five gangs with ten scamming every five or ten minutes or so for eight hours every day. Giving them a couple of days off for a rest and some sunbathing time the organizers stand to make a gross profit of between £20,000 and £30,000 in a two-week period.

The cost of the counterfeit notes varies according to quality. Good fakes that will pass an ultraviolet lamp detector can sell, at the height of the season, for nearly half their face value. The organizers clear at least £5000 per week on that scam. Who said crime doesn't pay? These criminals are making big money whilst taking very little personal risk.

At the end of the fortnight the teenage villains are flown home, a few hundred pounds better off and having enjoyed a working holiday. If they are caught they can usually talk their way out of a tricky situation, but even if they are arrested the worst they can look forward to is being thrown out of the country. So there is virtually no deterrent to either the petty criminals at the sharp end of the operation or to the organizers who reap their ill-gotten gains with apparent impunity.

After his discourse Benson sat back again in his chair looking like the cat that had got the cream. He went on to tell us that he was a middleman operating between the London counterfeiters and the organizers based in Spain. He himself did not operate the gangs of youths, but he claimed he made a profit by handling the bulk packages of notes that were delivered from the UK, splitting down the packages and passing them on to the local organizers. Presumably he must have known where the main consignment of notes was stored, which I thought was quite a heavy responsibility.

After unburdening himself Benson began to play down his role, saying that he had only a minor involvement. His main business was dealing in cars and caravans, but he saw this as an opportunity to make a few pounds on the side. Looking at him, he didn't appear to be the archetypal villain. He was a businessman with a family and a large circle of friends, and it was easy to believe he was just playing on the edges of the counterfeiting racket and was not one of its prime movers and shakers.

I didn't want to give the impression that we were shocked by Benson's revelations, and that afternoon we had a few more drinks and a bite to eat with him. I finished off the meeting by telling him that we were travelling back to the UK within a week. Quick as a flash he asked if I would pick up the proceeds of another car deal for him, this time from the London area. Thinking of the expenses money, I agreed. He told me I was to collect £10,000 from a man called Jim, and he gave me Jim's telephone number and asked me to call him and make specific arrangements when I was back in the UK.

I didn't know it then, but Benson had just asked me to contact directly a man who was on every policing agency's wanted list. He was a priority target, a known heavy with drug and firearms connections that spread deep into the London criminal underworld. I was going to meet him like a lamb to the slaughter.

4

HM Customs & Excise
Drugbusters

The tourist season was by now well under way in Europe. The roads were busy, and there were many touring caravans, camper vans and motorbikes in evidence up and down the highways, clogging service areas and cross-Channel ferries alike. Arriving in Portsmouth again we disembarked from the ferry, and I decided to ring Colin's mate Jim so that I could collect the money on the drive up north. I telephoned him from the ferry port, and Jim was very accommodating. We made arrangements to meet the same day at the South Mimms service area on the M25. I phoned Kath and told her we would be home in time for tea.

The interior of the van was like an oven as we motored up the M3 and on to the M25 in brilliant sunshine. We did the long crawling swing through the widening scheme road works up to the M25 services, and when I got out there I soon spotted Jim in the small specialist coffee shop inside.

He was sitting with a very attractive and expensively dressed young lady. Jim himself was short and slim with a receding head of hair, and he spoke with a thick

London accent. He told me he was an electrician and had an interest in a second-hand car dealership, selling 'prestige motors, Jags, Beamers, Rollers and all that'. He added that he had known Colin for a few years and did a few deals with him. I tried to imagine Jim as a counterfeiter, but to my mind he didn't fit the image. I collected the money from him, wrapped in an unsealed Sainsbury's plastic carrier bag, and promised to deliver it as soon as I got back to Spain.

Jim was an interesting guy, and we sat through a couple of cups of coffee whilst I told him about my export and import business. I thought he seemed genuinely interested. Driving up the M1 later I felt more at ease. I must admit I had been slightly concerned about meeting Jim and had decided on the way up from Spain that if I thought he was dodgy then I wouldn't have anything more to do with Benson or his cohorts.

Nick and I sold more furniture at auctions and loaded up again with white goods we headed off to Spain. Whilst at home I had bought myself a Honda Goldwing motorbike. It was a beauty, nearly three years old with low mileage, and it had previously been owned by an older biker who had obviously treated it with loving care. There wasn't a mark on it. I planned to drive it down to Spain as soon as I could and use it for the summer.

A few weeks later back in Spain Benson asked me if I would deliver some packages for an old friend in Manchester on my next run home to the UK. Subject to having enough room in the van I agreed, and subsequently he delivered two sealed boxes. These were well wrapped, and each had an inventory fastened to the side. The lists claimed that the contents were business papers and stationery. As we loaded the boxes into the van Benson offered me £500 to deliver them into London.

Stop, I thought, this wasn't right. Nobody pays £500 for a delivery of two tea-chest size boxes. Any international removal company would deliver them both for £100 maximum. I jumped from the van and set about Benson. It was only when I threatened to open the boxes to check out the contents that he relented. He told me that each contained 10 kg of cannabis, or 'gear' as it is called. I went wild, but Benson just stood there looking at me as if it was the most normal thing in the world to inveigle someone into carrying drugs across international borders. He upped the offer to £1000 and said if I brought down the cash payment too then he would pay me £1500.

I was stunned. This guy was unreal. I backed off a little and calmed down. Sensing victory Benson said that I should think about £1500 profit and give him a call, after which he loaded the boxes back into his car, told me to call him later and then drove off. He seemed supremely confident. In his mind I suppose he had been testing me out by asking me to collect money, introducing me to his friends and then telling Nick and me about the counterfeit money operation.

I hadn't been too concerned about the counterfeit money. To my mind it didn't hurt anyone. You never saw a newspaper report about someone dying after spending it or because they had been given some in their change at a shop. Like many people I equated counterfeiting as a 'bit of a con' and not too important. Drugs were a different thing altogether. I'd never taken them myself — I get my kicks from a bottle — but I'd seen the effects they can have on the lives of ordinary folk. You could see ruined people every day in Benidorm, Alicante, Torremolinos and Fuengirola, in fact in any town on the Spanish Costas, and much of it was down to drugs.

Drugs are destructive. The effects are bad, and the penalties for people mixed up with them are very serious. No, sir, I did not want to get mixed up with drugs at any price. Benson obviously thought the offer of a couple of thousand pounds or so would be enough to buy off my initial fright. He had only seen one side of my life: a family man struggling to get a business off the ground by buying and selling second-hand equipment. He had not seen our home in the UK and didn't know anything of our history. We had never been involved in anything like this. Like many people I could look the other way if I were offered something cheap occasionally, but that was all.

I wouldn't say I had a strong social conscience or was a great moral crusader, but we all have our own values, and when we are put up against it, then we have to make a decision. I made mine right there and then.

I felt weak at the knees after Benson had left and quickly packed up the van, collected all the paperwork and drove into town to find Nick. Having spotted him chatting up a young hopeful I nearly dragged him into the van, and we then promptly set off towards Granada, our first route marker on the road back to the UK. During the first part of the journey I told Nick about what had transpired with Benson.

It was obvious to me now that I was in trouble here because to my mind all the money I had brought down for him was money for drugs. I had been used as a 'mule'.

Things started to drop into place. Benson's interest in my business and the number of trips I was making between the UK and Spain; routes I was taking; what happened when I was stopped. All these questions now seemed to make sense to me. It was a pretty pensive time during that journey back to the UK. Funnily enough we weren't stopped once for a check during the entire run.

Back home Kath and I sat down for some serious talking. As a mother and a nurse Kath has always been totally against drugs, although it wasn't something we had come up against as a family. We had seen plenty of people smoking hash in Benidorm years earlier, and we were familiar with the unique aroma that is given off from burning hash in a joint. Drugs were something other people did. We were distanced from them, and we had never been involved with any drug users, let alone drug dealers, as far as we knew. Now the situation had changed dramatically. We talked for hours and hours, far into the night. Finally we decided to call the police and tell them what had happened.

The next day I phoned the Manchester police drug squad. I spoke for a while with Helen, a policewoman, and explained to her my predicament. I soon realized she wasn't very interested and asked her why. She told me that drugs outside the country and their importation into the UK was a matter for Customs & Excise and not a police affair. So she gave me a London telephone number, and we left it at that.

I called the number in London, but there was no answer. As it was a Sunday, I decided to leave it until the following day. On Monday I called the London number again and had a long talk with the Customs officer who answered the phone. He was very interested in what I had to say, and the upshot of the conversation was that I should phone the Manchester number he gave me for the Northern Area Drug Investigation Unit.

When I called there, I spoke with a man called Rob. This was not like a regular civil-service line. For a start the phone was answered with 'Hello, can I help you?' There was no announcement of department or any other information. It all seemed a little spylike right from the outset.

Rob and I spoke on the phone at great length. I gave him my number, and he called me back at home. He said he would like to meet, and that he would bring along a colleague too. That was OK with me, and we made arrangements to meet up at the Hartshead services on the M62 the next day. Both Kath and I felt more relaxed about the situation now, and we continued throughout the day to make plans for the next trip to Spain. Naively I had thought that when I told the Customs guys what I knew they would arrest Benson and his mates, and that would be that. With the situation normal again I would be able to carry on with developing the business both in Spain and the UK.

In the middle of the afternoon the phone rang, and Kath answered it. After saying hello a few times and listening for a reply she hung up. 'Strange,' she said, 'I could hear breathing, but nobody spoke. How weird.'

About half an hour later both the dogs started barking, and a car drew part way up our long drive, blocking it completely. Two men got out and stood in the driveway behind the five-bar gate that led into the garden and house area. I noticed one of them had his hand in his pocket.

Not acquainted with either of them I said, 'Hello, can I help you?'

'You owe us ten grand, and we've come to collect,' one of them said. As soon as he spoke I recognized a London accent and thought to myself, This is trouble. The situation immediately crystallized for me. Benson's drug deals, carrying cash to Spain, London accents, car blocking the exit. Boy, we were in the shit.

'Just a minute,' I said and quickly turned round and went back into the house, shutting the door behind me. Outside our two German Shepherds continued barking furiously.

I rushed into the kitchen, picked up the phone and dialled 999. It seemed for ever before the operator answered. I asked for the police, and after quickly giving my number and so on they finally answered.

'There are some men in my driveway, and they're armed. They're Londoners, and they are demanding £10,000. You'd better get someone round here quickly,' I hissed urgently into the phone.

The operator was very calm and collected. 'Who are they? Do you know their names? Are they in a vehicle? What is its registration number?' I could answer none of this series of quick-fire questions. He must have realized then he was dealing with a dickhead and said calmly, 'Officers are on the way, sir. Try to remain calm and stay inside your house until they arrive.' I hung up.

It was too late, though, because Kath had gone out of the back door and was shouting at the men. 'Who do you think you are? What do you want? We don't owe you any money. You're a bunch of gangsters! Well, you can sod off. We've called the police and they're on their way now.' Brilliant, Kath! I thought, now they might shoot us just out of spite.

Instead the slightly bemused exchange they shared during Kath's tirade of abuse at them quickly changed to looks of concern. At this point they walked back towards the car. Belatedly I noted it was a big, burgundy Rover saloon. They climbed in shouting, 'We'll be back for our money, you bastards!' and underlining their threat by waving what looked like a shotgun in my direction, they reversed out of the drive at great speed and raced off, tyres squealing, down the road.

'Come on, Kath,' I urged, 'we're getting out of here.' Kath grabbed Natalie, and they quickly pulled on their coats and shoes whilst I called 999 again. I was quickly put through and got the same police operator again. 'It's OK. We told them the police were on the way, and they headed off in their car towards Gainsborough. They are driving a burgundy-coloured Rover saloon, and there seem to be four people in it. I'm sorry I didn't get the registration number, but they definitely have a shotgun.'

I could hear the operator relaying the car's description to someone else. 'We're getting out of here. I'll speak to you later,' I said and hung up again before he could reply.

With that Kath, Natalie and I jumped into Kath's car and hightailed it out of the drive. I took a back-lane route I knew, weaving circuitously between potato and sugar-beet fields, and headed for the motorway. One of the problems with living in a remote location is that you are isolated in the event of an emergency. Stories abound in the village pubs of the length of time it takes for the emergency services to arrive. The problem isn't helped by the lack of road- and street-name signs and the almost total lack of streetlighting. I knew it would take the police at least ten or fifteen minutes to arrive in the area and find our farm. By that time we were on the M180 motorway heading towards Leeds.

After a calming cigarette we assessed the situation. Natalie was crying, more with the shock of sudden events than with fear. Kath was shaking like a leaf and desperately trying not to cry herself. I myself was alternating between fear and a great tide of anger that was building up in my chest.

'Right, I've had enough of this shit,' I said, and I pulled off the motorway at the next exit and found a payphone. I called the Customs number in Manchester. 'Let me speak with Rob,' I said brusquely. Rob came to the phone almost immediately.

'Hi, Rob,' I said and went on to introduce myself. 'Listen, things are moving pretty damn fast here,' I announced, and I went on to relate to him the afternoon's events. 'I want to see you now, so that you can nail these bastards before someone gets seriously hurt.' By this time I was fuming.

'OK, John, calm down,' he urged. 'I can meet you about six o'clock tonight, where we agreed before. We will arrive in a dark-blue Orion, and we'll wait for you in the café area. See you then. Meanwhile I'll make some calls and check up on what's happening.'

With a curt 'Bye' I hung up. Back in the car I related the conversation to Kath, and we set off back towards the motorway. We arrived at the services rendezvous about an hour later and decided to book ourselves into the Travel Lodge motel on the site overnight. Luckily Kath had her credit cards with her.

the spanish connection

We checked in, and Kath bathed Natalie. Then we visited the cafeteria and had some food. The resilience of children to adapt to new and strange situations amazed me. Natalie seemed completely recovered from the ordeal and showed more interest in playing in the amusement arcade at the side of the café than in the afternoon's events. After the meal Natalie took herself off to the arcade, and Kath and I had another talk, whilst keeping a watchful eye on the arcade entrance for Natalie. We agreed that the day's turn of events were awful, and that I should assist the Customs, and as a consequence the police, in every way possible to have these criminals tracked down, arrested and taken off the streets.

Just before 6 pm Kath took Natalie to the motel room, and I went outside to watch out for the blue Orion. I waited for ages outside. After about half an hour it still hadn't arrived, and I was becoming increasingly pissed off. I went back into the café and had a look at all the new arrivals again as they sat there eating and drinking. No obvious contenders stood out. I went outside again and continued my vigil.

After a few minutes a guy in jeans and a black leather jacket walked up to me and said quietly, 'Hi, John, I'm Rob. Why don't we go for a chat in my car?'

I was amazed. I had noticed the same guy walking into the phone box from the car park, but he certainly hadn't arrived in a blue Orion. Now he walked me over to a red Sierra and opened the back door. I saw there was another man in the passenger seat. I hesitated. 'It's OK, John, this is my partner Steve. Sorry about the car thing. We just wanted to have a look at you. Make sure you were on the level, and that you weren't being

74

followed by anyone. Everything seems OK so you can get in the car, and we'll try and sort things out.' He smiled encouragingly at me.

I climbed numbly into the rear seat. Steve introduced himself and flashed a wallet at me, just like the cops do in American films. But, other than seeing his photo on a card, I didn't have a clue what it said. Steve seemed to understand, and he smiled and said, 'We're the good guys, John. Listen, rather than talk all squeezed together in the car, why don't we go into the café and grab a coffee? It'll be more relaxing all round.' Steve with his modulated public-school accent somehow immediately put me at ease, while Rob hadn't endeared himself to me in the first few minutes of conversation.

So off we went into the café where we sat down with steaming mugs of coffee. Rob pulled out a pad, and looking like three men just having a chat after work we started talking in earnest.

Apart from reading Len Deighton spy thrillers and watching the occasional TV film about undercover cops I had not had any contact with any semi-secret organizations before in my life. Nor had I known anyone else who had any experience of dealing with the police or Customs. The nearest I had been to a Customs officer was at Manchester airport in the days when the personal cigarettes and booze duty-free allowances were strictly enforced, and my baggage had been checked over late one night by a bored counter jockey.

I instinctively believed this was the real thing. These guys were pros; it was obvious from their demeanour and bearing. They were quietly spoken, confident and seemed to understand everything I was telling them. They nodded together in an almost hypnotic rhythm as if it were a story they had heard many times before. Rob took copious notes, while Steve kept the conversation rolling.

I developed a quick rapport with Steve, and in an almost good cop/bad cop routine Rob left the talking to him whilst I unburdened myself. I told them everything. From the failure of the staff agency because of the Gulf War up to the latest events of that day. I missed out nothing, occasionally stopping to light a cigarette whilst Rob caught up with his note-taking.

They told me I had done the right thing by contacting them. They confirmed the police wouldn't be interested in drug smuggling overseas, but that the Customs and police often worked together on jobs involving narcotics in the UK when it could be shown that the drugs had come from abroad. This seemed a bit daft to me. Everyone knows that most narcotics crops are grown in hot tropical climates, and so they surely had to be imported at some point in the chain. To me the obvious exception would be chemically manufactured drugs such as LSD or speed, and of course Ecstasy tablets. Rob just smiled knowingly at my comments. God! he was a dark horse all right.

After a couple of hours Rob went to the payphones. He was there for ages, talking and checking his notes and occasionally glancing over at Steve and me. When he returned he picked up on the conversation again.

'Right, John, I just need to confirm some of the names and addresses you have given me.'

We talked about Benson — his appearance,

distinguishing marks, tattoos, his lifestyle, friends, contacts I had met, cars he drove – it was like an observation game that you play at parties. I warmed to my task, and I'm sure I gave a good account of myself. Later Rob mentioned some other names and asked me if I knew them. I didn't. They then asked me what I knew about the drugs trade.

I told them about all I had seen years before in Benidorm and more recently my observations in Fuengirola as I'd sit watching the late-night antics of the tourists and drug pushers. That was the sum total of all my knowledge. Over the next two hours they increased what I knew by 100 per cent as they explained about the complex structures of the cannabis trade, from where it was grown in the Rif range of the Atlas mountains of Morocco through to its sale as cannabis resin in the towns and cities of Great Britain.

They advised me that I had become involved with a gang unknown to them but displaying nevertheless some of the classic dealing practices. Engendering trust, dummy runs, carrying small sums of money, big payments for the little work done and a gradual exposure of other criminal activities are the stock-in-trade tactics of the drug dealers' recruiting new staff.

They also told me that the car I was driving was almost certainly stolen, a conclusion I had reached myself earlier in the evening when mentally reviewing the day's events. The vehicle documents were in Spain, but I gave them the registration number, which Rob dutifully recorded. Bye, bye £7000, I thought, and I felt the knife of hatred for Benson turn a little deeper in my guts.

We discussed cigarette smuggling from Gibraltar, but

they weren't too interested in that. They were after drug dealers. Rob and Steve weren't judgmental at all – that wasn't their job – they just wanted names, dates and facts. They left the moralizing and judging to others.

The methods employed by the drug dealers to get their product into the UK are ingenious and successful. They make the running, and the Customs agents are constantly trailing behind, trying to catch up. The best weapon in the Customs armoury is the undercover informant. He or she is the person closest to the action and is usually up to date on the latest smuggling methods and routes. Sometimes the agents are members of a smuggling gang and as such ideally placed to provide up-to-the-minute information about a gang's activities and plans to their Customs 'handlers'.

We talked about informers and drug dealers, and I confirmed that subject to Kath's approval I would certainly help them, if I could, to obtain information about Benson and his operations. By now it was nearly eleven o'clock at night, and after the day's traumatic events and the lengthy meeting with the Customs I was exhausted. We agreed to knock it on the head and meet later the next day at the farm. I dragged my weary bones to the motel room aiming for some much needed shuteye.

Not able to sleep properly, Kath and I sat talking until the early hours of the morning. Whilst I was in discussion with the two Customs officers Kath had spoken by telephone to her son Anthony, who was at that time a butcher in a nearby village. Travelling home from work on the main road past the farm he had noticed the police activity there and naturally had called in to see what was happening.

Undaunted by my cancellation call the police had arrived at the house in force, and not able to raise an answer to their knocking they had used their discretionary powers to break into the house and conduct a thorough search of the farm and its outbuildings. Not finding any bodies they had then scoured the area of the surrounding fields. Later receiving a call from Customs & Excise updating them on the situation they decided it best to leave police officers at the farm all night in case of a return visit by the gun-toting gang. It was a waste of time because nobody showed up.

The next morning after a café breakfast we all travelled home again. I arranged for a joiner to fix the broken door, and we sat down to await the call from Customs. Rob phoned me at about 10 am and said they wanted to see me urgently, so I gave him directions to the farm and invited them to visit us later that day. Both Rob and Steve turned up at about 1 pm. Kath fixed sandwiches and drinks for us all, and we sat down for my induction into the world of Customs informants.

Steve opened the batting, whilst Rob again took notes. He told me that if I agreed to become an informant I would be involved in work for the public good, but my efforts would never be publicly acknowledged. I would, however, be paid if criminal convictions were obtained against people about whom I supplied information. Equally, if drugs were seized I would also receive a reward. Payments for drug seizures were not as high though as those for information that lead to arrests and subsequent convictions.

For my own protection I would be given a codename. It would be used in all my future dealings with HM Customs, and no one, including any superior officers, would have access to my true identity. That was a sacrosanct rule within the organization, obviously one put in place to protect informers for whom revelation of their real identity could open them up to threats or worse. The idea was also that an informant's true identity could never be disclosed by accident or through negligence.

I was to select my own codename because then I wouldn't forget it, and it would remain with me even under intense pressure. I thought about it for a while and finally decided to use the nickname that I'd been given at school. 'Benjy', I said. 'It's short, easily remembered and not likely to be used by anyone else.' OK. That was agreed. The name was adopted, and from that moment on both Rob and Steve called me by it, as if trying to impress upon me the seriousness of the situation.

Rob gave me a central London telephone number dedicated to a Customs hotline that was answered 24 hours a day by special operators who understood the problems that agents had to handle and with which they had to live. I could call the number any time and use my codename to obtain immediate contact with one of my 'handlers' or to leave a message for a later response. He told me never to write it down, even though it was ex-directory. Customs were aware that the big dealers had paid contacts in the police, and very possibly BT; these people could check out any telephone number or indeed any other information. To combat problems that might develop from this all the unlisted Customs phone numbers were registered to businesses unconnected to HM Customs & Excise. Steve gave me his bleeper number too, which I was permitted to write down. If it were to be investigated, this number also came back as registered to a business with no links to Customs & Excise.

That meeting with Rob and Steve lasted for more than four hours. We talked about everything to do with drugs and intelligence-gathering. Apparently they had checked out my story overnight and received confirmation that the names I had given them were genuine, indeed some of them were known to other agencies, such as the police.

They told me that I should try and get as close as possible to the drug gang leaders. They were not interested in the mules or carriers because they were catching them at the UK ports of entry every day. They were after the main dealers — the buyers and the sellers who paid for and organized the drug-smuggling runs. These were the guys who ultimately made fantastic profits from the illegal trade; all the others were just minions, who might earn a lot of money and were partaking in illegal activities but who were not making the vast sums accumulated by the organizers and buyers.

We agreed that I was to become a 'Confidential Informant'. That is an undercover agent who provides intelligence about drug-smuggling activities but only actively participates to a minor degree in any criminal activity. I was not to handle any drugs personally, and I wasn't to act as an *agent provocateur* which is to say that I wasn't allowed to provoke any person into committing an illegal act. Furthermore I had to report anything that seemed important, bearing in mind the prime objective of capturing the big boys. I was also supposed to relay to them any other illegal activity that I came across – counterfeit money operations and stolen car rings were activities that came immediately to mind.

In return for my assistance Customs & Excise would ensure that I did not have to appear in public court to give evidence for the prosecution against any dealers. This was very important to me. Having experienced a mild threat of potential violence I could all too easily imagine what would happen if I helped put dealers behind bars and they found out that it was my evidence that had helped to nail them. Their anger and subsequent retribution would know no limits, and they would simply kill me out of hand.

I had already read reports in Spanish newspapers of people disappearing only to be found washed up on a beach some weeks later, and of folk trapped in burning villas under questionable circumstances. More than one corpse had been found dumped in the hills overlooking Malaga. It didn't take a great leap of imagination to believe that these were the bodies of drug dealers or participants in the drug trade. That these were the men or women who had paid the ultimate price for deals gone wrong, or for rip-offs between rival gangs.

The Customs officers told me that there was also another policy in place to protect informants from exposure in the courts. If an informer's evidence were put before the court and the defence called for confirmation or the agent's cross-examination, Customs prosecutors would first discuss the matter in chambers with the trial judge. Usually the judge would rule that the informant did not have to be named. However, as sometimes happened, the judge might rule that the agent should appear in person, in which case Customs would offer no prosecution evidence, and the case against the defendants would be dropped. This was an expensive policy to implement in terms of finances and time, but to me it was the ultimate guarantee that I wouldn't be forced to appear in a criminal trial as a prosecution witness.

As I sat in the lounge of our home talking with Rob and Steve these risks seemed distant. The Customs guys were experts and knew exactly what they were doing. If it became necessary they had the power to protect not only me but also my family from any revenge attacks. If by chance anything went wrong and I were arrested whilst on an operation then I could rest assured that HM Customs would sort it out. This was normally done by a technical defect in the arresting procedure, placed there to enable any defending solicitor to get the charges against me dropped and allow me to walk away. The benefit of this technique was that the dealers wouldn't consider my release suspicious, but rather the result of police error. Apparently these knockouts over a technicality were not uncommon and would be accepted without any reservations by the drug gangs.

I was also told that I should not contact my handlers in any regular pattern, that I should vary the time and the place. When 'on the ground' in Spain I should only call when I had something important to say. They appreciated that active informants could be placed in difficult situations, and stressed that I should never risk compromising myself just to make a report. If I got into any major difficulties then no matter where I was at the time, whether in the UK or abroad, I should get along as quickly as possible to the nearest police station. If I were compromised by then working with the police, steps would be taken to protect my family, including our relocation and help with new identities.

During a natural break in the discussions Kath and I had a private chat in the kitchen. We both agreed that although the situation wasn't good – and certainly wasn't one that we would have wished for – there could be no doubt that Steve and Rob seemed to know exactly what they were doing and appeared to be dependable, stand-up guys. We decided that for the time being at least I would go ahead and work for them as an informant.

Later that afternoon we talked about what could have prompted the goons to turn up at the farm the day before, and Steve explained how a typical deal was done. A buyer, or a group of buyers, would send a 'tester' to Spain, usually to a known contact with whom there had been previous dealings. The tester was given some small samples of cannabis, which he would test carefully and give his opinion, usually by phone to his boss, over the next few days.

If the cannabis or 'gear' made the grade an order would be placed and agreed, and then the money, always in cash sterling, would be sent by courier to Spain. With a small outfit the head of the gang would travel to Spain and complete the deal to buy anything from 50 to 500 kg of gear. After paying for it the buyer had then to fork out for local storage, a wrapping service and transport back to the UK. These oncosts would be paid when the service was provided.

So, having bought the gear, it would be wrapped in layer upon layer of clingfilm or sealed in vacuum packets to defeat sniffer dogs. Then, depending on the buyer's preference, it would either be transported to the UK by a hired transport contractor or by the buyer's own transport and routing.

It was not unusual for a buyer to try and ship gear himself. If he proved successful he would increase his profits tremendously. But, if he were to fail, and the drugs were seized at a border crossing, the highest point of risk, then he stood to lose all his gear as well as the money already invested. In that scenario, using known contacts, the buyer would probably lose someone he knew personally with the attendant risk that they might tip off the police in order to negotiate a lower sentence.

Overall it was better for a buyer to use a third-party transport company. That way he didn't make as much on a shipment, but the risks to him and his gang members were minimal. Furthermore, because the competition for transport jobs was so fierce, the buyer could dictate payment terms.

The going rate for bulk shipments was £100 per kilo of drugs delivered within the UK, half paid up front as a deposit and the balance due on safe delivery. The downside of this transportation method is that the buyer hands over control of the goods previously guaranteed by his own trusted tester. Now there are other people involved – the storers and the baby-sitters, the wrappers and the couriers who do the actual smuggling.

Tampering with shipments is not uncommon. Partial loads might be stolen, or good quality cannabis swapped for something inferior, usually for gear contaminated with diesel fuel or 'let down', or mixed with wax, in the blending process. Sometimes the bars of hash, called 'soaps' and each weighing 250 gm, would be filed down slightly and 20 or so grams taken from each one. In this way the inside operator will steal about 20 per cent of the load. All in all there are many ways for a buyer to be ripped off.

When such shortages or losses occur the established buyer's revenge is extracted in a remarkably short space of time. If he knows who has ripped him off then he will arrange either through his own resources or by way of a hired team to hit back as soon as possible. This has two purposes. First, if the thief is hit fast and hard then the buyer may recover the goods or money, and the word on the street would make any other potential rip-off merchants think very carefully before making a move on that buyer. Second, if the buyer doesn't react swiftly then he may as well jack in drug dealing because everybody will rip him off all the time. So the jungle wars are swift and usually sure. Retribution is harsh, and the weakest fail.

It was more than likely that the money I had agreed to collect for Benson was the balance due following safe deliveries for Jim and his gang. But, when the gear had been sampled, it was possible that the quantity was short of the agreed load or the quality inferior, that is to say that all or some of the gear had been swapped.

Now Jim knew that I was only a mule carrying the money, but it made no difference to him. I was his last contact with the Benson gang, and he had handed me £10,000. I was the logical choice to squeeze first. If I came up with the money, all well and good; he could ignore the little difficulty with Benson and carry on business as usual. After all Benson could always get another mule. If I screamed when squeezed then Benson would hear and instigate a search for the real thief, either in his wrapping or delivery gang, or further back up the line among the storage boys.

Either way Jim was sending a message to Benson via me. What he couldn't and didn't know was that his squeeze operation had coincided with me contacting Customs about Benson anyway. All he had done was to convince both Kath and me that we weren't going to be walked over by those bastards. We were going to fight back and see them go down, one way or another.

Kath, Steve, Rob and I talked through every ramification. I even suggested they might let me have some gear seized elsewhere to replace that delivered by Benson's gang. This might lull them into a false sense of security. Rob laughed and said no, they could not allow such things to happen.

After several hours the meeting broke up amicably. I had agreed to work with HM Customs, not as a long-term informant but only so long as to ensnare Benson, his gang and other contacts. After a quick run-through of the business and a thumbnail training seminar we agreed that I should contact Benson to see how the land lay. No doubt he would have heard by now that I had phoned the police.

If the situation was still OK then I would travel back to Spain and go to work as an informer. But if he were frightened off then the matter was dead in the water, and I would continue to develop the import and export business and simply stay away from Benson and his cronies. Just before they left I told Rob I would phone him the next day. We all shook hands and as they drove away I noticed it was about six o'clock in the evening. We had been hard at it all afternoon.

Once again Kath and I sat up burning the midnight

oil, discussing the various options and possible consequences. We decided I should have to go through with it, certainly for the time being until I managed to extricate myself from the invisible web that Benson had contrived to weave around me. We decided that the situation was now potentially too risky to involve Nick. He would be a liability in Spain, so I would leave him at home where he could help Kath. He could still go out and buy white goods ready for the next trip. I would leave the van at the farm and travel to Spain on the Goldwing.

It meant that the business plan was on hold for the moment, but I didn't mind too much about that. We could always take up the reins again when we were ready. It wasn't yet the type of business that depended on repeat orders or customer loyalty; it was still a young, fledgling operation. No, I had no doubts about my priorities: look after my family, remove the threats, make some money and strive for a peaceful coexistence with my neighbours. Surely, I thought, that wasn't too much to ask.

We also had to look at how we should best adapt to events that might happen in our lives as a result of my new role as an undercover agent. Kath could forget travelling to Spain with Natalie, certainly for the time being. There would be a great deal of stress to be encountered and overcome, possibly with only moral support and the odd, brief telephone call. I could hardly say, 'Sorry, lads, Kath's upset so I'm shooting off home for a week or so.' That seemed a sure-fire way of arousing suspicion. We decided the risks were too great to tell the family what I was doing, just in case anything slipped out by accident. So Kath would have to cope with the strain of it all herself without a shoulder to cry on when things got rough.

As we were talking that night I looked over towards Kath in the dimly lit lounge. I could see she was upset, that tears weren't far away, but the angle at which she held her head, with her chin jutting out defiantly, revealed to me her complete determination. She was generally more passive than me, but I could tell she wouldn't allow these fuckers to break our dreams or threaten our lives. We would get through all right. Like they say, the female of the species is more deadly than the male. She would do for Benson and his mates if it came down to it.

We went to bed eventually, and both of us slept soundly. We had made our decision and had the resolve to see it through. Now it was time to go to work. Early the next morning I phoned Benson feeling hyper alert and ready for any comments he might make. He was very calm and listened to my story. I explained angrily about the visit from the Londoners and told him I believed they were connected with Jim and the money I had collected from him. I demanded to know what was going on.

In turn Benson himself wanted to know what happened with the police. I responded furiously that it wasn't every day that we had a visit from men with guns threatening us, but that I told the police it was a domestic dispute, and we had the matter in hand. He seemed a bit wary about this, but it was the best I could do under the circumstances.

I wound up the conversation by saying I would be down in Spain during the next week, and he had better square up the matter with Jim. I didn't want a repeat performance at the farm. What I didn't tell Benson was that Kath and I had agreed that she and Natalie would fly out to Spain the next week to be with me. That way if the issue weren't resolved then at least there would be nobody at the farm for them to have a go at.

Benson seemed happy that I had taken such a stance, and he said he would contact Jim straight away. I called Rob at the Manchester Customs office later that morning and told him what had transpired during my conversation with Benson. He agreed that it was probably safe to go back to Spain, and that the operation was on. I left it at that and promised to be in touch.

Two days later I set off on the Goldwing, loaded down to capacity. I remember it was glorious weather, the sun shining down from a bright blue, almost cloudless sky. Kath and Natalie waved me off from the farm drive. It was a tearful parting even though I already had their flight details tucked safely in my wallet, and we knew we would meet up again at Malaga airport in six days' time.

Now it was official, I was an informant for Her Majesty's Customs & Excise. I felt great. Wrapped in their protective armour I was about to lay waste all the scum drug dealers I could get my hands on. I felt tremendously invigorated, and a sense of peace washed over me. I would show the fuckers. I knew I would succeed. It was the only way to protect my family and put the crazy, law-ignoring bastards behind bars.

5

Living as a Smuggler

The trip down to Spain driving my Honda Goldwing was one of the best journeys I have ever made. The sun shone all the way. I sat bang in the middle of the road, wrapped in a cocoon of taped music, courtesy of the powerful stereo. It was superb. Other vehicles moved over for me, and at junctions they allowed me to cut in front of them.

Whenever I stopped for fuel, to take a leak or grab a cold drink a small group of admirers would wander over and gather round, smiling and gesticulating, I'm sure no one noticed me; it was the Goldwing they were all interested in. The bike seemed to engender warmth and friendliness from everyone. Or was it just my euphoria at the task in hand? I don't know, but it was a bloody good feeling.

When I reached the by now familiar Hendaye border crossing between France and Spain there was an almighty queue of tourist traffic awaiting entry into Spain. No problem! I passed slowly up the line and waited until another driver waved me into the line in front of him. At the guard kiosk I stopped, took out my passport and handed it to the guard. He waved me on and commented, 'Formidable, monsieur! Bonnes vacances.' He was such a nice guy. Similarly at the Spanish border a couple of hundred metres ahead the guard was more interested in looking at the bike than inspecting my documents. I was across in no time at all with no hint of a check on me or my papers.

The trip through the heartland of Spain was hot with daytime temperatures soaring into the mid-40s. I stopped a couple of times at garage forecourts and bought a bottle of mineral water from cooled dispensers. I would drink my fill and then pour a great dollop of icy water over my head, face and neck, pausing only thoroughly to wet the inside of my helmet before I was off again. It was no good, though, because within ten minutes the coolness from the impromptu shower had evaporated, and beads of sweat were running again into my eyes and making my sunglasses slip down my nose.

Meanwhile my legs, crotch and back were bathed in sweat, and my flesh was chafing with every little movement. I pulled off the road and took a bag of clothes from a side pannier. Ducking behind a bush I stripped off and changed into a tee shirt, shorts and trainers. Re-stowing the bag I set off again. Oh, heaven! I felt great. The sun was beating down, but the passage of air cooled me just enough. Riding a powerful bike along motorways in the afternoon sun for hour after hour ranks as a must-do experience.

In the distance I could see the heat haze and the black tarmac shimmering, while eagles swooped lazily overhead. Other drivers gave me a thumbs up, wagons hooted, and even police motorbikers dropped their customary disdainful expressions to smile and wave at me.

As is the way of all good things this all came to an end, and after a great journey I arrived back on the Costa del Sol. I drove straight to Carmen's pension in Fuengirola and checked in. Carmen was surprised to see me without Nick; she kept glancing behind me to the open doorway as we were talking. She was even more surprised when I showed her the bike. I think all the Latin women love their men to be macho. I could almost hear her changing gear and reappraising my potential in the new light of a superbike. Later, darling, I thought to myself, right now I've got work to do.

I showered and changed again, gave Carmen my dirty laundry for washing and drove into town to phone Kath and grab a bite to eat. As I suspected the bike drew lots of attention, especially from English tourists, many of whom shouted as I cruised posing down the seafront boulevard. Feigning ignorance of their envious glances I parked the bike right in front of a bar and nonchalantly locking the helmet on board I adjusted my shades and walked inside. After talking on the phone with Kath for a while I wasted the rest of the day just relaxing and gathering my thoughts.

I thought I knew what I was up against. I was sure that after thinking about it intensely over the past few days of my solitary journey I was more than ready for it and eager to begin.

The next morning I phoned Benson to check out the lie of the land.

'Hi, Colin, it's John. I've just got back, how's it going?' I asked lightly.

'OK,' he responded. 'I'm sorry about that bit of

bother you had, but I've squared it up now. Why don't you come up later on, and we'll have a chat?' he suggested.

'Okey-dokey, I'll see you about threeish. Cheers,' I said and hung up. Yes, the game was on. I phoned Rob in the Manchester office, and he sounded pleased to hear from me. I told him I was intending to visit Benson that afternoon. Rob warned me to be careful and not to take any chances.

That afternoon I drove up to Benson's villa in Cartama. Of course everyone came out and had a good look at the bike. Benson wanted to take it for a quick spin, and I let him, just to demonstrate there were no hard feelings. Later we sat alone on the shaded porch, a cold beer in front of each of us.

'Well, Colin, it seems like we have to get a few things straightened out between us,' I began, opening the discussion. He looked over at me, squinting against the glare behind me, and so we began to talk for more than an hour about the situation. I told him that he should have trusted me. I wasn't stupid, and I had realized how he made his money, which certainly wasn't from renting out kennels or selling the odd car and caravan. Besides people who had bought and sold cars didn't send round goons with guns to get their money back, they sent solicitors' letters and used the courts.

'No,' I said, 'you're involved in hooky money or drugs. Personally I'm not bothered which, but I wouldn't mind a piece of the action. Selling microwaves is a hard way to make a living.

'Besides I've got a good business head and could be a great organizer. I know the roads across Spain and France really well, and I'm used to the travelling. I know where the police hang out, and where they have roadside checks. Maybe, most importantly, I am totally clean – a good citizen without a record – I can stand up to any checks.'

'That's not such a good thing,' he temporized. 'Lot's of people prefer to work with known cons, someone who they can check up on easily.'

'Yeah,' I replied, 'so they have cons checking cons, and then you end with the sorts of problems you've obviously had with Jim. One of your trusted cons drives off into the sunset with your gear or your money. You need somebody straight who will work from the outside, sort of like a subcontractor.'

We also discussed the Land-Rover Discovery I had bought from him. When pushed Benson admitted it was stolen. In fact it had been stolen in France and put on to English plates by a gang operating out of a town near Salou on the Costa Brava. A printer in the UK turned out the fake Vehicle Registration Documents, and they really were indistinguishable from the real thing. Benson was proud of them and said they were the best available. As for the tax discs, they were original, stolen from various post offices in raids up and down the UK. Similarly MOT certificates were available for older cars, stolen from testing centres the length and breadth of the country.

So it went on for a couple of hours, but I didn't want to push it too far with him. I'd planted the seed, and that was enough for starters. As I stood up ready to leave he said to give him a few days, and then he would be in touch. No problem, I had plenty with which to occupy myself. I left and drove pensively over the hills down to the coast.

During the rest of the week I hung around likely haunts of drug dealers, shady Spanish bars and some of the rougher British ones. I made a few contacts and got on to nodding terms with a few dodgy-looking individuals.

A couple of days later Benson left a message for me at the pension. I phoned him and arranged to meet for a drink in Torremolinos. When we met he looked wary and couldn't settle. He told me that he had another hooky car for sale, a Ford Escort on English 'K' registration plates. He said I could have it for £1500 as it stood or £2000 with paperwork, logbook and tax disc. He obviously didn't want to talk about anything else, and so again I didn't push it. He looked like a man with problems.

I used that Escort as my ticket into the criminal fraternity. I talked to everyone who looked as if they might be the slightest bit interested, and it's a wonder I wasn't pulled in myself considering how I flaunted that knocked-off car. A few people mentioned that I might try a bar in Gibraltar, where hot items of property and other things were traded. Excellent, I thought, I'm finally making a bit of progress. The next morning I set off there.

Gibraltar is a strange place. A self-governed British dependency, the size of a small English market town, it holds a curious mixture of those of Italian, British, north African and Spanish origin as well as other generally cosmopolitan people who live cramped together in an atmosphere of repressed hysteria on what is effectively a small rocky peninsula at the southern tip of Spain. Its chief value is its strategic position on the Straits of Gibraltar, which makes it the gateway between the Mediterranean and the North

Atlantic Ocean. The seas of the Straits are notoriously dangerous at this point where two great bodies of water smash together through the narrow gap between two continents.

Gibraltar is famous for its British-style bobbies and circular red post boxes. It also has English money and English-style shopping centres. Woolworths and Marks & Spencer department stores stand in the main shopping street cheek by jowl with cheap tourist novelty shops selling china mugs, linen cloths and aprons decorated with blurred images of the Royal Family and Ye Olde English Tea Shoppes abound. There is a general air of seediness, of a place long past its prime. To my mind Gibraltar should have been closed down and handed back to the Spanish after the Second World War ended, though there is a strong pro-British lobby there.

Gibraltar's main asset now apart from its location is its duty-free shopping facilities. Tourists arrive in droves to buy 200 Silk Cut or Benson & Hedges cigarettes for less than the duty-free prices in international airports. Perfume, clothes, video cameras and electronic goods are all available at some of the cheapest prices to be found in Europe.

High on the small list of other things for which Gib has become famous is the well-kept tradition of smuggling, which the populace continue with vigour. Everyone does their bit. Tourists try to smuggle more than the tobacco or bottle allowance back on to mainland Spain, past the ever vigilant Spanish Customs guards, whilst the locals smuggle cigarettes by the speedboat load from Gibraltar to the beaches of nearby La Linea. They do so in a crazy game of cat and mouse with the local Guardia Civil, who ceaselessly patrol the area.

It is difficult to obtain a permit to reside in Gibraltar, and in any case property prices are sky high. Most of the better apartment blocks house the bankers and accountants that work in the Gibraltar-based offshore banking industry. Ordinary working-class people who are not in company-subsidized property live in La Linea, the Spanish border town that abuts the frontier with Gibraltar.

La Linea is a dirty, smelly run-down place. The roads are worn out, cratered and potholed with great mounds of sun-swollen tarmac that look like surreal fermenting dough. The streets seem largely to be populated by mangy-looking dogs, screaming, dirty kids and old women dressed in black who sit in shaded doorways. It's a hellhole with a pointless existence.

When I got to Gibraltar I headed straight for the bar to which I'd been recommended. Nearby there were other commercial units commonly known to be rented for storage by cigarette smugglers. Gibraltarian police and Customs officials know many of the smugglers by name and often stand by benignly to watch the nightly operations as the small black-hulled speedboats are fuelled up and loaded with boxes of duty-free cigarettes.

The smugglers are well organized and have accomplices in La Linea equipped with night-sight scopes and walkie-talkies. They sit around the beach and watch the roads, and when the coast is clear of police they radio the boats that have been hovering just around a blind corner of the cove. The drivers zip up the speedboats' throttle to maximum and zoom towards the beach at fantastic speeds. Once there the crew quickly throw their loads overboard to an awaiting group of perhaps 15 or 20 teenagers, who have materialized apparently from nowhere. They spirit away contraband up the beach, across the main road and into the warren of dirty little back streets to a safe house. It is all over and done with within five minutes of the boats' departure from La Linea harbour.

The contraband cigarettes are sold for £12 a carton for British-brand and Marlboro, and consequently hardly any of the locals buy cigarettes in the shops. It is in fact hard to purchase them in a shop in La Linea. Most shopkeepers just don't bother stocking them because they are so easy to obtain on the black market. Furthermore the Gibraltarian authorities don't much concern themselves with the tobacco smugglers. After all they are smuggling out of Gibraltar and not into it. Similarly there is a healthy trade in Scotch whisky, brandy and rum.

Obviously the Spanish are exceedingly unhappy with the nightly smuggling operations, which occur like clockwork unless there is an offshore wind that makes the sea too rough and stops the light speedboats from getting up and on to the beaches. The Spanish police try to stop the smugglers, but it is like trying to halt the tide. The rewards are just too good, and the risks minor. If caught the smugglers face a large fine or a small jail term, and the contraband and boat are confiscated.

Big deal! I know smugglers who treat the cigarette and alcohol smuggling as a proper business, even declaring the sales for tax in Gib and paying a levy on the profits. I have seen them fill up with gas at the small fuelling jetty and demand a receipt for the cost. This is then submitted as a legitimate expenses claim. This may seem to be turning smuggling into a fine art, but against this level of smuggling gall and expertise and Gibraltarian indifference the Spanish are fighting a losing battle. This is part of the reason why the Spanish are so tight on the land border and insist on stopping and searching every vehicle, which in summer can be a ballbreaker. It is no fun queuing up for two hours in the hot sun waiting to clear the Spanish checkpoint.

Once smuggled into La Linea the contraband cigarettes are either sold in the major Spanish holiday resorts, or bigger loads, concealed in packed container lorries, are shipped out to the rest of Europe and the UK. These are big operations with more than a million cigarettes smuggled out each time. I know that ocean-going yachts and small cruisers lie just off Gibraltar filled to capacity with cigarettes. When a cash price is paid in a local bar, the cigarettes are taken by boat to southern Ireland or Scotland. The carrying boat lies in international waters off a small harbour or deserted beach until rubber inflatables arrive to transport the light but bulky boxes to awaiting onshore vehicles. These milk runs are sophisticated smuggling operations that deal with millions of pounds worth of tobacco.

It was into this environment that I arrived hoping to sell the Escort that evening. I discovered the bar to which I'd been directed to be a strange establishment, populated by locals in denim shorts and flip-flops. Its atmosphere was noisy and crude, and the place was dirty and stank of stale beer. English beer adverts covered the walls, and the price list was in English with English prices, something of a shock after Spain.

The bar was in no way pretentious and obviously did not seek to attract the tourist trade, although it is only a five-minute walk from the centre of the main shopping areas.

I settled myself in at the bar and ordered a pint of Fosters. All around me there was the quiet, conspiratorial purr of deals being done. Before long I began a conversation with a guy about bikes. The pavement and small parking lot outside was filled with Gib-registered motorbikes of varying makes and vintages. Inside the atmosphere was highly charged, and within an hour I was told that a lad called Peter was after a new car and directed to one of the lock-up units further along the block, facing the jetty. This turned out to be my entry point into the whole game.

Strolling into the heartland of the smugglers' territory I tried to look unconcerned but inside I was shitting blood. I nodded at the few people who looked up at me from the boats just feet below. These were all filled up with contraband and ready to go, just awaiting the word from their mates in La Linea. It felt surreal to be in the thick of international smuggling operations and trying to sell a stolen car. I was giddy with excitement and hoped I could carry it through, because if I fucked up I would be lucky to escape with just a severe beating. These lads obviously played for keeps, and they were all young, slim and as fast as greyhounds.

I walked up to a unit with an open door. 'Hi, there, I'm looking for Peter,' I said to one of the older-looking guys inside. He just glanced at me before speaking quickly into a walkie-talkie that had been lying on top of a box of cigs. I heard him say the name Peter as he briefly stared at me again and listened distractedly to the tinny voice that came back to him.

'He's on the boat. He will be here in ten minutes,' he told me abruptly and turned away.

'OK, pal, thanks, I'll wait here,' I replied to his back. Feeling a bit like a spare wheel I turned and walked out of the storeroom and headed back to the jetty to watch the proceedings unfold. There were about eight boats against the jetty wall held there by lads hanging on to lengths of rope fastened to eyebolts in the jetty flooring. I noticed that all the boats were painted black, and each had two crew in the cockpit. The engines were turning over quietly, and little trails of bubbles popped regularly to the surface below each stern.

There was a sudden shout, and in unison the speedboat engines rose to scream pitch, and the boats lifted almost out of the water as they shot for the marina entrance, jockeying for position at high speed. Within seconds they were out of sight around the stone harbour wall and heading for the Spanish coves. I could just see the non-drivers waving and gesticulating at each other, and it all looked like a high-school prank to me as the echoes of the receding engines reverberated noisily around the marina. I looked upwards and saw observers with binoculars on the stone-built headlands, no doubt ensuring their loads were delivered safely.

Within five minutes the first of the boats were returning at high speed and slewing round expertly in tight U-turns to pull up at the jetty. Those on board were excited, shouting and jabbering madly at one another. Within ten minutes all the boats had returned safely, and the crews had jumped ship and on to the jetty, heading off for the storerooms. Young lads of about 14 or 15 now ran to and fro the boats with the next consignment of contraband to be stored, ready for the express delivery service.

I wandered back to the storeroom and asked again for Peter. In the half darkness a slim athletic-looking young man with blond hair and a sparkling white smile turned to me in response. 'I'm Peter, man,' he said. 'What do you want?'

I told him I had heard that he wanted a new car. I launched into my prepared spiel and offered him the car for sale as if it were an everyday event. He looked at me for a moment, weighing me up. 'Sure, man, I need a new car,' he said. 'Have you got it here?'

'No,' I replied, 'I don't drive it around because my name isn't on the Vehicle Registration Document. But I can bring it down to show you if you are interested,' I added helpfully.

Peter was thinking about this when the radio crackled into life again. He grabbed it and pointed in my direction. 'Can you swim?' he asked. Dumbly I nodded back at him. 'Come on then, let's see if you are a copper.' I could have died right there. This stupid bastard wanted me to go on the boat with him. 'Come on, man, let's go,' he shouted, already halfway back to his boat. All his mates were looking at me and watching my reaction. This, I felt, was it, shit or bust.

'OK, let's go,' I said and ran after him to the boat. He jumped in, and a young lad who was holding the steadying rope looked at me. Fuck, I thought, this is the way to do it. I jumped the couple of feet down into the boat and took the rope from the kid's hand.

Peter looked across at me and smiled as he spoke into the radio.

'Hey, man, what's your name?' he asked across the noise of the engines.

'John,' I replied and smiled back at him. 'How many years do we get if we are stopped?'

He shrugged. 'It's not the prison, it's the way they stop us now,' he smiled and motioned a man firing a rifle. Great, I thought, I could get shot by the Spanish just for being in this poxy boat.

Before I could reply the radio started to transmit instructions again, and without any warning to me to let go of the rope he pushed the throttle levers wide open. It was like being in an express elevator. The boat took off from the jetty like a Porsche, and I was still holding on to the rope and steadying the boat. Now I knew why everyone was wearing gloves, and so much for me thinking they didn't want to leave any fingerprints. It was more mundane than that. They just didn't want the skin burning off their hands.

I screamed into the dusk, but I'm still not sure whether or not it was from searing pain or the sheer exhilaration of riding in that ultrafast speedboat. It was like nothing on earth, a live thing, bucking and jumping over what looked from the shore like small waves but close up were too big for comfort. The boat took off and landed with a bone-jarring jump into every crest. Water shipped on board in chilling scoopfuls, and within seconds I was wet through.

We were about third in a line of boats, the propellers of those in front roiled up the sea behind them in turbulent little cross waves. I snatched a look at Peter, who was standing up and steering with one hand and trying to talk into the walkie-talkie with the other. What a dickhead! I was holding on to the steel grab handle fastened to the front bulkhead for dear life.

They tell me a good run is to be in and out within five or six minutes, but to me it seemed we were travelling for ever. Suddenly, without warning, the engines cut, and the boat seemed to stagger in the water. A large wave sloshed over the side, and sea water gurgled around my feet in the footwell. There was a crunching noise from underneath as we beached.

'Quick, come on,' Peter yelled. I turned and saw him heaving boxes overboard like a madman. I jumped into the back of the boat and stood amongst the cargo and started throwing it out on to the beach. A crowd of youngsters had gathered and stood holding out their arms for a box. We both worked like crazies, and in no time the back of the boat was empty.

'OK, man, let's go,' shouted Peter. I just nodded weakly, now knackered by the sudden exertion.

The boat had been lightened by the loss of cargo, and we were semi-floating on the incoming waves. Peter gunned the engine, and with a groan and squeak the boat backed into the water. He spun the wheel and turned the engine to full throttle again. We were off bucking, jumping and writhing across the surf and into the bay. Not too bad, I thought, as we careered towards Gibraltar.

The return trip was more of the same, with conversation an impossibility. I was cold and wet and frightened half to death. This was nothing like a sedate water-skiing cruise up a lake or in the lazy offshore swells in the sunshine. It was hard, fast and dangerous. The stakes went up by a factor of ten when Peter pointed back behind us towards the beach. I couldn't see anything until a blindingly bright searchlight cut in from the sky and danced over the water to connect with one of the boats behind us. The light dipped and swooped but held fast on the fleeing boat.

We obviously hadn't been travelling at full throttle for Peter immediately gave it everything, and the boat jumped in the water like a hot-rod car. We were literally travelling over the wavetops. I could feel the water tugging under the boat as if it were trying to grab it and pull us back down into the sea. The engines screamed like banshees as we veered into the marina entrance. Abruptly the searchlight was cut off, and the other boats followed us in, screaming towards the harbour wall through the silent port. Peter cut the engine at the right moment, and we slewed in to a perfect berthing. Nicely done, this guy should have been driving in the world championships. He could handle a boat like nobody else on earth.

Another youngster passed me the rope and leapt into the boat behind me. He was dressed like an urchin and laughing at me like a nutter. Peter slapped me on the back and boosted me up on to the harbour wall. I reeled a bit before I could walk in a straight line. Peter and his mates gathered round and laughed approvingly. 'Hey, John, grande cojones' he said, and some of his gang clapped. 'That's pretty good, eh?' he asked. 'A free ride and a profit too.'

I was too fucked to answer him, and it took me all my time not to throw up on to the jetty. We headed back to his storeroom. The other members of the team looked up when we entered and gathered round us, one of them throwing me a towel, which I used to rub my hair dry. An open can of beer was thrust at me, and I drank it greedily. I hadn't realized how thirsty I was.

Later Peter and I sat on the steps near the harbour entrance and discussed things. He told me they liked to test out new people in boats, giving them no chance of backing out once they were in. No police would take the chance of being a target in a smuggling boat. Little did he know that if I'd known I could get shot at then nothing on earth would got me into that boat. So I'd passed his test by default.

Peter said he often made five trips a night, but that night he was finished because the Guardia Civil had turned up in a helicopter, something they did from time to time. He explained they were really after the drug boats from Morocco, but while awaiting the druggies they would chase the tobacco smugglers. A few months earlier they had fired rubber bullets at a boat, one of which had hit a fuel tank. The resultant explosion wrecked the boat and killed the driver; the other crew member had been rescued by police helicopter but was immediately arrested and sentenced to six months in the local prison.

Finally we got on to the topic of the Escort. Peter liked the idea of a nearly new car for £1500, and he was keen to buy it. He offered to pay me in cigarettes, which I didn't really fancy though he said he would let me have them at trade price. This was £8 a carton, which I could sell on for £15, and he would introduce me to people who would take them off me in Marbella. That seemed like a good deal to me because it would allow me to make further contacts, and sooner or later I would come across drug dealers rather than cottage-industry tobacco smugglers.

After we swapped phone numbers I left Gib in the late evening and drove sedately up the road to the Marbella area. It had been interesting, and I had made some initial inroads into the drug-smuggling fraternity.

I collected the stolen Escort from Benson the next day and drove it down to La Linea. I parked on the roadway outside the Anglo-Spanish frontier amongst all the other vehicles of those who prefer to walk across the border rather than risk getting caught up in the interminable traffic queues. I followed the crowds across the road and the airstrip and went into a burger bar near the walled entrance to the old fortress town to telephone Peter.

Five minutes later an old Mercedes pulled up outside, and from it Peter shouted at me to jump in. The car was crowded with his mates; an older man who turned out to be his father, Henry, was driving. Peter introduced me to everyone. They all appeared to have heard about my boat trip the previous night, and there were smiles all around.

We drove off and up to the border, where on production of British-style passports we were quickly waved through. More surprisingly Peter's father started chatting in Spanish with the border guards. He was obviously well known to them. After a cursory look inside the boot we were off again.

Peter loved the Escort. He and his mates piled in and drove it around La Linea with the windows rolled down and the radio blaring. I waited by the Mercedes, trying to look cool as I chatted with his father. When they returned about 20 minutes later Peter confirmed he would take it. Without more ado we jumped back into the Mercedes and drove into a labyrinth of small streets. Parking up finally they gestured me inside a nearby house. The place was wall-to-wall cigarettes. There was hardly any furniture, just box upon box of Marlboro and Winston. It was an amazing sight.

'OK, John, you bring down some transport, and we'll load it with eight boxes of cigarettes. We can arrange for a friend called Ernesto to buy them off you at 4000 pesetas a carton. That will give you a good profit and help us with a transport problem we have at the moment,' said Henry. I noticed how Peter had slipped into the background, and the business dealings were being handled by the father. Family ties here were strong and deeply instilled. It was like dealing with the Mafia. I wasn't about to argue.

'What if we get stopped on the road from here to Marbella?' I asked.

'That is the risk you take if you want to make big profits, my friend. But if you plan carefully you can move all the cigarettes you want. All these boxes will be sent up the same road within two days. They will be sold in Malaga near the airport by the weekend,' Henry said and smiled knowingly at me, tapping the side of his nose. The crafty old goat knew how to move the tobacco without getting caught because he was more than likely paying bribes to the police. I would make a nice little offering to the police in return for a bit more peace and quiet for Henry and his family gang. Talk about cheeky, it was written on his face.

'Right,' I replied, 'I can supply transport, but I'll need you to lend me a driver for the van, because I'll be in front further up the road looking for Guardia patrols.' A nice answer, I thought. Henry couldn't refuse to help me, but he wasn't about to sacrifice one of his own gang.

He smiled at me shrewdly and said, 'OK, John, you call me when you have the transport ready in La Linea.' We shook hands and walked outside; suddenly everyone was all smiles again. These guys worked on the principle that their business offers weren't to be refused. I didn't like to dwell on what would have happened in that house if I hadn't agreed to the proposed deal.

I handed over the Escort's keys to Peter, and after he gave his name and address for the Vehicle Registration Document they arranged for one of the cousins to drive me back to Marbella. We all shook hands and wished each other well. I said I would be in contact very soon.

Later that day I sat at Benson's house telling a very different story. I made out that these were guys I had known for months through the motorbiking fraternity and that I was selling the car for £2500 of cigarettes at trade price. I could see Benson was well impressed. We arranged he would have the logbook prepared, and I told him I would pay him for the car within the next two to three days. He congratulated me on getting a good deal and said that he would at some point like to meet my friends in Gibraltar, to which I agreed when this job was over.

That night I called Kath and told her about what was happening. She sounded doubtful about the deal and didn't want me to get mixed up further with another gang of smugglers.

'This is cigarettes, love. It's part of a small industry,

and it's no big deal,' I told her. 'These guys are doing it every day and have done so for years. They have all the bases covered, so there is little risk. Most importantly it's my entry ticket to Benson and his mates.' Kath still wasn't convinced by the time we'd finished talking. From where she stood she could see me dropping into a circle of criminals and smugglers who traded stolen vehicles and smuggled contraband. It was a far cry from anything else we'd ever done and was no doubt scary for her. As for me, I was hyper alert and living on my nerves. My stomach was in constant turmoil, and my appetite had dried up.

I called the Customs and gave Rob a précis of what had transpired. I had passed on the registration number of the stolen Escort and a description of Peter and his father, whose full names I had also clocked on their passports. Rob was noncommittal; he didn't say don't do it. He was pragmatic and accepted that I had to have some form of initiation into the smuggling fraternity to prove that I was *bona fide*. But with no encouragement from him I felt very down and sat late into the night musing on the situation.

I was in the middle, that was clear, and I could feel myself teetering on the edge of the smuggling pool. There was no doubt I was now a known man, and I couldn't walk away from this deal and maintain any credibility at all. I had to carry it through or just forget any ideas about living in Spain once the Benson gang was locked up and safely out of the way. No, I would continue and see it through to the end.

Early the next morning I breakfasted in Fuengirola and

spent the morning recruiting some help. I visited the bars where I had tried to chip my way into the baddies' world, and in no time the offer of a 20,000 peseta cigarette-driving job soon had people interested. I picked Dave, a singlet-clad Welshman in his mid-20s. A friendly chap always with a ready smile he was rumoured to be lying low on the Costa after carrying out a few building-society robberies in the Cardiff area, topped off, he claimed, by one at a local Kwik Save supermarket on a Saturday. After that things had got too hot for him at home, and he was taking a few months off to enjoy the summer in Spain.

Dave was usually to be found lounging around the bars, or sitting on the terrace reading the *Sun* and drinking endless cups of coffee. He knew some of the local guys and sometimes disappeared for a couple of days, but I don't know if that was because he had pulled a bird, was nursing a hangover or was off on a 'job'. One thing was certain: he seemed to have lots of cash. As a result he wore the best designer clothes and had acquired a motor scooter, an inconspicuous mode of transport in the busy streets of the Costa.

Dave said he would drive my van, and we sat down outside as I laid out the deal. He would drive it down to Gib, count the cigarettes on board and accompany them to their dropping-off point in Marbella. He would also back me up when payment was being made, the point at which, it seemed to me, when the biggest risk might occur. Dave looked like he could take care of himself.

I called Peter on his mobile, and we guardedly made arrangements for the next day. Later I drove down to the builders' merchants in Marbella where the contraband was to be delivered. There I met Ernesto, a tall, hefty man of about 60, who was obviously the proprietor and who invited me into his office for a coffee. He had previously taken a call from Henry, who had informed him of our arrangements. It was a short, wary meeting in which we agreed the delivery would be made in the early evening. To accommodate any unforeseen delays Ernesto would wait until 10 pm for us to arrive; he would have the cash on him to pay me once the cigarettes were delivered into the yard. We swapped mobile numbers, and he wished me luck.

During the afternoon and early evening I again drove down towards La Linea and carefully observed the main road looking for police parking places and likely spots for roadblocks. By now I was feeling really tense and nervous. I wanted to get the job done and out of the way.

That night I met Dave in the London Bar in Fuengirola to make final plans. We decided to do the run in what passed for the rush-hour period when there was less likelihood of a roadblock, and the road would be busy with both commuter cars and tourist coaches heading back to the main resorts in time for tea. Dave had managed to borrow a mobile phone, and we agreed to stay in contact as much as possible so I could give him a running commentary on the state of play on the road ahead. I would drive the motorbike about a mile in front of him and hopefully give him enough advance warning to pull off the road if I saw a roadblock. If I was stopped there would be no problem because the motorbike and I were both legal, and I would have all my documents with me. The presence of a mobile phone marked me as a resident rather than a tourist, but that was of no real concern at that time.

In the morning we set off fairly early and travelled steadily down towards Gibraltar. Dave was driving my Mercedes van, which by now was back in Spain and empty of electrical goods, containing only some boxes and blankets to cover up the contraband. Once again it was a perfect day. The sun was high in a cloudless sky, and there was just a breath of wind off the sea. Driving along we were in constant communication, and I pointed out the various police checkpoints I had seen, and we checked for dead spots in the mobile's signal. Near to La Linea was a bad area for mobile phones, and reception was patchy at best. We would have to work through there as fast as we could. I had already shown Dave the route we would be taking. He seemed altogether confident and just wanted to get the job over and done with.

I phoned Peter at about 2 pm and told him to meet us in La Linea. We drove there uneventfully and parked up in the car park adjacent to the large outside community swimming pool, a meeting place for camper vans and people on touring holidays. The majority of the vehicles were UK registered, and we blended in well.

A few minutes later Peter phoned to say they were ready, and we set off in the direction of the storage house. In the small lane near to it a young lad ran into the road in front of me and directed us into a yard off a small alley intersection. I swung in, and Dave closed up behind me. A corrugated sheet-metal gate clanged shut behind us, and Peter appeared from a ramshackle storage shed. He was all smiles and full of bonhomie.

'John, man,' he announced, 'your ciggies are all here, and we have put a guy on the top of the hill watching for the Guardia.' This was, I realized, to protect their driver and not for my benefit. We quickly loaded the boxes into the back of the Mercedes and covered them with blankets, but there was no way they would escape discovery if the van were stopped and searched. A young man introduced as Javier was to be our driver. I had seen him on the jetty during the night of my speedboat ride. He was pleasant enough, notable mostly for chain-smoking and just saying 'No problem' all the time. When we were ready to go Peter asked me to call him as soon as the cigs were delivered.

We set off in a convoy: a small motorbike in front to check the roads in town and to lead me a back route out of La Linea; then me on the Goldwing with the van as tail-end Charlie and Javier driving with Dave in the passenger seat looking as if he hadn't a care in the world. My heart, however, was in my mouth. If we were stopped I chanced losing my van to the police; the cigarettes would be confiscated and I would still owe Benson for the stolen Escort. This was the period of maximum exposure for me, and my body was letting me know it. I was quickly developing a banging headache.

Up through the hills, leaving La Linea in the valley below, we made it to the main road without incident. The scooter peeled off and waved goodbye as he shot back down to the coast in a puff of blue smoke. I was speaking to Dave who still seemed totally laid back. I drove easily ahead of the lumbering diesel-engine van to establish a safe distance between us. The road was busy with other traffic, and we were travelling at about

40 mph, which was slow, but the van blended in nicely with the other traffic.

Sure enough, though, as we drove down a long gradient, I spotted a couple of police cars ahead parked on either side of the road, and I quickly warned Dave to be alert. As I got closer I noticed that there was no roadblock yet. The policemen were talking and smoking in a small circle, obviously preparing to set one up. I could see traffic cones piled in little heaps at the side of one of the cars.

I relayed this information to Dave, and they decided to continue rather than pull off the road for maybe an hour or more until the police removed the roadblock. Further up the road I parked up and watched as the white van drove serenely past the police who still hadn't made a move to establish the block. That was too close for comfort for me, and as I picked up the pace again, I asked myself for the thousandth time what was I doing here? This was a far cry from the safe world of contracts and subcontracts in the oil business. I must have been mad.

The rest of the journey was just as tense, but despite the presence of a few police jeeps on the road the trip passed without any problems. We reached Marbella about two hours after leaving Gibraltar, and I called Ernesto. As we drove around the final corner I saw with relief that the yard was clear, and a garage door was wide open for us. I parked over to one side, and the van drove into the gloomy interior.

We quickly unloaded the boxes into a rear storage area. Ernesto was happy to see us, and he and Javier launched into a conversation in Spanish. When we'd finished we all wandered into the inner office, and

Ernesto produced a bottle of local 103 brandy. It was like firewater, but it helped stop the churning low down in my guts.

'Now, my amigo, the money,' said Ernesto, pulling out an old petty-cash box from his desk drawer. He took out an envelope and handed it over. I counted the money. It was dead right. We all said we would do it again next week because it had been so easy, and after a few minutes of chat we left. Dave was to drive the van back to the Fuengirola car park, and Javier climbed on to the Goldwing behind me. He loved the ride back to La Linea as we shot down between the traffic like two maniacs; the radio was blasting, and we waved at all the girls, pretty or otherwise. When I stopped just near the Gibraltar border post he jumped off and thanked me for the ride before disappearing into the throng crossing the frontier. I called Peter and told him everything was OK and promised to visit him again soon when the Vehicle Registration Document was ready for delivery. He was in good spirits and said he looked forward to doing more business with me.

Feeling much more relaxed I turned the bike once again to the north and headed for home at Carmen's. Later that night after a shower and change of clothes I met Dave in the London Bar again. I paid him his wages and was pleased to discover that he had been spreading the word about our little job to his mates. Suddenly the other locals seemed more friendly and had started to nod at me. It was great. I was being accepted into their circle, although I had no doubt they would have turned on me like a pack of wild animals if they had suspected for one minute that I was an informant for HM Customs & Excise and was setting them up for a big sting operation that was calculated to put them all behind bars for a long, long time.

Before a late supper of cheese, bread and tuna and a few glasses of red wine in the 24-hour bar on the front I took time out to phone Kath, who had been patiently waiting at home for me to call her. She was worried that something had gone wrong, and her nervousness and anxiety flooded down the phone at me disguised as shouts of anger. I tried to pacify her, explaining I had been busy and in company all day and could not have phoned her earlier. She wasn't to be put off, though, and gave me a good tongue-lashing. Although I was dejected by her attitude, I could understand how very difficult it was for her at home, kept in the dark and dependent on calls from me at odd hours to enlighten her of my progress. But I felt she didn't understand my position either, mixing with smugglers and criminals and on constant guard every minute of the day, trying to juggle between good and evil whilst knowing that one mistake could well be my last.

Little did I know then that the stress and tension were only just beginning to play a part in the plan, and their combined effects would conspire nearly to wreck our marriage in the ensuing months. It was with a heavy heart that I crawled into bed that night, exhausted by the events of the day: the hours of driving in the relentless heat, the constant vigilance not only over police movements but also of people whom I didn't know and trusted not a whit.

But at the bottom of all the dejection I could feel a

little glow of satisfaction. I had done it. Albeit by
breaking the law a little, I had nevertheless taken the
first step into the world of the drug smuggler. Now I
could only go forward and do my level best to stuff
every last one of them with whom I came into
contact. I slept the sound sleep of the just that night.

6

Secret Agent

Within a couple of weeks I was on the way to becoming established as a free agent in the group of smugglers centred around Fuengirola. I made great efforts to be seen as reliable, sure and not too greedy, with a good knowledge of both the local roads and the main arterial routes up and down Europe.

The work started off with a request to ride shotgun in front of a shipment of tobacco, after which I was asked if I would do the same for a consignment of cannabis resin. The gear was being moved from La Linea to a storage villa just south of Marbella. That job went without a hitch, and I was paid £500 for half a day's work, which just goes to demonstrate the profits made by the drug barons who trade in any commodity so long as it is illegal, and there is money to be made.

They don't handle the goods themselves but just sit in the background organizing deals and shipments whilst their workers on the ground do the actual smuggling and take the risks. That way the barons can't get caught with their hands on any illicit gear and thereby ensure they are almost impervious to prosecution should any of their gangs get caught and turn against them to become prosecution witnesses.

I put myself about more and more, making sure that I kept in close contact with Benson. Every time we met I would drop a name into the conversation just to let him know I was dealing with the right crowd. It seemed I was on the go 24 hours a day, calling in at the different bars from Torremolinos down to Gibraltar during the day and doing the round of the bars, clubs and restaurants that served the night scene.

I quickly learnt a lot about drug smuggling: who was doing what, what the risks were, how packages were wrapped and prepared for shipment to the UK and all the rumours about who had been busted. I noticed that the professional smugglers had commercial vacuum-packing machines and used vast quantities of heavy food-grade plastic bags of varying sizes, of the type in which frozen meat joints are packed in supermarkets. These were the smugglers' main weapon against the sniffer dogs.

First two cannabis soaps are wrapped together in several layers of clingfilm. Then other layers are added, one of black pepper and another of coffee grains. After a final wrap of clingfilm the whole soap is placed in a plastic bag and sealed in a vacuum machine. The air is sucked out, and the bag shrink-wrapped around the contents in that familiar squashed-up look. The sealed bag is then cut to size and the open edge heat-sealed by the wrapping machine. The entire process takes about two or three minutes per soap for the experienced wrapper.

A consignment of a hundred kilos of cannabis contains on average 400 soaps, and the whole lot will be wrapped and stored within a full day. Cannabis resin is a dense product and doesn't take up much room; 50 kg can easily be hidden in an average family saloon such as a Ford Sierra.

The packers and wrappers are masters of misdirection and deceit. The wrapped cannabis is secreted under the back seat and in the door panels, not too much there though as the windows need room in the well of the doorframe to retract when wound open.

More product is hidden within the spare wheel itself and sometimes under the front bulkhead up in the heater area. The heaters are removed, the pipes sealed off, and the hot-air blower motors are taken out. At a casual glance the bulkhead looks identical to any other car, but it is only a metal and plastic shell covering. Cannabis replaces the guts of the heating system.

I have even seen cannabis placed in windscreen-washer bottles and air-filter boxes. Storing it in the engine compartment is tricky, though, because if the car breaks down then the drug could well be unearthed by a mechanic. There are the tales, jokingly passed around, of smugglers whose car engines have overheated and ignited the slow-burning resin. The resultant clouds of blue smoke have passed through the ventilation ducts and into the passenger compartment, affecting everyone in the car. Pleasantly stoned presumably no one cared about being arrested until the next day's sober realization of their predicament.

There are specialists who live on the Costas who professionally fix up cars just for the smugglers. The way in which they work is to obtain a vehicle, usually one on UK plates that hasn't been stolen, and doctor it. They remove the rear seats and sometimes the front ones too, the cloth facings and the padding, and fit in as much cannabis as possible into the seat frames. The padding is cut down and refitted, and then the facing material is also refitted and stitched back in place. It is a professional job, and it is hard to distinguish a cannabis-laden seat from one that has not been tampered with.

If the model of car has a steel partition between the boot and the rear-seat back then that steelwork is carefully cut away. This reveals an open space, which is filled with cannabis. Later the steel is welded back into place and then resprayed in a colour match. Finally the joints are sealed with mastic that exactly replicates the manufacturer's so as to end up with a perfect-looking concealment job. Sometimes a fire-extinguisher or first-aid kit is screwed on to the steelwork to add a touch of authenticity.

These cars are driven back to the UK by experienced operators who charge anything up to £10,000 per trip. The drivers apply for new papers for the car from DVLA in Swansea, take out motor insurance and buy a green card for European travel. Their documents are complete and accurate in every detail and will stand up to any check. Then they recruit passengers for the journey. There are husband and wife teams who, along with their children, regularly do the run between the Spanish Costas and the Channel ports.

In 1994 I heard about an English man and woman in their late 50s who were stopped and searched by French Customs officers on the Hash Highway in the south of France. They had their two young grandchildren in the back of the car who were found to be sitting on 40 kilos of high-quality cannabis resin. The grandparents were arrested, and the children taken into state care, until their parents travelled down from

England to collect them. The grandparents are still in prison, serving a six-year sentence in addition to a massive Customs fine or the option of another two years inside.

I do not feel sorry for such people. They are not just naive old grannies caught up in a web of deceit but professional and experienced smugglers who carefully weigh up the risks before getting involved. They don't just walk into a bar in Spain and say, 'Hi, does anybody want me to smuggle some cannabis back to England for them?' That's an unlikely scenario. No, these people make a career of it and have probably already successfully netted thousands of pounds from previous trips.

For the experienced packer other great concealment opportunities are offered by camper vans and towed caravans. Cassette toilets are emptied, and the heavy plastic waste receptacles cut in half. They are filled with cannabis and sealed with plastic welding machines. This effectively forms a tank within a tank, after which the chemical toilet fluids are poured into the top tank. The cannabis-charged cassette unit is refitted into the caravan, and hey presto! there is both a useable toilet and a cache of hidden drugs. It's a brave Customs officer who rakes around in the shit tank just for a quick look-see. The only way to be sure whether or not there are concealed drugs is to weigh the empty cassette unit and measure the depth of the cassette from the exterior as opposed to the interior. This is a nasty, smelly job that, for obvious reasons, will not be undertaken unless the authorities have a very strong suspicion that there are drugs on board the caravan.

Calor gas and propane gas bottles are also used for concealment purposes. A bottle is completely emptied of gas and carefully cut around the middle seam weld into its two component halves. The bottom half of the bottle is filled with 10 kilo of cannabis and then a sheet of light-gauge tin is welded over the top. Finally the two halves of the tank are welded together again and spray-painted before the gas bottle is refilled.

The useable and partly filled bottle is placed in the caravan stowage compartment and connected up to the gas supply. The bottle now functions correctly, and if a Customs officer were to light the gas stove it would work. Alternatively if the official were to disconnect the gas bottle from the small regulator and open the handwheel valve he would get a blast of high-pressure butane gas in his face, another classic trick that is frequently used.

In touring caravans the whole of an interior wall may well be stripped out and the interior foam and polystyrene-type insulation removed. Packets of wrapped cannabis are carefully packed inside the outer skin and secured by tapes stapled to the wooden strengthening supports. The inner wood-grain or pastel-shade veneers are refitted very carefully, and all the accessories wired back into place. Both sides of a caravan receive the same treatment so that it sits levelly on the suspension. If experienced interior fitters are used it is impossible to tell that the walls have been disturbed in any way, although there can easily be 100kg of cannabis, worth £300,000, concealed within an average family-size caravan.

Professionals don't stash cannabis in cupboards or on shelves under clothes or in biscuit tins or coffee or sugar jars. They hide the gear in such a way that no casual check could ever uncover it. These packers secrete the gear in such a fashion that damage must be done to the fabric of the storage vehicle, be it car, van or caravan, before the cannabis is revealed.

Bear in mind that the gear is wrapped so carefully no sniffer dog would discover the cache and lead his handler to a location. It is a brave Customs officer therefore who would systematically remove the wall from a caravan or cut open a toilet cassette or remove the welded plastic fascia of a caravan fridge or the plastic panelling in a shower enclosure just on a suspicion that there may be drugs stored on board. A normal border or port inspection consists of a sniffer dog inspection of the interior whilst a couple of Customs men open drawers and check shelves and cupboards.

A classic piece of misdirection is to secrete ten or so cartons of cigarettes in a remote, inaccessible cupboard, which are invariably found during an inspection. The surprised smugglers then offer to pay duty on their uncovered tax-free haul of tobacco, whilst the Customs men are satisfied they have found a family bringing back some extra duty-free goods. The offenders either pay the extra duty or escape with a stern lecture about the correct use of green and red Customs zones before shamefacedly driving through the inspection sheds and out to deliver the caravan full of cannabis a couple of days later to their colleagues in crime.

The Customs drugs units work mainly from information from registered informants or tip-offs from the public. They can't start dismantling every vehicle going through the various Channel entry ports into the

UK. Abroad in France and Spain there are temporary roadblocks set up along the Hash Highway. These often discover the cannabis hidden by amateurs in the obvious hidey-holes, but they are not equipped to start taking vehicles apart. Any contraband that will pass the sniffer dogs and is well secreted will get past them, assuming of course that the roadblocks actually stop the smugglers in the first place. Most consignments travelling up the Hash Highway are minded by baby-sitters at the front, who are in constant contact with the loaded vehicle. Sometimes there is another vehicle behind providing a rear security screen and acting as overwatch for the main men back in Spain. Every effort is made to ensure that nobody has any clever ideas about taking a wrong turn and making off with maybe half a million pounds worth of easily saleable merchandise.

In 1994 and 1995 there was a growing trend to use motorbikes to carry cannabis. The ever vigilant smugglers had discovered that they were rarely stopped at border crossing points or by roadblocks. By their very nature there cannot be any large quantities of drugs concealed on a bike, unless the gear is stowed in the side panniers or back box, but either way it would be uncovered very quickly.

The smugglers quickly exploited this apparently laissez-faire policy towards motorcycles and put their carriers on to cruising bikes, and thereby sending hundreds of kilos of cannabis over to the UK during the following two summers. The sight of half a dozen bikers, not long-haired yobbos but more mature, respectable citizens riding quality motorcycles such as BMWs, Yamahas, Hondas and the like, does not attract a lot of attention from police or Customs officers. Furthermore, at the British entry ports bikers are the first group of travellers to be disembarked from the ferries, quickly let through immigration and Customs with no more than a cursory glance at the driver's passport.

There are more and more lone operators who regularly smuggle small amounts of gear for themselves. These guys and girls are usually successful because nobody is going to tip off the authorities about them. They keep their departure dates and itineraries to themselves and travel by constantly varying the routes and modes of transport. If they are caught it is usually by chance. Sniffer dogs may catch them because they don't have access to the vacuum-packing machines that are the foolproof method used by the professional gangs.

I knew several lone operators, each of whom did well from their illegal trade, and as far as I know they are still in business. One young couple, Andy and Jane, were very, very good. When I knew them they had been bang at it for two years. It was their stated intention to carry on until they had sufficient money to buy a house in Wales. In their mid-20s they weren't saving up for a deposit and a white wedding, they were actually going to buy a place for cash.

Andy was smallish and wiry. Fair skinned, he coloured up like a lobster in the sun and was always to be seen wearing a hat. He wore jeans, cut-offs in summer, a Granddad-vest tee shirt and tennis shoes. He was amiable enough in a distant sort of way. Personally I thought there was a lot going on behind his dopey-looking mask.

Jane looked just the opposite. Slightly taller than Andy, she was bubbly and vivacious, always on the go. She had dark skin and tanned to a really good colour under the Mediterranean sun. She looked a real goer and flirted shamelessly with everyone in sight, all part of a carefully contrived image.

With the looks and the body she used both shamelessly to disarm people, effortlessly deflecting questions by 'accidentally' showing off her well-developed tits as she bent down to take a pack of cigarettes from her bag conveniently located on the floor near her feet. She would bend down and fiddle around and then look up with big, innocent green eyes, as if to say, 'Yes, I know what you've been looking at.' She was a bloody good actress who played Jeff to Andy's Mutt, and I'd hear them later, laughing about it.

Andy and Jane appeared quite hippie-ish but not at all rough. They were certainly well spoken, though she had a tinge of a Geordie accent when she was especially animated. They both smoked and drank a tad too much, but with all the stress in their lives that was probably no wonder. They were an ambitious couple who knew what they wanted and were apparently well on their way to achieving it.

I first met them in a known smugglers' bar in Fuengirola. When I'd been seen to prove my credentials by consorting with some of the local hard men they started warming to me, and we began to talk. Once again the Goldwing was something of an icebreaker, and we chatted for a while about bikes. This led inevitably to a discussion about routes from the UK to Spain and then turned to the pros and cons of different border crossings, the best days and times to try the crossings and so forth.

Over time I had many such conversations with lots of different people in all sorts of strange and exotic locations. Although often drugs were not discussed specifically it would be unreal to think that ordinary people could be so preoccupied with frontier crossings and roadblock locations if they were only carrying an extra bottle of brandy or carton of cigarettes.

Andy and Jane became quite chatty once we had made friends. They didn't discuss their supplier or where they sold the gear, but they openly traded information about the different itineraries they had used, and they were interested in learning more about new and to them untried routes and methods of smuggling. They lived for a month or so at a time in a Dodge camper van based on a little site near Marbella. They were well prepared for their chosen money-making venture: they owned the van outright and had genuine paperwork, green cards, Caravan Club travel dockets and every bit of paper you could want.

The van itself was a diesel-engine professional camper-van conversion. The double-wheel high-top was old but in good condition with very little rust and obviously well cared for with an American-style shiny alloy spare-wheel cover and a chrome ladder leading up to a safari-type luggage rack. Alloy wheels and caged spotlights completed the picture.

During the spring, through summer and up to the middle of September the pair would travel monthly between Spain and England smuggling cannabis-resin soaps. They claimed they always bought from the same dealer and paid top money for the best product. They packed the gear themselves, and their concealment method was apparently always successful. The van's luggage rack held a windsurf board and sail and two Malibu surfboards. The drugs were hidden in one of the boards, which was split lengthways down the fibreglass-moulded side seam. The interior polystyrene was carefully cut away in sections, sized to accept the cannabis soaps, 20 or so of which filled up just over half the length of the board.

When the soaps were wrapped and packed they were sprayed with an aerosol can of cavity-wall fire-retardant spray, the stuff that is used by plumbers to fill holes in walls where pipes pass through. This spray held the soaps in place and stopped any rattles from inside the board. Finally the two halves of the board were put back together and sealed with a fibreglass car-body repair kit. Andy would sit outside the camper van under the awning, a glass of beer at his side as he repaired his damaged surfboard, and nobody paid him the slightest interest.

When the board was 'repaired' he would carefully paint over the newly sealed area. It would then be waxed and left in wet sand overnight prior to being fastened on to the luggage rack with bungee cords. For all the world it looked as if the board had been loaded up without being washed, with grains of sand still in evidence in the cracks and around the protruding skeg.

If they were unlucky and got pulled the van would of course be searched, but there was not even so much as a joint there, and a search of the interior would come up dry. Likewise the spare-wheel stowage, which cried out to be examined, was clean. If the surfboards were taken off and checked the repair was bang on, allowing for the different lengths and thicknesses the board weights were more or less the same. It was a perfect method of concealment. Again it would have to be a brave Customs officer or copper who started cutting up surfboards at random on a chance he might discover some illicit drugs.

On the other hand if they were caught they wouldn't receive such a heavy penalty: first offence, no previous record, of good character and only five kilos of product. Hardly *News at Ten* stuff, so they probably wouldn't even get a custodial sentence the first time around. They would make a profit of £10,000–£12,000 a trip, and that meant that with roughly six trips a year they weren't doing badly. They were also enjoying a hell of a lifestyle while they were doing their work. That young couple, Andy and Jane, were a classic example of how drug dealers make crime pay. They weren't big time, but they were breaking exactly the same laws as the drug barons, and they had carefully weighed up all the odds before getting involved in the business. They'll probably end up as Conservative MPs in a few years' time.

Andy and Jane were independent operators who received some respect from the bigger-known dealers. But they were only two of the many smaller operators, some of whom were successful while others got caught. It was all down to ingenuity, skill and a little bit of luck.

There were lots of wannabe smugglers. Some were dope heads who asked around to find out who had some product for sale, as if it were hard to come by. They wanted a couple of kilos as a first-time run to make enough to get a good start as proper smugglers.

It was obvious they only had a few grand to spend, and they behaved as if they were shopping in a supermarket, always hunting around to try and shave off a couple of hundred pounds from the sale price. If they'd had any experience they would have known it isn't the buying price that is important. The trick is to get hold of good-quality uncontaminated gear, have it properly wrapped and then smuggle it back into the UK. The profits per kilo far outweigh any small differential in buying price. By asking around continually for cheap gear and hanging about for days or weeks on end they marked themselves as amateurs. Then they became easy prey for the hustlers who worked the bars.

A couple of hard-looking men had come from a village in Wales, near Cardiff, to buy a few kilos of gear. They were ex-miners, redundant, thanks to an uncaring and short-sighted Tory government policy. They didn't fancy retraining as sole proprietors of a decorating business or taxi company, so they decided to invest some of their redundancy money in the drug game. Like most newcomers they were tempted by the fantastic profits that could be snatched by the successful smuggler.

These two were a joke. Aged about 40ish they couldn't get over the availability of cheap booze and all the young female flesh on offer in the tourist areas and drug zones of Spain. Most of the time they were either half pissed and swaggering around with a young big-titted girl on their arm or sitting in cafes nursing hangovers and a coffee. They were a desperate, comical pair, who reminded me of characters from *Boys from the Blackstuff*.

I spoke with them several times, and they were friendly in their blunt rural way, used to life down a coal mine and drinking in village union social clubs. They were hard men in their own fashion and would have no doubt been good one-on-one fighters. They were no match, however, for some of the hard-eyed youngsters roaming the Costa del Sol, as they were destined to find to their cost.

The hangers-on and hustlers who infest the Costa del Sol are the bottom of the human pile. With their backs constantly against the wall, they would glass a tourist, casually walk away and eat a McDonald's burger without any thought of the carnage they had left behind them. The miners were from a different school altogether and just weren't equipped to deal with the scum of the earth gathered from all the cesspools of Europe. It was an accident waiting to happen, and I had the misfortune to see it all develop like a bizarre cabaret in front of me.

The two miners, I never did get their real names, used to hang around a few different bars touting for ideas and waiting to bump into 'Mr Big' so that they could do a deal. What dickheads! The bigger of the two constantly carried a beach bag with him. I later learnt he carried a few thousand pounds in it, presumably in readiness to do a deal on a street corner. How daft can you get?

Well, the accident happened one quiet weekend. They had arranged to buy a few kilos from a street dealer, a gypsy-type with a horrible gap in his front teeth who spoke with a lisp. Spanish and broken English spoken thus is something hard to understand or to take seriously. They agreed to meet in a late-night bar in

Torremolinos. There Manolo the gypsy was to introduce the miners to his friend who would supply a sample of gear for quality control.

Things went to plan until the sample was handed over for testing. Unused to smoking cannabis the miners had hired a local guy to test the gear for them, rolling him a joint from the sample. That in itself was a remarkable display of stupidity on their part, because obviously the local would declare the product to be of good quality, whatever its true state, so that he would get a kickback from the guys selling the drugs.

The sample was pronounced OK, and the miners agreed to buy a few kilos of cannabis to smuggle home. The most dangerous time in drug dealing is when the money and the drugs are in the same room. That deal fell apart at that juncture. Having taken the money and handed over a few kilos of cannabis soaps in an apartment in the rougher area of Torremolinos I heard the buyers and their new mates the miners had a bit of a party whilst they talked about future business deals. The miners no doubt fantasized about the road to super riches, egged on by a couple of dolly birds, the exotic, erotic location and the booze.

When they left the apartment block late in the night they were jumped by a waiting gang of hoodlums who promptly relieved them of the bag containing the gear. In the ensuing fight one of the miners was knifed in the stomach. The muggers departed with the drugs, and the Guardia Civil duly arrived to pick up the pieces.

The two miners claimed they had been mugged, but they were well off the tourist trail, and the police must have been suspicious. The injured miner was taken off to hospital and his pal for questioning. He must have been seething, but he kept his cool and was released the next day. By this time everyone in town was talking about the hold-up; it certainly made the next edition of the local English-language newspaper.

The miner who had been knifed had a damaged spleen and was in intensive care. Later that night his uninjured mate, who had by then put two and two together and realized the mugging was no casual attack, was making a nuisance of himself going from bar to bar looking for the dealers. Unsuccessful in searching out his enemies he started drinking hard. He claimed he was going to the apartment to get the money back.

I sat in the bar and listened to his impassioned ravings to a little Irish girl serving drinks. She tried to talk him out of it, but she could have saved her breath for it was obvious his mind was made up. When I left the bar he was still working himself up and fuelling his anger by drinking tequila slammers. Nobody had ever told him in his local pub at home that alcohol affected the sensibilities, and in that rage was similar to sex: the spirit might be willing, but the flesh was weakened by too much booze.

Sure enough the drunken miner returned to the apartment looking for revenge and his money. Unfortunately rage and alcohol combine as sweetly seductive but unholy bed sisters, and the Spanish have a beautiful phrase: 'Revenge is a dish best served cold.' The macho bit is OK in the cinema, but in real life it's a good way to get yourself killed.

The next morning as I sat eating bacon and eggs in a pavement cafe I learnt that a drunken tourist had fallen to his death in Torremolinos. The stupid fool, he should have slept on his ire for a few days. Instead he went home in a coffin and his mate in a wheelchair. They had lost several thousand pounds and stuffed their families' chances of getting out of an impending life of grinding poverty in a Welsh pit village, where the only source of work had closed its doors.

They would have been better off starting a decorating business or a taxi company in their mining community. Instead one family is now without a father, and one man has a damaged spleen and no money. This sad tale has a moral behind it somewhere. It is a harsh demonstration of what can really happen in the high-rolling world of illegal narcotics at its most basic level. I took it to heart as a lesson. If I were found out as a Customs informant I too would be going home in a coffin, that was if they ever recovered my body.

* * *

The miners' episode wasn't an isolated story. In the summer it was happening almost weekly. The place was full of hustlers, peddlers of dodgy gear, informers, robbers and, according to rumour, undercover cops. But still the dealers arrived with bags bulging with buying money, ready to take their chances in the drug-smuggling lottery.

A favourite trick of the established well-known and well-heeled smugglers was to climb down from their pedestals and sell a smallish quantity of gear to a new wannabe, usually by using a locally known dealer as an intermediary. The new buyers would be pleased that such and such a body was dealing with them. The dealer would be solicitous and advise them how best to get the drugs back into the UK, sometimes even supplying vacuum-packing services for them. The buyers would swagger around for a few days mouthing off about their business prowess in dealing with one of the bigger dealers.

Off they would go, dutifully following the route set out for them by the nice Mr Big. Meanwhile Mr Big had sent a bigger delivery up the same route, a few miles behind the new guys. When they were safely in the queue awaiting their turn to board the cross-Channel ferry a phone call would be made to either the British police or the Customs.

The new guys were about to be sacrificed to the authorities by Mr Big to increase the chances that his own delivery was not intercepted on the same ferry. Can you imagine the surprise and gut-wrenching fear as the new guys pulled up in the Customs shed at Dover or Portsmouth? They didn't know it but their car registration number was already logged on the Customs officers clipboard. 'Good afternoon, can you pull into that bay over there please, sir?' They must have shit themselves.

Of course the new guys didn't have access to the professional vehicle packers, and so the drugs would be uncovered stashed in the spare-wheel housing or under the seats. Bingo! Go straight to jail, do not pass Go and do not collect your drug profits. Another set of losers in the lottery. Meanwhile Mr Big's load of drugs has headed safely up the motorway to the delivery drop-off point. Who cares about the sacrifice suckers? They were lucky. At least they are still alive.

I passed details of many amateur runs on to the Customs, but they weren't really interested. They were more concerned with netting the major suppliers, the barons. One 500-plus kilo snatch would equal more than 50 of the smaller amateurish-size drug runners. So they were usually left to chance inspections at the ferry ports. It became obvious to me that I should concentrate on getting close to and dealing with the longer established dealers who had access to the barons.

The bigger loads of cannabis, 500 kilos and more, are handled in a completely different and more professional style. These quantities are the province of the really big players, drugs barons and overlords, all dangerous men who have millions of pounds invested in their illegal businesses. Because of the sheer volume of product carried they cannot afford the time or trouble to split loads and secrete everything carefully in cars and caravans. They are in the bulk transportation business, and they need a fast, reliable service shuttling back and forth to the UK on a regular basis.

These guys use the fruit and vegetable packing houses in the Barcelona and Alicante regions. Open wagons containing 20 tonnes or more of fruit and vegetables, usually oranges, are their preferred method of transport. Some massive bribes are paid to stash say 500 kilos of cannabis in the loading bed of a steel tipper truck. Oranges are poured on top, and the gear is concealed under 20 tonnes of fresh fruit. The wagons, with two crew on board, drive for 24 hours nonstop and arrive at the French Channel ports after stopping only to refuel and for calls of nature. The lorries are given priority at the ports because of their fresh-produce cargo. They are rarely detained by the Customs who have to process literally millions of shipments of foodstuffs, chemicals, household products and manufactured items of every type during a year.

Each 500-kilo load successfully delivered by the smugglers represents £1.85 million in sales. Taking into account a purchase price of £300,000 and delivery costs of about £50,000 the drug barons stand to make a profit of nearly £1.5 million per delivery. In 1996 Customs & Excise seized 46,000 kilos of cannabis resin in the UK, mainly at the point of entry, yet they acknowledge that figure represents a seizure rate estimated at only ten per cent of the total amount of the drug entering the country. It is easy to imagine the sheer volume of drugs and the profits made thereon arriving in Great Britain each week.

Another route the big boys use is the tourist coach. Drivers are suborned by offers of large cash payments. The coaches, owned sometimes by major tour operators, drop off their loads of tourists at their holiday destinations and then have a couple of spare days waiting to return to the UK with other homeward-bound, sunburned tourists. The coaches travel to local coach parks, where they are overhauled, washed, cleaned internally, restocked with drinks and so forth. During that time a nondescript van draws up and overall-clad workers transfer a number of suitcases and holdalls into the cavernous cargo and baggage holds located under the aisleway and passenger seating areas.

Days later when the coach collects the home-bound tourists no one would ever question that there are already some ten or twelve suitcases and bags already loaded. The driver heads home knowing that as a tour coach they are unlikely to be stopped and searched by Customs. At frontier crossing points immigration officers may enter the coach to check passports, but they are very unlikely to insist that all baggage is unpacked and checked. Of course all the drugs are carefully wrapped and sealed and so would be undetectable by the sniffer dogs.

At the English entry ports some work a system whereby coaches arrive and pass through the Customs with the passengers and baggage still on board. So the illegal shipment sails straight through the checking area, and another 400 or 500 kilos enters the country with nobody any the wiser. Except the smugglers and the driver.

The driver may be paid up to £20,000 for his part in the operation, which he may split with his co-driver, and there is little risk for either of them. If the drugs are discovered they can simply claim that they didn't see the bags loaded; that they were loaded at the coach park by a local courier firm. They're in the clear and are very unlikely to be successfully prosecuted. Meanwhile if the drugs do pass into the country then the smugglers have made another million pounds or so.

An alternative route used by the big boys is one with which I quickly became closely involved. I was asked to baby-sit a load of drugs being moved from a villa located in the hills outside La Linea to a small working harbour further down the main coastal road, south of Gibraltar.

The drugs were concealed in an old-looking Seat panel van, and I led them down the hour-long journey there without any problems. I drove into the harbour and as per instructions went into a small bar inside the marina. It was a cheap little place with a scarred counter and cracked tile flooring. Sitting at a small side table were two Brits. I recognized them from a British pub in Gibraltar, also frequented by drug dealers. I bought a Coke and sat down with them. One of them, Gerry, was openly rolling a joint, whilst his mate looked on. They seemed quite unconcerned and obviously felt secure in their surroundings.

We chatted for a few minutes while Gerry got his joint going. He told me he was from Northamptonshire, and his mate Vince was from Sheffield. Vince looked a real nutter. Gerry pointed out through the dirty window overlooking the harbour to a pretty sail boat.

'That's the baby, the *Ocean Spray*,' he said. 'She'll sail us back to the UK in no time, and then we drop off the gear and return home for a nice quiet year after so much hard work.' Both he and Vince fell about laughing at this. Whether it was a private joke or they were stoned I don't know, but it amused them no end.

After a while I reminded them there was a van parked around the corner and that the driver was probably having kittens by now.

'No sweat, John boy,' said Gerry. 'Come on, then, let's do it,' and with that he gathered together his bits and pieces and sauntered towards the door. The barman watched us leave with an impassive, blank look on his face. I could just imagine him picking up the phone immediately after we left his bar. I mentioned this to Gerry who laughed out loud.

'No way, Johnny, he's well paid for watching the boat for us,' he said. So the barman was a part of the gang too. It seemed to me that wherever I turned I tripped over a drug dealer or someone in their pay. No wonder these guys were so unconcerned. They had their arses covered on every side.

We climbed on to the boat, and I had a good look around. It was very pretty and clean both inside and out. I know nothing to speak of about sailing boats, but I noticed it had a sturdy rubber boat with a powerful outboard fastened to some bright steel davits on the stern. All the deck ropes were neatly coiled and tidy looking; all in all it appeared a functional, businesslike piece of kit. I surreptitiously paced its length at about 18 metres and noted that it was made of wood, had two masts and seemed to have all brass or steel fittings. It was not unlike another hundred boats lying in the marinas up and down each holiday resort on the Spanish Costas.

I called the Seat driver on the mobile, and shortly afterwards the van crept quietly up the concrete jetty to the boat and stopped alongside. The driver and two passengers got out and stretched. They obviously knew their way around and sauntered off casually to the bar for a drink and a piss.

My job was now done, but I hung around for a while talking with Gerry and Vince, who, it transpired, had jumped Crown Court bail whilst awaiting trial on possession and trafficking charges. For this, he claimed, he would have gone down for a couple of years. 'It's far better to be here in Spain with all the birds and booze,' was his philosophy.

Gerry told me the boat would leave within the next two or three days. They were waiting for a replacement part for the autopilot and would sail as soon as that was delivered and fitted by a marine engineer. By this time the sun was starting to go down, and I took my leave of them as they contemplated loading the drugs on to the boat under cover of darkness.

This opportunity was too good to pass up. It was my chance to land a really good catch for Customs. I had already discussed it with Rob and Steve, and now I had all the information I needed to pass along to them. I knew sufficient details: the name of the boat, her description, port of origin, destination and the amount of drugs on board. The names of the crew were incidental to the operation; the main objective was to stop 2000 kg of cannabis resin from hitting the streets and to catch the organizers.

Everything was set, and I flew back to England to discuss the situation with Customs. We met up at Hartshead services on the M62 again. I bought a copy of a boating magazine at the shop there and searched out a photograph of a boat like the *Ocean Spray* for the lads. I gave them all the information I had and advised them the boat was due to leave as soon as the autopilot was repaired and would probably depart within the week.

Customs were very happy with what I told them and asked me to return to Spain and report back to them as soon as the boat left. I had time for a quick overnight visit home, a meal and a few drinks in a local restaurant, and then off to Manchester airport for Malaga, from where I immediately drove down to the port. It was early afternoon when I pulled in to the harbour, and the boat was still there, glistening in the baking sunshine. By this time the boys were getting really pissed off with hanging about waiting for the repair to be completed.

Gerry seemed a bit suspicious of my interest, and I did not want to push it too far or appear too obvious, so I made up a story of having left a special Zippo lighter there last week. Driving in the area I had thought to call in and see if they had it. Later Gerry gave me his mobile number, and I promised to call him and visit with some beers the next night if they were still there.

That evening I called the Customs 24-hour number and asked for Rob. I had to give my codename to the male operator, who took my message and told me it would be passed on within the hour. It all seemed very James Bond-ish. I confirmed the boat was still in the harbour.

That night I stayed in a small pension nearby, a few miles off the main road. I took no chances and parked the Goldwing well back and away from the road behind some ramshackle outbuildings. I didn't want Gerry or his mates spotting the bike and putting two and two together. I had a solitary meal of ham, cheese and an olive and tomato salad and a few beers. The pension was clean, cheap and restful. After all the running about over the last few days I was knackered so I slept really well.

The next day I phoned Gerry on the mobile number he had given me, but there was no answer. I drove down to the harbour and stopped at a garage to buy a couple of packs of beer. Driving into the port I was surprised that the boat had gone. There was no sign she had ever been there, just an empty berth, the oily harbour water moving listlessly in the bright sunlight.

The guys in the bar were a bit reluctant to talk and would not be drawn into conversation. I sat around outside for a while and drank a few of the beers I had brought with me so that I didn't seem in too much of a hurry to leave. I remembered that the bar owner was in the firm and might well put in a call back to Marbella after I left. A couple of hot hours in the sun drinking beer seemed to me to be a small price to pay for security and peace of mind.

Driving back up to Carmen's pension in Fuengirola I called Customs again and advised them that the boat had left, that the operation was on. I could detect a quickening of interest over the phone. Steve double-checked the description again with me and told me I had done a good job. He suggested I should forget it for now, and they would let me know of any definite developments. I was only too happy to move on. I was a busy boy, and I had a lot more work yet to do.

7

Life in the Fast Lane

The drug dealers on the Spanish Costas live in a manner that cannot be likened to anything akin to normal existence. Initially it is important to understand they are mostly from the criminal classes and consequently operate by a different set of rules to other, more law-abiding members of society. These people are human predators, and they cruise through different levels of society like sharks in the ocean. Similar to their marine counterparts they are ruthless, amoral, efficient machines. They feel no loyalty, have no regrets and display no real emotion other than anger when things don't run on track.

If the bigger players are caught and convicted they are rarely rehabilitated as full members of society. They often remain outcasts and will never conform; almost like serial killers they have to reoffend. They are in fact serial drug dealers, and no sooner are they released from prison than they slip back into the netherworld of drugs, sex and violence. They find themselves drawn to the massive illegal profits to be made there like moths to a flame.

They know society cannot really harm them and feel themselves safe from any meaningful retribution that would be a proper deterrent. They certainly don't fear policemen, Customs officers, judges or any judicial process. If caught or informed upon and charged with conspiracy they simply divert funds from overseas banks into the accounts of the best legal minds they can buy. State prosecutors, the Director of Public Prosecutions (DPP) and the Crown Prosecution Service (CPS), are only ordinary, workaday solicitors; these guys employ the best defendants money can buy. Unless they are caught with their hands on the drugs, which happens very very rarely, they usually walk free.

There is no effective deterrent that will stop them from buying, shipping and selling drugs. The only thing they fear are others of their ilk. Drug wars flare up and die away with monotonous regularity, like armies skirmishing along a disputed border. It may be over an imagined slight or a clash between two opposing dealers when buying or selling. Sometimes money carriers are ripped off, or they may tip off the police about each other either out of spite or for gain. It's a classic, capitalist world model, where battles are fought without rules, and any tactics are acceptable. The barons display all the moral attributes of Attila the Hun.

One day after I had been working freelance for a couple of months Colin Benson asked me to meet his son, also called Colin. I had heard a lot about this guy, most of which added up to what I can only describe as a really nasty piece of work. He was 28 years old, unmarried and looked like his father except for his rather feminine-looking mouth and bright pink lips and tongue. Short, fat and prematurely balding, he had black, greasy hair that lay thin and flat against his shiny scalp.

Ostensibly a dealer in the luxury used-car market he was every corpulent inch a successful-looking spiv. With a big diamond signet ring, a gold diamond-encrusted Rolex and top-quality leisure clothes he looked the part. He spoke with a gratingly nasal voice that complemented his image perfectly. Not one for social niceties he talked loudly and used gutter language continually, no matter in whose company or where he was. He would mouth off, belch or fart just as the mood took him, in a bar or restaurant or just walking down the street. He was a Lancashire version of a 1930s' Chicago street hoodlum.

I learnt from his proud father that Colin Jr was deeply mixed up with a London Greek gang heavily into heroin and cocaine dealing; he was a northern England connection for them. He was known to the police and had several minor busts behind him. Early one morning they raided him again after having had him under surveillance for some time and discovered a holdall containing several kilos of cocaine in his wardrobe. Caught bang to rights, he had been arrested and was refused police bail; the local magistrates' court jailed him on remand pending trial.

I was told that his London associates put up a substantial sum of cash for a rather dumb villain to tell the police the bag didn't belong to Benson but to him. Unsurprisingly the police were not taken in by this rather flimsy story, but it was enough of an argument when advanced by Benson's top-flight barrister to convince a judge in a private meeting in chambers that Benson Jr should be granted bail.

Although on bail he continued trading as before until the week of his trial. In the middle of the proceedings, when his barrister told him he would probably be convicted and go to prison for a considerable time, he decided to abscond. One day he just didn't turn up for court. On the run, he headed down to Spain's infamous Costa del Crime. By this time he had acquired some cash, a false passport and some contact phone numbers.

Young Benson arrived on the Costa del Sol looking for somewhere discreet to hide out. Because of my contacts with a couple of estate agents from when I was seeking industrial units for the import business, Benson phoned me and asked if I could locate a quiet, out-of-the-way place, not known to anyone, in which his son could lay low for a while. I told him I would think about it and get back to him. Of course I immediately told the Customs what I then knew about Benson Jr. They were interested and asked me to get closer to him.

I soon met up with both the Bensons. They really were like two peas in a pod. In the three or four days since I had spoken to Colin Benson his son had established himself in a luxury apartment near Puerto Banus, an upmarket development of high-quality shops, villas and apartments centred around a millionaires' boating marina south of Marbella. Puerto Banus is where the megarich go out to play whilst staying on the Costa del Sol. Several movie icons and pop stars, Adnan Khashoggi the gun dealer and Arab oil playboys use the marine as a base. The value of the yachts in the small harbour would pay off a large portion of the Spanish national debt.

It was in this centre of ostentatious wealth that young Benson had picked a ground-floor luxury apartment for himself, a three-bedroom apartment for £1500 per month, with a two-month deposit. The place was tremendous. A large ornate front door led to a neo-Roman lounge complete with black and white marble tiles and floor-to-ceiling fluted columns. The lounge contained a pond with a fountain, a posh bar with an ice-making machine and a small disco-style dance floor. The furniture was old and heavy with an array of white leather chairs and settees around a massive coffee table with a solid crystal glass top. There was also a space-age kitchen, four bathrooms, a games room with a pool table and large French windows opening on to a tile patio overlooking a kidney-shaped community pool.

It really was quite incredible, and all that was missing was a drawer full of gold chains and a condom machine. As is customary in Spain the apartment was furnished down to the last detail, and all Colin Jr needed to do was to move in his clothing. Everything else came with the property: bed linen, table napkins, towels and his and hers bath sheets were all provided.

This was living millionaire style, and it was beyond the reach of most people. Yet this bloke had jumped bail, driven through Europe in a nicked car and less than a week later was luxuriating in a superrich lifestyle. But it had to be paid for, and he was the lad to organize the money-gathering. When I was first introduced to him by his father he wanted me to escort a shipment of 100 kilos of cannabis from Malaga up to a mate of his in Benidorm. He offered me £3000 for the trip and pulled a thousand out of his pocket there and then. I thought this was a good one for the Customs, and so I nodded at him in agreement.

'Right, well, you'll be going tomorrow night, so you can stay here with me tonight, and we'll have a few drinks together,' he said. So much for me immediately tipping off the Customs. I quickly found out that dealing with this guy was not like playing around with his father or any of the others in Fuengirola. This boy meant business, and he was as paranoid as a nun at a whores' convention. I immediately sensed a feeling of mistrust in him, and I resolved to tread very carefully.

I told him I would go out for a drink that night, but first I would have to return to my digs to shower and change my clothes. He smiled and offered to drive me there so that we could chat. There was no way I could refuse without it seeming suspicious. So we all piled into his car, a nearly new Mercedes with air conditioning, leather seats and dark-tinted windows, and went off to collect my kit.

It was always the same with Benson Jr: instant decisions, immediate action and sod the consequences. He should have been a City trader, and he certainly lived the lifestyle of a well-born and moneyed young executive. But because he was the new boy on the block he had to do some of the dirty work himself, and he would turn up unannounced at the sharp end from time to time.

After he had been in Spain for only a few weeks already he had acquired a small circle of friends, one of whom always carried a small automatic gun. It wasn't a Dirty Harry magnum-size showstopper, but it was enough to put a few holes in anyone who ripped off

Benson or any of his mates. The frightening thing was not only that the gun was so easily available but also that he was probably stupid enough to use it. I didn't want any target practice on me.

* * *

I had visited Benidorm and the general area of the Costa Blanca many times in my life. Since living there during the abortive period when we had owned a bar in the old town we had returned frequently to visit my parents and on quick-break holidays. Whilst we hadn't formed any firm friendships in that town with its largely transient population we did know plenty of the old-timers, that is the people who have lived there for more than two or three years.

I certainly knew some of the dodgier hang-outs frequented by drug users, and it didn't take a great leap of the imagination to work out that the drug dealers were located in the same locales. I had used my Benidorm knowledge as part of my credibility-building factor with Benson, and now it was being called upon by his son.

The day of the Malaga–Benidorm run I met some English guys at Benson's apartment, and we planned out a route up to Benidorm. Really it was simple: follow the coast road towards Almeria, branch inland to pick up the motorway and carry straight on towards Alicante. It was a hell of a run, but actually safe enough. The Guardia were more likely to be looking for drug shipments heading towards the French border than any running along the coast roads.

The drugs were stashed in a butcher's van packed

solid with trays of chicken, beef and so on. The vehicle was refri-gerated and bloody cold inside the rear compartment. Of course the idea was that the chill factor would defeat a casual search; no copper would make a driver and his mate empty out a full load of frozen but quickly melting foodstuffs at the roadside. That was the theory at any rate.

The van was based on a Seat diesel. A Seat is a Spanish-built Fiat, and like all Italian-bred vehicles it could really motor. The two English guys, George the driver and Alf his mate, were obviously well known to Benson, and I had the feeling I was going to be under scrutiny the whole trip. Anyway we all checked the batteries in our mobiles, agreed stopping points along the route, and then we were off.

It was a beautiful day, and we made good time along the road up past Fuengirola, Torremolinos and past the outskirts of Malaga itself. We swung inland for a while and then settled on to the motorway-like road through some stunning scenery, cliffs and coves that flew past at a good rate.

I arrived at the first stopping point a good ten minutes in front of the van and had a drink and a cigarette leaning against a wall as I watched the oncoming traffic. When the van pulled in the two lads disappeared inside the café cum garage without acknowledging me, though they had surely seen me and the Goldwing, both of us were in plain view. It seemed to me that for the first time I was working alongside a gang who seemed to have an idea of what they were about. I set off while they were still inside and motored further up the road in front of them.

Driving that motorbike around in a hot climate, with

the sun shining down and not too much traffic, is better than riding in cold, wet England. There is no need for sets of leathers, scarves, gloves, boots and all the other warm and wet-weather paraphernalia. You can drive in shorts, shirt and trainers, though, of course, the safety purists argue that you need all the Kevlar protective gear whatever the weather. My view is that if you are dicing with death every day whilst acting as a drug informant the chances of being injured in a motorbike pile-up fade into insignificance. So there I was cruising up the road listening to a tape of Queen and Freddie Mercury singing 'Radio Ga Ga' and thinking that everything was pretty cool.

By now I was missing Kath and Natalie and wanted to get home for a few weeks to relax with my family. But I knew that by now I was deeply enmeshed in the drugs scene and that if I did anything so obviously out of step with the drug gangs' philosophy it would cause needless suspicion. So I resolved not to go back to the UK for a few more weeks at least. There was nothing for it but to continue on the road and try and find time to contact the Customs as soon as possible.

We drove for six hours that day, stopping every hour for a ten-minute break, mainly for my benefit. There's nothing like a thrumming bike seat to give you a numb bum. At first it's just uncomfortable, but if you ignore it the cramps set in, and it can be bloody dangerous. So we pulled over and had a cigarette and a drink from time to time and filled up with fuel. Other than a few words on the mobile there was no sign of recognition among us.

Towards tea time we passed through the sprawling town of Elche, and I knew we were on the last leg of the journey. On the bypass there I saw the first Guardia Civil car of the day travelling in our direction. The boys inside were smoking the inevitable Ducados and talking to each other, and they didn't seem like much of a threat to anyone. Up beyond Elche, then the area capital of Alicante, to Alicante airport, we kept to the motorway and didn't drive along the pretty, wide boulevards of the town. Then past Villajoyosa and its squalid roadside brothels and the short jag up to Benidorm, one of those places, like Miami, that always look good in the distance; it's when you see it up close and smell it that the magic starts to break down fast.

The van drivers and I had a short meeting at the motorway services outside Benidorm and worked out where we were to leave the van for collection by the other gang. We decided on a supermarket car park near La Nucia. Back on the motorway we drove for about ten minutes until we hit the Benidorm exit. We could see the town twinkling off to our right, and it looked great in the evening twilight. Instead of turning off towards it we took the exit up towards La Nucia. I watched as the van passed safely by the exit toll booth manned by an elderly woman.

Near La Nucia we drove through the roadside lemon groves; the aroma was enchanting. Soon we came to a supermarket and small parade of shops on the right-hand side, which had only just closed. We pulled off separately into the car park, the boys parking the van discreetly at the rear amongst the rubbish skips and empty pallets. It looked innocuous there, as if it were waiting till the next morning to make a delivery.

We got out, and the boys tossed to see who was sleeping with the van. George won, and after a quick call to young Benson we left Alf sulking with a cold pack of beer and some sandwiches before setting off on the Goldwing for the lights of Benidorm. We headed for town over the bumpy Lemon Express train lines and drove into the Ruzafa, one of the main streets in the old town.

We parked the bike alongside a million mopeds and some go-faster 125cc screamers, locked up the helmets, set the alarm, collected our mobiles, and we were off. I said we should check out the accommodation situation and visit some of the bars I knew.

Near the headland in the small pedestrian precinct of Calle La Palma, known more accurately by the locals as the Street of 1000 Arseholes, is the Playboy Bar. From the outside it resembles an old sweetshop, inside it is all dark wood and red upholstery with a spotlit bar and heavy Andalusian furniture. Tourists are encouraged and provide a welcome diversion from the locals bemoaning their lack of funds. The Playboy specializes in mixing weird and exotic cocktail drinks: the Banana Cow is a house speciality. The music is rock *à la* Jimi Hendrix and Bruce Springsteen. Eddie the bar owner, a tall, slim ex-Brummie, is discreet; a part of the old Benidorm establishment set, he is a good friend and drinking partner of Ray the Chippy, Benidorm's original fish and chip shop proprietor.

Eddie doesn't do drugs, but he watches the cavorting and shuffling throngs in his bar and sticks to offering a sympathetic ear to the never ending tales of woe. He learnt his bar trade in New Orleans and copies the Swiss style of management, knowing what goes on but happy to be a neutral observer and pocket the profits of selling drinks to winners and losers alike. Eddie is ageing now, with a few grey hairs creeping into his immaculate black pelt. He is respected in the town, and there is never any trouble in the bar; you get the feeling that it wouln't be a good move to argue with Eddie: he has presence.

The Playboy has the best-stocked bar in Benidorm, offering more varieties of whisky than can be found anywhere else in the town. The up-market locals meet in Eddie's for a few drinks and a gossip on Saturday afternoons and on Sundays before taking their families for Sunday lunch at the Broadway or whichever other eating joint is in vogue that season.

When we walked into the Playboy that night it was as if I had only been there earlier in the week. Eddie didn't raise an eyebrow, he just nodded and said, 'You look a bit thirsty. What'll it be? San Miguel or Mahou?' We settled for a bottle of Mahou each; no glasses, thanks, we're locals and eschew such niceties. It was close and hot inside, and Eddie was obviously economizing with the air con again, so we wandered outside and leaned against the wall watching the street activity.

Not far from the Playboy is The Castilian. A Spanish bar not for the faint-hearted, there are never many tourists in The Castilian. Years ago it was a small open-all-hours walk-in establishment with a minuscule bar area and a large grill where Carlos would cook a wicked *pincho* or burger with blue cheese and garlic filling.

Now after taking over and spreading into Harry's Bar next door, it is bigger and boasts separate male and female toilets, but the atmosphere is still overtly mid-80s, Spanish hippy. Walk in anytime after 10 pm and the noise will deafen you. Leather-jacketed locals use the place as their supply house. The whisky of choice is straight Ballantynes *con hielo*, and cannabis is available from a number of suppliers who frequent the place. As in most of Spain there is a regular supply of good-quality gear at good prices.

Generally a quiet, moody bar you can on occasion be treated to an impromptu flamenco show. But don't get upset if the dancer stumbles and crashes into your table – in keeping with the spirit of the place just shout a little, playfully, and offer the artiste a drink from your bottle, or you can always join in if you're so minded. The guy slouched at the end of the bar staring into the mirror behind the bar could be the local undercover narc. He won't bother the locals, but he has been known from time to time to pull a tourist and demand an on-the-spot 'fine', especially at the end of the month.

Brash, brassy Benidorm is like an old, careworn whore with a false smile and bleached hair, but I always feel comfortable there. I know all the nooks and crannies, the ups and downs and the places to avoid. That night though I was tired and just wanted a room, shower and bed. But it wasn't to be.

My mobile started ringing; it was young Benson. He wanted us to locate the guys who were collecting the van and hand it over to them. He told us he would be up in the morning to pick up his money for the delivery. This guy's arrogance was unbelievable. Everyone else was guarded in conversations when they were talking over open telephone lines, but he didn't seem to care a toss one way or the other. I kept the conversation as short and neutral as possible and promised to call him back later.

We walked to some phone boxes near the Plaza Triangular, near to where the Avenida Mediterraneo runs out of the narrow streets of the old town down the dual carriageway thoroughfare towards the Rincon de Loinx of the New Benidorm with its skyscrapers, McDonald's burger bars and night-club scene. We waited amongst the ETs – tourists phoning home – until a cabin came free. I stood outside whilst George called the local contact and made arrangements to meet. He grinned and gave me a thumbs up, and we returned to the bike and headed out of town back towards La Nucia and the parked van.

We found Alf fast asleep. We could have nicked the van from under him without him knowing what was happening. After a bit of piss-taking and another can of beer each an old-looking estate car on Alicante plates rolled into the car park. George and Alf seemed to recognize its two occupants and walked over towards them. Friendly nods and greetings were exchanged, and then the leader of the two newcomers looked over at me. He was about 35 years old with a broad Scots accent and wearing a baseball cap and blue jeans. A grubby-looking, baby-faced individual he looked as if he were in need of a good tubbing with disinfectant and carbolic soap.

'Who are you then, friend?' he asked me. 'I'm showing these two the quietest routes and baby-sitting the van for Colin,' I replied, looking straight at him.

'I don't know you. You could be a narc for all I know,' he replied.

I knew he was just sounding off and couldn't possibly have a clue about my real role, but instinctively I felt my guts clench tight. This was just the kind of shit I didn't want.

'Well, mate,' I said, 'I don't know you either, but I'm

not having kittens about it. You know Alf and George, and that's good enough for me.'

'Yeah, leave it, our Keith,' said George. 'John's OK. He's running with Colin now. He's just earning a few bob doing a little work on the side.'

Keith nodded, but I could sense a feeling of mistrust; he was obviously a careful man. We all walked over to the freezer van, and Keith said, 'Let's have a look at this gear then.' I thought he was joking, but George and Alf immediately opened the rear doors and started pulling out the trays of frozen food.

'What the fuck are you doing?' I almost shouted. 'We can't unload everything here. If the coppers drive past we'll all be busted.' George looked at me as if he hadn't considered the stupidity of unloading a freezer van full of frozen meat products in the dark at the back of a supermarket.

He nodded slowly. 'Yeah, John's right,' he said. 'We'll show you at your place.'

Keith nodded as if we'd just passed some sort of test, maybe it was a dope test. 'Yeah, OK, we'll take the van and see you boys in the morning.'

That seemed a better solution to me, because if anyone were going to get screwed it wasn't me. We quickly agreed to meet up at noon the next day, and Keith and his silent pal would drop George and Alf off down in Benidorm before shoving off to their hide-out. Quickly we mounted our respective rides and set off into town. I could feel my ears burning and could easily imagine the sort of conversation they were having in the estate car about me.

After the two Benidorm dealers had gone, Alf, George and I decided to have a last drink before finding a room. It was then I realized that the two of them seemed extraordinarily happy. The daft pillocks had both dropped an E courtesy of Keith and his mate during their short car ride. There was nothing I could do about it, they were set for a night on the town, dancing the night away. I made my excuses, pleading I was tired after the long drive from Malaga and slunk off to find a hotel. The boys weren't upset. I could see their feet itching as they jigged about impatient to be on with the night's entertainment. We said our goodbyes, and then I left them to it, silly idiots.

The next day Colin Benson arrived along with two more of his henchmen. He seemed to have an inexhaustible supply of them. They completed the final deal with Keith the Benidorm dealer, but by that time I was on the bike and headed back to the Costa del Sol. I had stopped at the first motorway services and put in a long call to my Customs handlers. Of course by then it was all after the event information, but it was of interest to them to have details of how the cannabis was moved between the coastal areas and the method of transport, as well as the names of the players involved.

I never did discover the final outcome, but a few months later I overheard that the regular shipment up to Benidorm had been busted. No one ever told me if that was a result of my information. Dealing with the Customs is rather like talking to a sponge: they take it all in, but never give back any information.

Benson Snr had been in discussions with a gang based in Liverpool. His son effected the introductions to mates he had picked up during his time on remand. From conversations I heard it seems that remand prison is a form of employment bureau for villains; as soon as they are let out there is a job ready for them.

This gang were regular shippers of hundreds of kilos of cannabis and some cocaine. Recently they had lost a few loads, and because they weren't sure if it were either just dumb bad luck or the suppliers or shippers had an informer in their midst they wanted to try a new route and a new shipping contractor. Benson was ready made for this type of operation. I was in contact with my Customs handlers from day one on this shipment, and we were all set up and prepared.

The plan was that Benson would arrange to ship 65 kilos into Liverpool as a trial; if that were successful then he would organize 300 kilos a month along the same route for a six-month period. I don't know what he was due to be paid per kilo, but the thought of it was enough to make his eyes water. He spent thousands of pounds setting up his operation on the strength of profits to come.

Advertisements were placed in newspapers in the UK, the Costa Blanca and around the Malaga region offering furniture removal, shipping and export and import services. Offices were rented, letterheads produced and staff employed. A nearly new Mercedes box van was bought legally in England, sign written and driven to Spain.

There is a constant stream of people moving from England to live in Spain, and a line of folk returning in the opposite direction, of families beaten by the harsh economics of business, of lives ruined by booze or relationships shattered by infidelity. Spain is the absolute testing ground for partnerships and dreams.

the spanish connection

Many of these treks back and forth require an accompanying house move, and international furniture removers have, so I am told, a great and thriving business as a result.

Benson's idea was to graft a drug-smuggling organization on to an existing outfit. He started a business and got it off the ground very quickly. This was not as hard as it sounds because Benson succeeded by cutting prices to the absolute minimum and giving all sorts of guarantees about deliveries and free breakage insurance and so forth. His real competitors must have sat there scratching their heads and wondering how he could do it.

He dispatched several loads to England without any drugs on board just to test the Customs systems at frontiers and check out the roadblock inspections. I saw the consignments of furniture and household possessions leave. Everything was done properly: all the boxes were marked with collection and delivery addresses; there were typed inventories and multicopies of all paperwork. It was a dream to behold.

Eventually Benson and his paymasters deemed themselves satisfied and were ready to try a smuggling run. Furniture and household effects were collected from addresses in and around the Fuengirola area, all destined for the UK. The idea was that the drugs would be concealed in boxes in the middle of the household items. As insurance against the drugs being found the van driver would have an inventory that showed he had collected the boxes from an apartment in central Fuengirola.

This apartment actually existed, but it was a studio holiday-let for cash on a weekly basis. Two girls had rented it, had given false ID to the flat's caretaker who was really only interested in the proffered pile of pesetas he'd received from the skimpily clad young women. The pair just disappeared after the boxes were collected. I remember how the driver and labourer laughed about the fact that the caretaker had helped them load up. If questioned subsequently, however, he would not remember anything out of place or dubious about the exercise.

The boxes were inventoried and placed carefully amongst the genuine delivery. Each box was identified by a mark that confirmed it had been supplied closed and sealed by the customer, so the company were taking their client's word that the inventory was accurate. George, of the Benidorm run, was to be the driver again. I was to be paid £1000 cash to escort him as a baby-sitter to the Channel port.

A week before the operation was due to take off I returned to England. I met up with Rob and Steve, my Customs handlers, at another clandestine rendezvous in a motorway services, and we went through the operation in detail. I told them that I was to accompany the van carrying the cannabis up to the ferry port and then ring Benson to tell him it was on board. He would have another passenger on the ferry to check it went through British customs all right. Rob wanted me to phone him with the description and registration number of the van, which I said I would do as soon as the van was loaded. I had noticed, however, that Benson had become increasingly tense as the planned departure time approached. He was behaving in a very paranoid fashion and going to extreme lengths to keep the operation a secret, even from his normal circle of friends. Unbeknown to me he might arrange for a last-minute switch of vehicle. Nevertheless our tactics were agreed, and we parted. I returned to Spain, explaining my absence by the fact that Kath was ill and would have to go into hospital for treatment.

Two days later we set off. George drove the Mercedes van filled with furniture and the drug shipment, and I rode the Goldwing out front. We were in constant contact by way of mobile phones. From Malaga to Madrid the trip went like a dream. We stopped every two or so hours for the usual quick break, piss, drink and fuel up, then we were off again. The first night we reached a small town on the outskirts of the northern edge of Madrid. I pulled into a small motel just as dusk was falling and checked in and paid in advance for one night. Whilst unloading my overnight bag from the bike's panniers outside I called George and told him where I was.

A few minutes later he pulled into the car park and, ignoring me, walked in to the motel and booked himself in. After a shower I went into the bar cum restaurant and ordered a drink. George was sitting further up the bar nursing a beer, and we struck up a conversation and decided to have a meal together. To any observer we would have seemed just like two Brits travelling on the same road who after a chance meeting decided to chew the fat together. Outside on the patio drinking brandy and cokes we had a more private chat. I felt a little sorry for George, because if all went to plan he would be locked up the next night. Our drink together could very well be his last taste of brandy for a few years to come, if only he did but know it.

A few hundred yards up the road in what passes for next door on those Spanish international routes I could see the brightly lit, flashing neon signs of a Whiskeria. Ostensibly a late-night drinking club this is often a front for a brothel in Spain. I suggested to George that as he hadn't had a Spanish bird he should go along and try it out. Not speaking the language he was loath to go on his own and wanted me to accompany him.

So at about ten o'clock there we were walking into a brothel in northern Madrid. Inside it was dimly lit with red lights and spotlights on a small, raised stage area. Most of the customers were obviously transport drivers and local farmer types, a friendly enough bunch. We wandered over to the bar and ordered two beers from a bare-breasted girl behind the bar. Things were looking up.

Two beers and two whiskies of indeterminate manufacture were pushed across the bar. After much shouting back and forth over the loud 80s' dance music I learnt that every drink order had to include a whisky. The round of drinks cost 4000 pesetas, approximately £20, to include a free floorshow. A quick glance round the other patrons showed that they too all had small whisky shot glasses in front of them, so the rip-off was not just limited to us foreigners.

We made our way towards an empty table and chairs and within a minute of sitting down two 'ladies' wandered over and sat down too, smiling ingratiatingly at us. George beamed at me. Silly sod! he thought he'd pulled a bird already. I leaned across and explained the situation to him as directly as I could. These girls were workers, who would sit and entertain us, but we would be expected to buy a bottle of exorbitantly priced house champagne for the privilege. Later you could take the girl of your choice upstairs to one of the bedrooms for an agreed rate.

George seemed all for this but was badly hampered by his lack of Spanish: he was hard pressed to order a sandwich and a beer, so chat-up lines were way out of his vocabulary range. We were well off the normal tourist routes, and the girls, though willing, didn't speak much English. So I sat there like a big brother translating all sorts of shit whilst the women sat there grinning and drinking the £25-pound bottle of lookalike champagne as if they had been parched in a desert all day.

I was rapidly becoming pissed off with the situation and regretting I'd advised him to visit in the first place. I'm game for a laugh with the best of them, but I draw the line at screwing some roadhouse hooker who has probably been had by more men than I've had hot dinners. No, thanks, I wasn't that desperate.

I went for a piss, and when I returned George and his girl had disappeared, I couldn't see them dancing so unless they had gone outside for a walk they were no doubt upstairs making conversation. His lack of vocabulary hadn't slowed him down at all, still I suppose some subjects just cut right through the language barrier. I made my excuses to my intended and left.

The next morning George wasn't around for breakfast, but I couldn't really go and knock him up as we weren't supposed to know each other. No doubt he had been playing out till late with his new girlfriend and had overslept. I dawdled as much as I could with breakfast and then spent time ostensibly checking my route on a large map I spread over the breakfast table.

George appeared eventually. He looked bloody

rough, his eyes screwed up against the sunlight streaming into the room, obviously nursing a daddy of a hangover. Over coffee he told me he had phoned Benson who had given him a change of plan. Rather than head up through France to the Channel ports we were to go to Santander or Bilbao. These are sea ports on the northern Spanish coast, both of which receive ferries directly from the UK. They have a longer sea crossing of 24 hours, and sailing the Bay of Biscay in winter can be a bit hairy. But these routes have the advantage of missing out France completely, thereby cutting out the risk of the Franco-Spanish border, the internal Customs checks, roadblocks and sometimes overvigilant police at the ferry ports.

On the other hand the Customs in Britain tend to concentrate on the Spanish-originated ferries as they know that all the vehicles have come directly from Spain. It was a risky decision for Benson to take and to me only a further demonstration of his paranoia. George had no idea about any of this and in his state was looking forward to the shorter drive.

We set off ten minutes apart and headed towards Santander. After we had passed Burgos and were in the high mountain passes that separate the northern coast from the great Spanish plains we stopped for a coffee. George was by now looking green around the gills. I was surprised when he pulled Brittany Ferries' Santander to Portsmouth timetable from his pocket. Maybe Benson was checking me out, and it had been their intention to take that route all the time. Now my paranoia kicked into overdrive.

George called the ferry terminal only to be told the next boat was fully booked, and there would be no room for him until a crossing in two days' time. He then tried P&O in Bilbao and learnt there was space for the four o'clock sailing. We would have to hustle but decided to go for it anyway. There was no sign of any police activity along even the busier routes. George drove as fast as the van was capable, while I just cruised nicely on the bike all the way into Bilbao.

At Bilbao we were late, but we parked up on the hill overlooking the port and watched the commercials being loaded on to the ferry. Benson's instructions had been explicit on this point: George was to wait until the last possible moment before boarding as Benson believed the Customs were less likely thoroughly to check a vehicle that was holding up departure. Maybe Benson was right, because as I sat alone later at the top of the hill I saw the Mercedes waved straight through the Spanish Customs checkpoint to join the last of the vehicles waiting to embark.

I drove into Bilbao and found a small bar, from where I phoned the Manchester Customs number. I quickly got put through to Rob. 'Hi, Rob, it's Benjy,' I said.

'Hi, Benjy, how's it going?' Rob's northern burr came back at me.

'OK. I've just watched our friend drive on to the P&O ferry at Bilbao. He'll be docking at Portsmouth sometime in the next 24 hours or so.' I gave him the van details and the registration number.

'Great work, Benjy,' said Rob and read the number back for checking, 'but I thought you said it would be Cherbourg,' he countered.

'Yeah, I know,' I replied, 'but Benson's been acting really strange over this one, and by pulling this change of route at the last minute he's really cut down the potential for anybody knowing where the shipment is going through. If anything happens he'll suspect me or George, and if George's been banged up he'll twig pretty quickly that it can't have been him.

'I suggest you let this load through. You can easily follow it into Liverpool and pull it there. But really, you know, this is only a trial run. If this gets through there are plans already made to send a 200- or 300-kilo shipment through in the next two weeks. Maybe it would be safer if you let this one go and grab the big prize next time.'

Rob was silent for a moment as he considered my proposal. 'I don't know, Benjy, it's not my decision. I'll tell my boss of your problem and see if we can't work out some solution that doesn't expose you to Benson,' he said.

'What do you mean, you'll try and work out a solution? This isn't a game of chess. If you get it wrong, and Benson susses me out then I'm dead,' I said down the phone. I could feel my ire rising at Rob's seeming indifference to my plight. If Benson discovered what was going on I would have a very short career from here on.

'Leave it with me, John,' said Rob, forgetting my codename for the moment. 'We'll work something out. Call me back later tonight or tomorrow,' and he hung up before I could protest further.

I felt as if I had just been fucked over. There was a definite awareness that now they had the information they wanted I was on my own. I sat down heavily and ordered a coffee and brandy. I had some serious thinking to do before I made any more moves.

I phoned Benson's home, but he wasn't in, so I told his

girlfriend, Susan, that I would phone back later. Then I called his son's mobile number, which was answered by Alf, a supposedly trusted gang member, with whom I'd done the Benidorm job.

'Hi, Alf, it's John the bike here,' I said, using my identifying name given because there were so many Johns involved in the gang and amongst their mates.

'Hi, Johnny, what do you want?' he answered.

'I'm looking for either of the two Colins,' I said. 'It's a bit urgent.'

'I'm in the bar playing pool with some of the lads. They're not here at the minute, mate. Do you want to leave a message?' Alf asked.

Sucker, I thought to myself. 'Yeah, tell Colin that I've just left our friend at Bilbao. Everything went as sweet as a nut. I'll speak to him later.'

I felt a bit better. By spreading the message I had lessened my own accountability by increasing the number of people who knew about the route. If push came to shove it might get me out of a sticky situation. If other people knew what was going on I could only be blamed for breaking security and not for being an informer. At least that was my theory. Wrapped in that weak protective armour I turned the bike and pointed south towards Malaga again.

It was a long, pensive drive back. I stopped for the night this time near the Toledo exit off the main highway and checked in at another hotel. I grabbed a handful of change and went off to find a call box to phone the Customs. I didn't want anybody checking my room phone later and finding a surprise on the telephone call register.

It was early evening and allowing for the time

difference the Customs office would be closed, so I called the London emergency number. I identified myself, gave them the phone number and asked them to have Rob call me back as soon as possible. He rang me within five minutes.

'Hi, Benjy, how y'doing?' he asked, all bright and breezy.

'I'm really concerned, Rob,' I told him. 'Have you decided to play it straight up or are you going to stuff me?' I asked hastily. I was feeling really worked up by now.

'Well, we had a long meeting about it, and we've decided to take no action at this end; except to cover ourselves we've had to notify the Portsmouth office that a consignment is due in sometime soon. We weren't any more specific than that,' Rob explained.

'OK, I can live with that,' I said. 'If they pull the gear then it's more a question of bad luck rather than just targeting the wrong van.'

'Yeah, that's about the size of it,' said Rob, 'so you can stop worrying and go back there with an easy conscience. You are in the clear.'

'Thanks, Rob,' I said. 'You can always take out the next bigger load.'

With that I signed off, and after phoning Kath and updating her on the latest events I went back to the motel. I had a few drinks that night and went to bed half pissed to sleep fitfully dreaming of Benson and his mates attacking me with iron bars. The next morning I felt awful, with a raging headache and all the familiar symptoms of the high blood pressure that plagued me from time to time. I resolved to see the doctor when I returned to England.

After a long, hard drive I arrived back in Fuengirola late that night, tired, hot and dusty. I phoned Benson to check in. He sounded concerned and told me he hadn't yet heard from George. My heart dropped into my boots and then shot straight up to my throat.

'Oh, shit! You don't think he's been pulled do you?' I asked in a voice laden with dread.

'I fucking hope not,' he said menacingly. 'You'd better come up here in the morning.'

'Sure thing! I've just got back, and I'm knackered, so I'll see you about eleven,' I said.

'OK,' he grunted and hung up, obviously not a happy teddy.

I phoned the Customs and went through the usual rigmarole before asking for Rob to phone me. Ten minutes later the call-box phone rang, and I snatched up the receiver.

'Rob, it's Benjy. Listen, Benson has just told me that the van driver, George, hasn't called him. Did the van get pulled by the Customs in Portsmouth?' I gabbled.

'Relax, John. I've had no reports that the van was stopped. The driver's probably going to phone in the morning. If he's got any sense he'll be in bed or having a drink in a club. Leave it until tomorrow, and I'll check up then.'

Rob seemed so confident that I did relax. He was the professional, he could weigh up the risks in an operation. Yes, I'd leave it until tomorrow. George would ring then. I went to bed that night certain I was in safe hands, which just goes to show what a bad judge of character I am.

8

Feel the Pressure

The next few weeks of that long, hot summer were both busy and scary times for me. After the Bilbao operation when, despite my warnings and fears for my security, British Customs had busted George in Portsmouth, I was sure I was being watched carefully by many of the boys in the various gangs. George had been pulled at Portsmouth ferry port, and 65 kilos of cannabis were discovered by a sniffer dog. He, of course, had played the innocent claiming that he hadn't inspected the contents of each box before they were all loaded into the van.

His story was obviously not believed by Customs, because he was charged with importation of controlled substances and held on remand in Winchester prison. A few weeks later a Crown Court judge released him on bail.

Luckily for me his phone conversations with Benson convinced the Spanish end of the operation that his pull was the result of bad luck; he was sure that he hadn't been 'grassed up'. That conversation between Benson and George may have saved my life, because I know for certain that there was a palpable lifting of tension that everyone involved could feel. Still I was very careful around Benson and his mates for a few weeks after that.

I considered that it might be a good idea to lay low for a while. The school holidays were on us, and so I decided to bring Kath and Natalie out to Spain for a few weeks' break, especially as the continued prolonged tension had started to play on Kath's nerves, maybe more than on mine. She was pale and nervy looking and had developed a short temper that would flare up for no apparent reason, even trivial domestic problems were getting her down. By now we had dropped into a state of almost permanent cold war, and our telephone conversations were getting shorter, louder and more acidic each day that went by.

It was the moment for a bit of rest and relaxation. Time perhaps to switch off and enjoy the Costa del Sol as a holiday haven rather than view it solely as the drugs capital of southern Europe. So for three idyllic weeks we stayed at the beach-front hotel Las Palmeras in Fuengirola and lived quietly in a small suite overlooking the glorious Mediterranean. We swam in the hotel's pool, played on the beach, borrowed a fast speedboat from one of my new work colleagues and coast-hopped to Benalmadena, Torremolinos and back down as far as Puerto Banus. We took trips into the countryside and ate at small isolated restaurants.

By night we watched the hotel cabaret and sat having a few drinks whilst Natalie spent her time with the other holidaying children watching the flamenco, cabaret or magic shows. Later she would dance till she dropped at the hotel disco, and I had the job of leading her tearful, tired and sunburned from the dance floor and carrying her to our room.

Kath and I sat on the balcony each night talking about the situation and the unforeseen problems that had cropped up. We had many things to put to rights. You cannot sustain a relationship under constant pressure by a series of short, cryptic telephone conversations. There are too many things left unsaid, and we needed a period together to repair our relationship and pour balm on each other's damaged ego and character.

In many ways it was a blissful period, and time flew by all too quickly. From our hotel I had been able to keep a weather eye on the bars where the action was, and I spotted many of the dealers and carriers as we walked along the sea front and around the town.

One night Benson Snr and his live-in girlfriend, Susan, invited us for an evening meal. Kath didn't want to go to the house, and so we met them in central Torremolinos and dined in a mock Tudor-style restaurant. Luckily Benson was at his most affable and charming, and the evening passed without any major incidents, although I could feel Kath ticking like a time bomb, and I was seriously on edge, hoping that she wouln't sound off at him.

Sitting back and watching Benson perform it was hard to believe he was anything but a middle-aged semi-retired rough diamond who liked to tell tall stories and enjoy a few too many drinks. His benign smile hid his thoroughly vicious, bullying nature. I realized that night that I had passed through mere contempt and had begun actually to hate this evil man. Without both him and his son, the world would be a better place.

The night before Kath was due to return home to England with Natalie we sat up nearly all night talking and planning. Things were becoming good between us again, and we felt enough confidence to make plans for our future. We were both determined to move on and put the drugs, Customs, accompanying dangers and the rest behind us and settle down to the life we wanted in Spain. It was becoming time for someone else to pick up the torch, as we were growing tired of the constant stress, lies and crosschecking.

I had heard from Benson that two of his son's mates wanted him to move 300 kilos of cannabis from Spain to the UK by a new route. He was impatient to start the operation and made it obvious he wanted Kath out of the way so I would be free to help him. I agreed with Kath that I would help Customs out on that job, but if nothing came of it and Benson was still free at the end of it, then, sod it! – they could find someone else to do their dirty work.

The next day I drove my wife and daughter to Malaga airport and waited with them until their flight was called. I walked up to the chrome barrier in front of passport control and waved them all the way through the baggage check and into the departure lounge. I was sad to see them go and unaccountably felt extremely upset, as if I sensed that I wouldn't be seeing them for a long time, certainly not for a relaxing family holiday.

Alone again I went into the first-floor restaurant and bought a coffee and a large brandy, which I sat drinking while pondering on the situation in which we found ourselves. Finally after weighing up all the pros and cons for a while, I definitely decided that I would help Customs with this upcoming operation and then that would be it – I was getting out, retiring and getting back to and on with my own life.

So far I had given Customs & Excise a straight five months of my own life as well as my family's. We had put all our plans on hold, forfeited our dreams of starting a business and moving to Spain, placed ourselves under immeasurable amounts of pressure, and, up to now, we had nothing to show in return apart from promises of payments when and if the authorities successfully prosecuted anyone because of direct leads I had given them. This was a double-edge sword because as a Confidential Informant I operated on the basis that I would not be called into court as a prosecution witness. This could make a successful prosecution more difficult because Customs could only work with my information behind the scenes. They claimed they couldn't act overtly as I might be compromised.

To me it was a crock of shit. Benson and the other big operators would never be taken off the streets unless they were actually caught with their hands on the drugs. But that was something they never did. They had minions to do that work for them. So how, I wondered, could the drug barons ever be caught? Well, it wasn't my problem. I would honour my commitment, and then – stuff it! – I was getting off this crazy roundabout.

* * *

A few days after Kath had returned to England I went up to see Benson Snr at his villa. It was now getting towards the back end of the summer, and although the days were still hot, the nights were drawing in. It was a great time to sit on the patio with a drink listening to all the whistling and croaking wildlife that inhabited the garden shrubs and hedges.

Benson and I sat relaxing in cane easy chairs on his patio, each of us holding a tumbler of good malt whisky with the bottle on a table near to hand. The air was filled with the scent of nearby pine trees and the expensive aroma of Benson's big fat cigar. During the ensuing couple of hours Benson described how two of his son's mates, Paul and Tony, both big movers of gear, had recently lost a couple of loads in Irun, a town in northern Spain. They now wanted to use the Benson gang to transport their product up to the UK.

We talked about methods and routes and names of possible drivers. It was agreed that I would travel back to the UK and meet up with Paul and Tony to arrange the shipment. Benson had a novel idea that was supposed to defeat the army of informers that everyone suspected was operating in Spain. He was sure they noted details of departing suspicious vehicles and forwarded this information back to their paymasters in England. His strategy to overcome this obstacle was to change the carrier vehicle in France. He claimed to have discussed his proposals already with Paul and Tony.

The idea was to pack the gear in the Marbella area and then drive it as far as northern France. There the gear would be taken to a safe house and switched into another clean delivery vehicle brought over from England on a day-return ticket. The registration number of the second delivery vehicle would already be on a ferry manifest and would have been logged into the Customs' computer, therefore it would not excite suspicion as it re-entered England.

Benson said that he already had a place in mind for a safe house, that he would organize the delivery for the first leg of the trip and that his son would bring in a reliable driver. I was to check out the French delivery address and confirm the details of the operation with

Paul and Tony. After that I was to return to Spain ready to act as baby-sitter for the shipment.

It all seemed feasible to me, and I couldn't wait to get back to the UK to talk about it with Customs. We parted late that night on good terms, and I drove a little unsteadily over the hills back to Carmen's pension in Fuengirola.

Nursing a hangover, I called the Customs in Manchester the next morning and had a long chat with them, laying out the gist of my discussions with Benson. I concluded by advising him I would be returning to the UK later that week. By now it was the first week of October, and I wanted to get back home before the weather broke and winter paraded its wet and windy wares across Europe.

My trip home was awful. It rained almost nonstop from just north of Madrid to Bayonne over the border in France. There aren't many activities that rate as low as driving a motorbike for hour after interminable hour in those conditions, and when I stopped for an early-evening meal and a shower I was wet through and chilled to the bone. The motorbike looked as though it had been washed down with a muddy hosepipe, its chrome and bright trimmings dull and dirty looking. I decided to turn in for the night and hope the weather improved the next day.

The following morning dawned bright and clear with a strong wind that had set in and blown the clouds across to the horizon. It was blustery and cold, but at least I would be dry. I pulled on my warm leathers and set off for Cherbourg. The journey was uneventful, and I caught the late-afternoon ferry. I arrived home the following morning to a joyful if wary family reunion; I hadn't warned Kath I was returning as I'd wanted to surprise her. Surprise her I did, as she immediately thought something had gone wrong and went into a flat-spin panic.

Her reaction demonstrated the kind of pressure we were both living under, and it increased my resolve to get out of this crazy situation as soon as possible. After I'd explained to Kath what was happening I had a long shower and then spent the rest of the day in bed cementing relationships.

Early the next morning Benson called me at home. There had been a change of plan, and he now asked me to travel to France to meet Paul and Tony at Nantes airport. I was to go with them to check out the suitability of an address for receipt and storage of the shipment there until its collection by the second van for the UK.

It was obvious to me that Benson had been thinking about his contacts in France and about how he could get the operation under way as quickly as possible whilst keeping his costs down, thereby maximizing his profit from the job. Using me for recce purposes meant that he could sit safely at home, well away from the scene of operations if anything went wrong later.

He reminded me about Eric and Jill, a British couple who lived in France and whom I had met twice before at his villa in Spain. This was a surprise to me, because I had thought of them merely as users of hash; I had them marked down as overage hippies. I didn't think they took part in smuggling activities.

Benson laughed when I voiced my doubts. 'I've known Eric a long time,' he told me. 'Just go and have a chat with him and see if it will be OK to move the gear up to his place.' He gave me their address, which was somewhere south of Nantes, and so I made arrangements to travel to France.

The next day I took the Honda and travelled down to Southampton, where I bought a day return on the Brittany Ferries' crossing to St Malo in Brittany. The voyage passed uneventfully until the ferry had docked and I was on the car deck unfastening the bike strapping. Feeling I was being watched I looked up. Bloody hell! You could have knocked me down with a feather, because there, right in front of me, stood Eric and Jill.

My paranoia kicked into hyper drive. How the hell could they have known I was going to be travelling on that particular ferry that day? The odds of meeting by chance were astronomical. Again I felt a flash of fear. Just how much did these jokers know about what was really going on? Who exactly was watching who?

Putting on the social mask we all said what a surprise it was to see each other. After some other friendly exchanges we agreed to meet after disembarkation. I rolled off the ferry and quickly passed straight through the unmanned French immigration and Customs post.

I met Eric and Jill in the ferry-terminal car park, and we had a chat. I told them I was on my way to visit them at their house, and I noticed they didn't seem too surprised. They explained that they had been to Britain to sort out a problem with Eric's pension, and I had caught them on their return journey. Yeah, I thought, pull the other one it's got bells on. I explained what Benson had proposed and that I would need to visit their home in the company of two major players called Paul and Tony. I was watching them very carefully for their reactions.

If someone whom I knew vaguely from a couple of summer barbecues had asked me to accept and store 300 kilos of drugs at my place of residence I would have been damn more surprised than that pair seemed to be. They accepted the deal with such equanimity that I was sure they had been in contact with Benson and had been expecting me. I wondered if this was another example of how dealers kept a close eye on their minions, checking constantly for any signs of disloyalty.

In any event it made by job easier, and that was my main interest. I left Eric and Jill in the car park at St Malo and headed south past Rennes to pick up the N137 towards Nantes airport. In overcast weather I drove rapidly down through Brittany, stopping only for a quickly eaten baguette at a roadside cafe near a Second World War museum. It was hard to believe that towards the end of the war this area of France had been contested so fiercely by the Germans when the Allies were advancing. Now it just seemed peaceful, green countryside populated by lazy-looking cows chewing the cud in the watery late-morning sunlight.

It was lunchtime before I had negotiated the Nantes ring road and found my way into the airport, a futuristic tinted-glass and concrete structure surrounded by acres of car-parking space. Eschewing it I parked right outside the arrivals hall sliding doors, and after locking up the bike I went inside.

Two hours later the last plane due that day from England had landed, and all its incoming passengers had departed. The arrivals hall was almost deserted, and I was standing out like a nun in a sex shop. Obviously

Paul and Tony weren't coming today. Angry and frustrated, I called Benson's home in Spain, from where his girlfriend told me he was out and not expected home until late that night.

I then called his son, who despite the hour was still in bed, no doubt with another bimbo keeping him warm. The ensuing, rather cryptic conversation wasn't helpful, and I decided to check out the Eric and Jill location on my own. I left the airport at a rate of knots and headed down the Route Nationale 137. It was a busy road with road works seemingly every couple of miles. I persevered and made good time by driving down the middle of the trunk road between the oncoming vehicles and the slow-moving southbound traffic.

I followed the instructions Eric had given me and turned off the main route on to a small back road. This was rural France, just like the movies. I almost expected to see a German tank appear from behind one of the hedgerows, but all I saw were fields and duckponds.

Eric and Jill's house appeared, and I quickly pulled into their driveway and parked at the side of their old camper van. After the second round of introductions that day they seemed as upset as I was that Paul and Tony hadn't arrived at the airport. We had a quick cup of tea, and I had a look around the outbuildings to check out their suitability. Everything seemed OK, and wishing to catch the ferry home that night I didn't hang around chewing the fat. I told them that the operation would be on within the month, and the next time they saw me I would arrive with the gear. To my mind they seemed incredibly laid back about the whole matter.

It was by now early evening, and I burned some

rubber as I headed back up the N137 towards the Channel coast. I missed the St Malo ferry, though, and so headed to Caen where I caught the midnight boat departing for Portsmouth. When I eventually arrived home late the next morning I was completely knackered. There had to be easier ways to live.

Two days later I met with Rob and Steve, my Customs handlers, at Hartshead services again. After some preliminary chat over a cup of coffee we left the cafeteria and sat in their dark-blue Orion for more privacy. Rob produced some photos of dodgy-looking individuals and asked me if I recognized any of them. I pointed out to them a man whom I knew as Garry, an ecstasy dealer whom I had met earlier in the summer during a visit to England with Benson.

It wasn't an operation that was of great concern to me as it had been a deal done by Benson and his son, and I had really only gone along for the ride and to be nosy. Benson had arranged for 10,000 ecstasy tablets manufactured in Holland to be smuggled into England. Garry was apparently a well-known northern-based dealer and a 'face' in the north of England nightclub scene. I had reported the whole matter to the Customs, who had passed it on to the police, but they had decided to take no action in the interests of public security.

Now that Customs were showing me his photograph it became obvious he was a high-profile target of theirs, and I wished I had taken more interest in the ecstasy operation. Rob confirmed they knew him and that he was a major player, but there was little further I could offer them on that subject. I could confirm that Garry had agreed to pay £4 per tablet, which meant he'd paid Benson £40,000 for the shipment.

I told them about the Benson plan for the French operation and his request that I arrange a meeting with Paul and Tony in Nantes. I told them that the two dealers hadn't shown and that I had visited the proposed delivery address alone. By now I had told Benson that his buddies had failed to show up at Nantes airport, and he had given me a mobile phone number for Paul, which I gave to Rob and Steve. They agreed I should set up a meeting with Paul and Tony. They said they would use the opportunity to organize a covert surveillance operation to obtain photographs and check out the car they arrived in.

I made the call on my mobile phone and got hold of Tony. He apologized for missing the rendezvous at Nantes airport but didn't seem cut up about it. I arranged a meeting with him and Paul at Hartshead services for three days later. Customs were happy with the arrangements and promised they would be in touch to give me instructions beforehand.

We then spent some time talking about the stolen car operations that were becoming ever more popular in southern Spain. I was able to identify more than 20 such cars circulating in the Malaga area alone, with more cars arriving weekly. Most of the vehicles were 'ringed' or 'twinned up', in that their identity was concealed, and they were nearly all luxury-market motors: Mercedes, Jaguars, Volvos, BMWs and the larger Fords were the most popular. Hardly a day went by but I would be offered a 5-series BMW or a Granada for a couple of thousand pounds.

These cars were invariably delivered with a complete DVLA registration certificate and a tax disc bearing an official-looking post-office stamp and the false vehicle registration number. I noticed a distinct lack of interest by the Customs in relation to stolen vehicles and the gangs who were delivering them to order. I rationalized this to myself with the knowledge that Customs were only interested in the illegal importation of drugs; stolen cars were a police matter and nothing to do with them. In my view it was a classic example of interagency non-cooperation.

The day before the meeting with Paul and Tony was due to take place Rob phoned me at home to give me precise instructions about what to do. He wanted me to sit outside the café in a picnic area overlooking the main car park. I was to position myself side on to the car park, reading a newspaper. When the two drug dealers arrived I should stand up and shake hands with each of them. He told me Customs would be waiting in a parked vehicle from where they would take their photographs. Everything was organized so he advised me to relax and try to act as naturally as possible. I agreed with him and resolved to give a good performance.

The next day I arrived early at the motorway services, and after buying a coffee and a newspaper I sat down as instructed. I was feeling intensely nervous. These guys were really hard men and potential killers, and if they suspected any funny business they would have no hesitation in bumping me off. While I was committed and prepared to do my bit, I just hoped my back-up was armed and watching carefully.

The plan hadn't taken account of the weather, though, and when I arrived the sky was leaden with low cloud. Just before the meeting was timed to begin it started raining pretty hard. Paul and Tony were late, and I was sitting outside in the rain with a newspaper that was quickly turning to pulp. Anybody with any sense would have been inside the nice warm cafe, so how could I sit here steaming in the pouring rain and try to look natural? I looked like a fucking idiot, so much for planning by the professionals.

Paul and Tony eventually arrived. They looked as hard as I'd feared, and I felt nothing but loathing for these two lowlifes. I was pleased to be of help in putting them away. They wanted to know why I was sat outside in the rain, which seemed a pretty fair question. I explained that it was more private here and that we wouldn't be overheard. Paul just said, 'Bollocks, we'll get piss wet through,' and that was that, inside we went. I hoped the Customs had taken all the photographs they needed.

Inside the cafe the meeting lasted for the duration of a couple of cups of coffee and a few cigarettes. They explained that the proposed French operation would be the first on a new route, which if it went to plan would be used for about six trips. They had heavy goods transport that travelled from England to France regularly on a weekly basis. They claimed this transport was good and legitimate and had never been stopped. Benson's job was to collect the gear from Malaga and then ship it to the French farm. They would pay him £100 per kilo delivered, so I knew Benson stood to make £30,000 for his part in the operation.

They asked me what role I would play, and I told them I would be the baby-sitter on a motorbike in front of the load. They seemed pleased by this. After warning me of the consequences for all concerned if anything went wrong, they wished me luck and said they would soon be in touch with Colin in Spain.

I left the café, and as previously agreed with my

handlers I climbed into my car and drove home without making any calls or seeing anybody else. The next day I had an extensive debrief with Rob over the phone. I related everything that had transpired, and for his part he confirmed they had taken some good photographs. I was very pleased with the operation, and that night Kath and I went out for a little private celebration to a Chinese restaurant in Retford.

Over the next few days I received at home a series of phone calls from Benson, Paul and Tony. In effect I became the linkman, coordinating the shipment. Therefore I was privy to most of the planning details, even down to knowing the name of the van driver. I spoke several times to Customs, and we decided to have one final meeting, which we set for the last day of October 1994 at Birch services on the M62 near to Heywood in north Manchester. The three of us met there late in the afternoon.

It was looking as if this job were shaping up to be the big one, the operation that would net both Bensons and two major north of England dealers as well as remove 300 kilos of drugs from the streets. This operation, I decided, was to be my swan song. With Benson out of the way we could get on with our own lives and move a little nearer to achieving our own ambitions.

It had been raining hard on my trip over the Pennines, and I was very wet when I joined Rob and Steve, who were already seated and drinking coffee. We got right down to business. Rob had brought along a map of northern France for me to pinpoint the exact location of the delivery address, but it didn't cover a sufficiently large area, so I went into the services shop and bought a road map of France.

We sat in the cafe poring over the map, and I showed them exactly where the farmhouse was to be found. I also sketched out the proposed route we would be taking across Spain and up through France to the drop-off point. I described the layout of the farm and gave them its full postal address including the postcode.

By now Customs had everything they needed for the operation. They knew the names of the buyers, the Spanish-based organizers and shippers, the type and volume of drugs to be smuggled and a timescale for the operation. Obviously they were aware that my intended role was to drive in front of the shipment on my motorbike acting as a front-runner escort and baby-sitter. For this Benson had promised me £10,000. Most importantly they knew that the intended plan included an exchange of carrying vehicles. This was where my input was critical, because I was the only one who could identify the second vehicle coming from England and report its details and registration number back to the Customs.

Rob and Steve appeared pleased with my assistance and offered me £500 to help with my 'running expenses'. I had to sign a receipt in the name of 'Benjy' for the cash. They warned me to be careful and not to break the law. This was delivered straightfaced by Rob, but I just sat there and looked at them incredulously. What a farce! Here we were, discussing the ways and means of smuggling 300 kilos of illegal drugs worth £1 million across at least two international frontiers and over nearly 1500 miles of roadways, yet he had the nerve to sit there and tell me not to do anything illegal.

I was so incensed by the transparent naivety of his statement that I said straight out that this was to be my last job for Customs. I let rip a little and told them what I really thought of their operations, how the drug dealers were laughing at their attempts to stem the tide of drugs being smuggled into the country. The smugglers are ruthlessly efficient operators backed up by well-paid organizations that can quickly adapt to changing circumstance and move the goalposts at will. On the other hand Customs were constantly playing catch up with the smugglers, hamstrung by policies and outdated policing methods that had never been designed to deal with international drug trafficking on such a major scale.

The dealers and barons could move about freely, crossing borders with ease as many as five times per smuggling trip. Customs, however, had to liaise with several different policing authorities. Each subject to their own internal agendas and local politics, the competition between the policing agencies was fierce. The interservice cooperation promulgated by the politicians and media spokesmen was a joke that wasn't taken seriously by either the authorities or the smugglers, it was just so much hot air.

I recall that Rob and Steve sat there in silence as I continued with my diatribe, but they certainly didn't disagree with me. After I had finished I gave them the last titbit of information I had about the upcoming operation. Benson had told me that the first carrier vehicle to be used on the Spanish–French leg of the operation was a Mercedes van stolen from a Hertz rent-a-van depot in Britain. Hertz's corporate livery was a distinctive bright yellow, and I thought it would stand out like a spare prick at a nun's wedding. To me there didn't seem much future in using a vehicle that was begging to be stopped and checked by every passing police car.

We agreed that the next time I would make contact with them would be when the drugs had arrived safely in France, and I had the details of the van coming from England to collect them. It was a cordial parting, but I felt that much of the earlier friendliness had dissipated. This I put down to my criticism of their employers.

Kath and I decided to move our plans forward a piece. I was so convinced that Benson and his cohorts would soon be out of the way, she was going to travel out to Spain and start searching out a property for us. We decided to all fly out together as soon as possible.

I contacted a local guy I knew in Sheffield who had previously organized a driver for Benson and asked him to fix me up with a driver. The idea was to put the motorbike in the back of a trailer and have it driven down to Spain. This would allow me to travel to Malaga with Kath and Natalie, and I would be there quicker to keep an eye on developments. The weather was really shitty and I didn't facing spending three days driving to Spain when I could travel it in three hours. I had done a lot of travelling around Europe in the last couple of months, and I was getting really tired and worn down. A nice warm trip in an aeroplane drinking wine and looking down on the snowy mountain tops seemed just right to me at that moment.

The next day I took a call from a guy called Barry, who had been put up for the driving job. I invited him to our farm, and he seemed all right. He was an ex-army cook, single and looked as if he could handle himself.

He came highly recommended by our mutual contact, and I was told he was trustworthy enough to drive a trailer down to Malaga. We agreed terms, and the next day we loaded the motorbike and some other bits and pieces into the back of a covered trailer, and he set off in his Orion towing the trailer, destination Spain. Meanwhile Kath, Natalie and I set off for Birmingham airport, from where he had booked tickets for the flight to Malaga.

The following day we checked in again at the hotel Las Palmeras in Fuengirola, and Kath and Natalie started to renew their acquaintances with the local shops and cafes. It was now early November, and the weather had turned, but it was still warm compared with the late English autumn we had left behind us, so much so that young Natalie spent an hour or so each day in the hotel pool.

Meanwhile I was busy with Benson, making sure that everything was ready for the forthcoming trip. I inspected the Hertz van and expressed my reservations over its vivid colour, which Benson ignored. Of course he wasn't the sucker who was going to be driving it, so his concern was limited to financial aspects.

A couple of days later Barry arrived on the coast with the trailer. I met him near the brewery adjacent to Malaga airport and escorted him up to Benson's villa, where the trailer was to be stored temporarily until Barry returned to the UK. By now I had learnt that Barry was unhappy with his lot as proprietor of a small cafe and intended to look around in Torremolinos and Fuengirola for some winter work in one of the hotels, restaurants or bars.

As we drove into Benson's villa Barry's eyes were

popping. It is easy to become inured to ostentatious luxury and grandiose lifestyles, because after a while you take it for granted, and it doesn't really register any more. But a newcomer introduced into the circle always stepped back in amazement. It was rather like walking on to the set of *Dallas*, and these surroundings seemed to imbue Benson with a sense of potency and enhance his charisma. It's really no wonder he was such a success with women.

We unloaded the bike, and Barry, with Jack, one of Benson's handymen, parked the trailer away with the caravans on the lower patch of ground. Benson took me aside and told me quietly that we would be on for the operation within two or three days. Then, because we were lacking a spare motorbike helmet, he volunteered to drive Barry down to the coast.

I saw the glint in Benson's eye and knew that he was going to sound out Barry for future use. That was how all the dealers worked. They cultivated an ever increasing circle of contacts hoping that one day one of them would come in useful. Still I wasn't Barry's keeper, so I left them to it and drove back to Fuengirola to have my evening meal with my family. That night we sat again and watched the hotel cabaret until Natalie was too tired to keep her eyes open, then it was a quick supper of ham and cheese at the 24-hour bar and off to bed and more relationship cementing. I was starting to feel like a bloody builder.

The next afternoon we were walking around the shops in Malaga's main shopping area when Benson called me on my mobile phone. He was in a right state and insisted he wanted to see me as soon as possible. I agreed to meet him after dinner. Later at his villa he told me that the van driver they had organized had failed to turn up there as agreed. So what? I thought. It wasn't my man or my arrangement, and it meant little or nothing to me. But the problem went deeper. The driver had taken the Hertz van the previous day to fuel it up and check tyre pressures and so on. He had parked it up, but now he had disappeared, and so had the van keys, which presumably were in his pocket.

This was a problem because it is not so easy to obtain spare keys for Mercedes vehicles. Apparently each one is tagged into a central computer and can be linked back to a specific vehicle. The risk was that if one of Benson's men called into Mercedes' main dealership in Marbella then they would soon know he was trying to obtain keys for a stolen vehicle. For obvious reasons this was a chance Benson didn't want to take.

I could see all my plans evaporating in front of me, as I thought about the problem for a while. If Benson didn't go ahead with the scheduled delivery then he would escape the elaborate net that was now set for him. All my own and Kath's dreams would come to nought again as we couldn't countenance moving into the area with the two Bensons hanging around free as birds.

I offered him the use of my old Mercedes van, which I had used for the import and export trials in what seemed a couple of centuries ago. Parked up nearby it was still in good nick and had the advantage of being white, a less conspicuous colour than the Hertz bright yellow. Another big bonus from Benson's viewpoint was that, although old, the van was legal, and all the papers were authentic.

I felt there was no material risk posed to me or to my van by this change in detail. The main players remained the same, we were still smuggling the same amount of drugs to the same address in France, in effect all that had changed was that I'd allowed my vehicle to be used.

Benson then told me that he had done a deal with Barry, who would now be driving the van. Even if the original driver turned up he would not be going with the shipment. Instead he would be lucky to escape with an assortment of broken limbs to show him that he couldn't piss about with Benson and his gang. A sort of grisly example to keep the minions in line.

Barry must have figured something pretty strange was going on when he first saw all the opulence around him, and no doubt he had readily understood when Benson explained the secret of the source of all the cash. Using Barry as a replacement driver wasn't a problem for me. He had said he was looking for a job, and I supposed this seemed an easy way for him to get some quick cash. I heard that he had been offered £4000 to drive the van up to France, but I don't know if that was an accurate figure.

Barry was a minor player in the operation, and I had previously reported many such small fry to Customs, who had taken no action against them, declaring their prime interest was in catching the main men. Therefore I couldn't see there was going to be any problem with the change of the driver, and I certainly didn't think it was up to me to report such a detail to Customs at this late stage. In a way it was a typical piece of drug smuggling, more like organized chaos than anything else. The smugglers were making absolute fortunes, but most of them couldn't organize a piss up in a brewery.

Later during that meeting Benson told us he had decided to load the drugs into the van the next day in readiness for departure. He asked me to help in the collection of the drugs from Fuengirola and to take them up to the packing house. At last, I thought, we can get this bloody show on the road. It was a good move as the constant strain was by now really telling on me. I was short tempered, irritable and often my blood pressure was giving me blinding headaches. Most of the time I had a nagging sort of background headache, which I had learnt to live with.

I invited Barry to join us at the cabaret session that night in Fuengirola. He seemed pleased to get the offer and have a valid excuse to leave Benson behind. I took Benson off to one side and told him I would keep an eye on Barry, giving Benson the nod to impart a special insiders' meaning to my words. It was little asides like this that made Benson feel he was in command of a situation. He was always happier thinking he had people watching each other for signs of disloyalty.

We played happy families again that night, Kath, Natalie, Barry and I laughing and joking at the comedian. Barry was warily swigging lager from a bottle of San Miguel whilst his eyes kept scanning the audience. I didn't know if he was looking for a bird to try his luck with or if he was expecting a horde of policemen to jump out of the crowd. He looked decidedly unhappy, and I figured he hadn't been involved in anything remotely like this before.

The next day Barry and I spent a few hours getting my van ready for the trip, fuelling up, checking oil and tyre pressures and so on. Later in the afternoon I delivered Barry up to Mijas Jardins where the drugs were to be wrapped by Benson's man Jack and someone else supplied by Paul and Tony's organization, who was no doubt keeping his eye on his master's drugs. He would be ensuring that there was no switching of product and that none of the 1200 soaps of cannabis disappeared into the wrong hands.

I knew we would be going sometime the next day, and so that night the three of us went out for a special peaceful meal on our own. It was the calm before the storm and was to be the last time I would sit down with my family for more than half a year.

The next morning it was all go, packing clothes, bike leathers, wet-weather gear, toothbrush, razor and other personal kit. Considering it was the first week in November the weather was fine with a watery sun just hot enough to dispel the sea mist and break up the high clouds. Barry came down and joined us for a massive English breakfast at one of my favourite bars. After eating we sat around drinking coffee and making small talk while Natalie wandered about in one of the nearby gift shops, watched by an eagle-eyed shop assistant.

Barry confided that he was going to use his pay-off this run to start a café or bar in one of the coastal resorts. I choked back a splutter of laughter. What was it with people? They could see the evidence of failing businesses all around them, intense competition was driving even the moderately successful bars out of business, and yet newcomers kept coming and plonking their money down, determined to show all the others how it should be done. It was like watching a tide of lemmings dropping off the edge of a cliff. Still who was I to laugh? I'd been convinced I could do just the same in Benidorm all those years ago.

About noon Benson called me on the mobile, and I knew the show was on. Barry went to collect his bag from his room. Kath was going out to meet a firm of estate agents that afternoon and intended to visit some properties to see what was on the market. I promised to phone her as soon as I could and let her know how we were doing. Just in case anything went wrong I made her repeat the Customs emergency number back to me a couple of times, I didn't want her to write it down anywhere. By now we were both running in a constant state of high tension, and no precautions seemed too outrageous to us.

Barry arrived back, and we all walked up to the Honda. I turned the engine over, and Barry and I climbed aboard. We waved our goodbyes, and with the throbbing beat of a Rod Stewart hit dancing behind us we swung up the road and headed towards Cartama village and Benson's villa again.

We set off on the journey at roughly three o'clock that afternoon. Me in the front leading the way, and Barry driving my Mercedes-Benz van at a steady 55 miles per hour. I was covering twice as much distance as Barry, powering three or four miles up the road and then doubling back to check he was OK. At the first agreed stopping point I had to tell him not to flash his lights whenever he saw me, a dead giveaway to any cops who might see him. Powerful bikes and old diesel vans were not conventional fellow travellers, and it would certainly arouse suspicion and a degree of interest that we wouldn't like.

We continued onwards, heading up the excellent

N321 road through Antequera, climbing continually to the ancient city of Granada perched high up in the Sierra Nevada mountains. After playing cat and mouse with the congested traffic around the city we were headed dead north through Jaen and the beautiful countryside to Bailen, one of the main junction towns in southern Spain. There are always plenty of Guardia Civil around that area, watching the traffic and pulling both cars and commercial vehicles over for spot checks, seemingly at random.

I stayed close in front of Barry, and sure enough I could see a couple of jeeps used by the Guardia near the Repsol garage in the centre of the route interchange. I drove over towards them and made a big show of climbing off the bike and pulling a road map from the rear box. Engaging them in a mimelike conversation I checked I was on the right road for Madrid, the coppers were only too pleased to help me and pointed vigorously to the north saying, 'Madrid, Madrid'. I thanked them and tinkered with the stereo on the bike as Barry swung past, I could see him gaping at me through the windscreen. He obviously thought I'd been pulled up, but he did the right thing by driving on and ignoring the little sideshow being played out at the roadside.

I climbed aboard the bike, and waving at my new friends I pulled off smoothly towards Madrid. I easily passed Barry within a couple of minutes, the relief on his face as I roared past giving him the finger was clear to see. We settled down for the next leg of the long journey. On the large three-lane dual carriageway European E5 route we passed through Valdepenas, home of some excellent Spanish wine, and ploughed on steadily towards Ocana, where the main road forks back off towards Cartegena and Murcia.

We hit the Madrid ring-road system just after darkness had fallen, but at least we missed most of the traffic. Barry was sticking to the job faithfully, and we circumvented Madrid without taking any wrong turns, a memorable feat late at night. An hour north of the capital we pulled off the road and checked into a motel for the night. We were not far away from where I'd stayed with George during the Bilbao operation earlier that summer, but I wasn't interested in brothels and hookers. I'd been in the saddle for a long time and was suffering from a severely numb bum.

We didn't bother with the pretence of not knowing each other, because the place was crowded with travellers, and it was obvious that nobody gave a shit about two more weary souls crawling in from the dark. I left Barry downstairs in the bar trying to order a beer and went to my room, where I took a long hot shower. Later we ate a good meal with lots of crusty bread and copious amounts of beer before retiring early for a good sleep.

The next morning we were up and off early. I was feeling as stiff as a board and wasn't looking forward to another ten-hour stretch on the bike, but it had to be done. By mid-morning we were on the outskirts of Burgos, a large commercial town nestling in the middle of a mountain chain that runs all the way up to the northern coast near to Bilbao. We ran along the top of the range heading towards the Vitoria pass. By now it had turned really cold, and snow lay on the hills. There was a cold, stinging rain, and I was feeling wet and miserable and envious of Barry nice and dry and warm in the Mercedes behind me.

Dropping down the appalling road through Vitoria was always hazardous, but now the route was wet and slick with oil and diesel and especially tricky and treacherous. A heavy mist came down, and hairpin bends loomed up without any warning. I had to take it slowly and steadily, and by now I was becoming really pissed off by this because we needed to get a move on to cross the French border before darkness fell. Like cockroaches the French Customs came out to prey on commercial vehicles after dark.

We headed for the dirty industrial town of Irun just next to the border. This area was thick with police like fleas, they seemed to be on every corner. The only thing to do was to keep on and tough it out, but I could imagine Barry was crapping himself by now.

Eventually we passed through Irun and headed the couple of miles up to the small town of Hendaye. The main motorway was on a causeway high above our heads, and we could hear the constant roar of traffic passing by. I had plenty of butterflies batting about in my stomach now, and the tension was giving me a headache. It was little comfort to think that UK Customs should have OK'd the route with the Spanish and the French, this was major bottle-twitching time. I wouldn't have been surprised if Barry had pulled up and left the van before catching the next bus home.

I saw the small border crossing ahead and drove up for a look-see. Unbelievably it was unmanned, except for one guard on the Spanish side who was sitting in his glass kiosk reading a newspaper. I about turned quickly and went back to spread the good word to Barry. I discovered him creeping up the road as slowly as he could, obviously working up his courage to attempt the crossing. I swung round in front of him and gave him a big thumbs up whilst waving him on. I could hear the old van accelerate gamely behind me.

I drove slowly across the frontier, and it was definitely unmanned. Safely in France I pulled to the roadside parking area and watched as Barry negotiated his way round the series of barriers and chicanes. It was now gloomy dusk, but I could clearly see a big grin stretched across his face from ear to ear. He was through.

Without hanging about we headed up the small coast road to St Jean-de-Luz, a seaside resort. The place was too small for our needs, and we continued now in the pitch darkness towards the upmarket resort of Biarritz. We passed a local airport full of parked-up millionaires' toys and found a small chain motel on the outskirts of the town that was admirable for our purposes. We quickly checked in, changed clothes and hit the bar. The border-crossing tension surge on top of the long drive had left us both tired, but we managed to sink a good few beers and brandy chasers before devouring a plate of sandwiches made up for us by a kindly night porter. That night we eventually turned in completely tired out and the worse for drink.

I was looking forward to the next day. I knew we would arrive at the farmhouse drop-off at about teatime, and then hopefully the day after the van would arrive from England. A quick phone call to Rob or Steve at the Customs and the show would be over, in more ways than one. Well, the show was about to be over all right, I just didn't realize how it was going to end.

9

The French Connection

The trip up from Biarritz was largely uneventful. We travelled north up the N137 passing through several small towns in the Cognac region. Driving all day with breaks for fuel when we would grab a cigarette, a drink and a sandwich bought from petrol-station shops we arrived at our departure point from the Route Nationale at about six o'clock in the evening.

I had gradually increased my distance in front of Barry in the van as I began to search for a suitable place to leave him parked up whilst I checked out the farmhouse refuge. Not far from the main crossroads where our route turned off the main road I saw a deserted garage. There were no lights in the building, and the car park seemed to be full of broken-down cars, some of which, minus wheels, were perched on blocks. This seemed an ideal location to me. As a bonus, in between the car park and the pavement, there was a telephone kiosk.

I quickly doubled back and soon saw Barry ploughing steadily up towards me. I U-turned and overtook him and pulling to the roadside told him my plan. I led him to the garage, and he pulled into a corner and switched off his engine and lights. I instructed him to await my return and walked over to the phone box. Once inside I dialled Manchester Customs' number but received only a buzzing noise from the handset. I tried again with the London contact number but got the same result.

This was getting beyond a joke, obviously the poxy French phone wasn't working. Tired out with concentrating after the long journey I decided to try again the next day, after we'd dropped off the van and got a good night's sleep. By this time I was knackered, I had been in the driving seat for nearly 14 hours already, and the day wasn't yet over.

Leaving Barry behind at the garage I continued up the road to the traffic lights where I would turn off. The junction was obviously the centre of town, and there were various local shops cheek by jowl with a new school, a community car park and some sort of public building flying the French flag. I quickly passed through the town and turned off into the country down a D-category road. I passed through a copse with a large lake on the right-hand side. A flight of ducks disturbed by the echoing sound of the bike's exhaust took flight, squawking their annoyance at the unwarranted disturbance.

I knew I was in the close vicinity of the safe-house rendezvous and carefully scanned the hedges for the concealed driveway. Concentrating on finding the farm I didn't see the cow dung dropped from a farmer's trailer until I was on top of it. I felt the squelch of a six-inch pile of shit at the same time as the front wheel started to slide into a skid. Quickly I decelerated and hauling the front wheel back upright I managed to regain control, shouting a curse that must have been heard everywhere.

Still recovering from the near accident and wobbling a little I saw the farmhouse ahead. I pulled around the side road and parked the bike at the side of a muddy path, and I remember emitting a long, relieved sigh, we had made it. To have got so far and then nearly come to grief just outside the delivery point was a bit much. I dismounted and noticed that my legs were trembling with effort and fatigue. I realized I was more tired than I thought as I pulled off my helmet and gloves. My movements seemed disjointed and slightly out of synch, like being tipsy without drinking any alcohol.

I opened the little wrought-iron gate and walked up the drive past the kitchen window. Before I could knock at the old stained front door it was pulled open, and I was blinded by the bright light pouring through.

'Hey, Jill, look what the cat's dragged in,' a man shouted over his shoulder back into the kitchen. No problem it was Eric, and he waved me in.

'Hi, Eric,' I said. 'Any chance of a cup of tea?'

'Course there is, me cock sparrer,' Eric replied. 'Come in, and Jill'll put the kettle on.'

Inside the heat of the kitchen hit me like a blow. After travelling all day in the cold November weather I was tired out and chilled to the bone. It wasn't long though before I was sitting cradling a mug of steaming hot tea. I noticed that Eric and Jill didn't seem very surprised to see me, maybe I was correct in assuming they had a direct line back to Colin. They had been expecting me, but I felt that they needed reminding of the quantity we were carrying. Despite their previous agreement, Jill didn't seem too happy at the thought of 300 kilos of cannabis being parked overnight in her driveway. Eric was up for it, but he wanted payment in kind, straight away that night.

After a bit of haggling for effect we agreed that he would be paid one kilo of gear, worth about £3000, for minding the storage van overnight and until the pick-up vehicle arrived from the UK, supposedly early the next day. Having sorted out the storage details I left to collect Barry and the van. As I climbed wearily back on to the bike, I noticed my back and thigh muscles were starting to complain. Back at the garage I found Barry asleep in the driver's seat. What a dickhead! I woke him, and he started the van up and made to follow me into the dark countryside.

So that he could keep up I drove back at a snail's pace towards the farm. I noticed a car with yellow headlights behind the van that made no attempt to overtake even though we were travelling so slowly. I put the driver's reluctance to pass down to the narrowness of the country lanes and the tight bends along the route. When we reached the farm I saw Eric had opened the drive gates and moved both his car and his camper van out of the way. I parked up and watched as Barry reversed into the driveway right up to the garage door, leaving the van at the top of the drive next to the camper van. It seemed safe enough to me.

In the house I made the introductions and dropped it on Barry that Eric wanted a kilo of gear that night before he would allow us to leave the van on his premises. After a lot of moaning about the dark and the fact that all the gear was concealed in the middle of the load Barry agreed to fetch it. Meanwhile in the kitchen Jill was warming some homemade soup.

Amid a lot of banging, crashing and swearing Barry

finally located the cannabis in the van. He emerged to ask for a knife and eventually resurfaced nursing a nasty cut on his hand and four blocks of cannabis. 'There you go, mate,' he said, 'don't smoke it all at once.' He gave the soaps to Eric who inspected them individually and then took them into the house.

Barry and I closed up the van and went into the kitchen. Jill offered us some soup and lovely crispy bread she hacked off a long French stick. The meal was excellent, both Barry and I were starving. Soon Eric returned and sat down to his soup; he asked us about the trip through Spain and France and when we would be leaving. I noticed he seemed very cool about the whole deal and that he didn't mention Benson particularly, which I thought more than a little suspicious.

As we talked I became more confident that he had been in touch with Benson and knew more about our plans than he was letting on. It would have been typical of Benson to have let Eric, who was a buddy of his, know what was going on without my knowledge. These sort of built-in security details are important in the world of drug smuggling for they allow the organizers or buyers to monitor the movement of shipments and maintain security whilst not being close to the product at any time.

Eric told us we couldn't stay at the farm as they had no spare beds, but he directed us to a hotel in a town a few miles away. We did not suggest that we might sleep on the settees or the floor, because it seemed to me that Eric wanted us out of the way. Perhaps he was intending to make a few phone calls of his own after we had gone. Barry borrowed a spare bike helmet, and soon after we both left for town on the motorbike.

The hotel was old fashioned but clean and warm. We had missed the evening meal hours ago, but they made us a large plate of cheese and ham sandwiches, which we quickly demolished along with a couple of beers. After a coffee we returned to our separate rooms for a shower and a change of clothes. I put a call through to Benson and confirmed our safe arrival. I told him the van had been left with Eric and Jill, and advised him of the payment terms I'd agreed with them, all of which he seemed to think were OK. I added that we would be at the farm tomorrow ready for the switch over.

'The collection van will be there about 11 am,' Benson said. 'They have bang-on directions, I gave them myself this afternoon,' OK, I thought, the job's a goer. I was pleased because I was sure that Benson and the English buyers would all soon be in the bag.

After speaking to Benson I put a call through to Kath at her hotel in Fuengirola, but there was no answer. I decided, she was probably watching the nightly cabaret show with Natalie in the lounge, so I thought I'd catch her the next day. I briefly contemplated phoning the Customs in the UK, but the hour was late, and I would have to ring the London number and wait for them to call me back, which could have been a bit tricky with Barry hanging around. Besides I had nothing new to tell them yet. The Customs part of the operation would start tomorrow when I got the number of the collection van.

I returned to the bar where Barry was now waiting. It was very quiet there, and we couldn't talk without being overheard so we decided to go for a drink in the town. Many French small towns seem to die when the sun goes down, and this one was no exception. We walked around for ages, but the whole place looked deserted, with shutters closed on all the houses and shops. We had almost given up trying to find anywhere when we heard the sound of a jukebox playing on the night breeze. We tracked back and discovered a tiny open bar in an alleyway.

Inside it reeked of strong French tobacco and beer. The bar was a students' haunt, full of leather-jacketed youths and fresh-faced large-breasted girls who all seemed to be wearing tight-fitting woollen sweaters that reminded me of the beatnik scene of the 60s. We sat at the counter, and after pantomiming our need for two beers we turned to watch the scenery whilst enjoying our drink.

Some lads were playing pool on a massive table, while their mates were enjoying old-fashioned bar football, the sort of wooden box game with two teams of players fastened to shafts and operated by handles, a machine found now usually in old greasy-spoon transport cafes. It was obviously all the rage there, and the players and onlookers were laughing and joking and whooping loudly when one of the teams scored a goal. All good stuff. Barry and I turned back to our drinks and surveyed the talent.

The jukebox kicked in with a French version of a heavy metal hit, which to our ears was absolute crap, but the French kids seemed to like it. Soon fed up with the watery beer, the smell and the overwhelming noise, the idea of another drink waned quickly, so I paid the tab, and we left. After the noise of the bar the streets seemed as silent as the grave. Back at our hotel we went straight to bed. During the walk back to the hotel I had said to Barry that tomorrow would be a long day. I didn't know how right I was.

The next morning was cold, bright and clear with a cutting wind. After a breakfast of croissants and coffee we set off on the bike for the farm. I could feel Barry shivering in his thin jacket. The wind was buffeting the bike pretty badly, and each gust had him gripping me harder. I'd end up with bruised hips if he carried on.

We arrived at the farm about ten o'clock. Barry jumped off the bike quickly. 'Bloody hell, that was cold,' he complained. His nose was red and his eyes were watering with the wind. Without gloves his hands were frozen. After a lot of knocking on the door Eric finally arrived. 'Morning, lads,' he said, 'that's a good bit of shit you've got there.' He looked wrecked with eyes like pissholes in the snow, he'd obviously had a good sampling session last night.

'Morning, Eric,' I said, 'get the coffee on before Barry kicks the bucket. He's bloody freezing.'

We went into the old-fashioned kitchen, and Eric filled a kettle and placed it on top of the Aga hotplate. He opened the firedoor and raked about inside before adding a log from a wicker basket. 'It won't be long boiling,' he informed us. 'What's the plan today then?'

'It all depends what time the van arrives,' I said. 'As soon as it gets here we'll swap the gear over, and that's it, we're off back to Spain, where it's a damn sight warmer than it is here.'

Just then Jill walked in wearing a long woollen dressing gown and heavy slippers; she too looked like she'd had a night on the tiles. She nodded a good morning to us and sat down at the kitchen table. Over a mug of coffee Eric explained that they grew their own marijuana and offered to show us his plants, I wasn't bothered but went with him anyway just to have a look and a nosey. He had several marijuana plants each over six foot tall growing in a little coalshed at the far end of the garden. He had removed the old tiled roof and installed clear plastic sheeting so that the sunlight shone directly on to the plants, it was like a greenhouse in there. The plants certainly looked healthy enough and the atmosphere in the small room smelled sweet and heavy. Eric showed us how he collected the younger leaves because they made the strongest smoke when dried out.

The farmhouse itself was very old and full of strange hippie- type objets d'art. Pine furniture and woven rugs were the order of the day, with wicker baskets occupying many table tops and odd corners. Dried flower arrangements gave an air of Laura Ashley's Rural Collection. The folksy image was at odds with a large poster tacked to a door depicting a faintly-smiling Mona Lisa smoking a joint as big as a carrot. I had noticed a similar picture of the Queen appearing to be smoking a joint in ceremonial dress behind the bathroom door. Overgrown hippies, I thought to myself.

As the time approached 1 pm I became restless, the van should have arrived by now. I walked out into the lane and wandered in the direction of the main road. I strained my ears but couldn't detect the sound of a commercial engine. I would have to phone Benson to get an update. I hoped there were no problems with the second van, the whole operation hinged on its arrival. Eric and Jill didn't have a phone in the house, and my mobile didn't work in France, so I clothed up and drove down the road into the village. I located a phone box in the market square and called Benson. He sounded as frustrated as me.

'There's been a delay,' he told me. 'Can you get Barry or Eric to drive the van further up towards the coast?'

'No chance,' I told him. 'Barry wants to get back off to Spain, and Eric is scared of his own shadow.'

'Tell Eric, it's worth another kilo to him,' said Benson.

'Look, Colin, what time's the van going to arrive?' I asked him. 'If it's going to be much longer there's going to be some serious bottling here.'

'Just hang on, and if it hasn't arrived by three o'clock give me a call,' he said.

'OK,' I said and hung up. Shit, I could feel the operation starting to slip away. I knew I had to ring the Customs at some stage today, hopefully before they all buggered off home.

I returned to the farm and asked Barry and Eric if either of them would be prepared to drive the van towards the French Channel ports. They both knew that security increased closer to the coast with roving Custom patrols stopping vehicles at random. They were not interested in moving the gear another inch.

Barry said he wanted to return to Spain. I thought he was looking frightened by now. I've noticed before that action of any kind is OK, it's during periods of inactivity that people seem really to think about what they're doing, and that's when they lose their bottle. Barry's part in the job was finished, so I agreed that we would get him off as soon as possible. Before he could go we would have to unload all the gear into the garage, but this didn't seem to be a problem to me as we would have to move it from the van it was now in to the one coming from the UK anyway. It would save us time later.

Eric agreed we could use his garage, so the three of us set out to unload the gear. When the job was under way I left them to ring Benson again and spring the news on him that the van wouldn't be going anywhere nearer the Channel coast. By now I was really concerned about the delays and told Benson that unless the second van arrived soon both Barry and I would leave the gear on the garage floor and return to Spain, leaving him to sort out the mess himself.

Benson went apeshit, he threatened me with a beating and said if the gear was lost he would have me shot. What a stiff! He was over a 1000 miles away and still shouting the odds, but I knew that nothing would induce him to travel up here where the action was. He wanted to sit in his villa and rake in the profits from his illegal trade whilst other suckers carried out the dirty work. There was no way I was going to leave the gear and return to Spain because I needed the registration number of the van coming from the UK, but I hoped that my putting pressure on Benson might hurry the situation along a little. Eventually he promised to get an update on the van and said I should phone him back at four o'clock.

When I returned to the farm all the gear was stacked in the garage. In the process of unloading some of the packages had split open, and there were cannabis soaps strewn all over the floor. The air was redolent with the heavy, spicy aroma of the drug. Eric dreamily surveyed the nearly half a ton of cannabis. I could see his mind ticking over: that amount of gear would bring in about a million pounds' cash when it was sold at street value and in a city or big town it would disappear within a week. We were looking at a tremendous tax-free retirement bundle.

His face clouded, and I knew that reality had set in. If he tried to get the gear himself he would be dead within the week, such is the threat of violence in the subculture of the world of drugs. Almost as bad was the thought of the crippling jail sentence he would receive if the police became aware of its presence at his farmhouse. I knew it was a sobering thought for him, I could read it clearly all over his face. He shook his head and walked back into the farm kitchen. Barry and I left him and Jill alone for a few minutes, but it was too cold just hanging around in an unheated garage so we went back into the kitchen.

Eric made yet another cup of tea, and we discussed the situation. Jill had disappeared into the lounge where she was ironing clothes, she seemed to be adopting an ostrich-like strategy of ignoring the situation and pretending that we weren't there. We agreed that I should phone Benson again, and then we would wait until five o'clock before Barry and I left. I intended to phone the Customs at that point and tell them something had gone wrong; the van hadn't arrived as planned, they could make the final decision as to what to do. I had a suspicion that there wasn't going to be a van arriving at all, the arrangements about the collection seemed too loose. It was not the way of things to leave 300 kilos of gear lying around awaiting collection. I thought that maybe Benson had contracted with the owners to have the gear shipped directly into the UK and had decided to wait until we were committed to the run before telling us of the final phase of his plans.

I came to a decision and decided to phone Benson back early. I put on my jacket and helmet and went outside. Barry was in the garage, Eric was talking to me as I walked up the driveway, and Jill was still ironing. As

I sat on the bike in the drive talking to Eric I heard the noise of a car engine screaming along the lane outside. A dark-blue car skidded to a halt across the driveway in a spray of mud and soil.

Before we could react four men dressed in black bulky jackets and ski masks jumped out of the car and ran towards us, leaping the garden gate. I was stunned to see they were pointing big pistols at us. Just then a helicopter descended from the sky and a loudspeaker cut in shouting something deafening and unintelligible in French. More black-suited men vaulted the hedge, and rolling in the grass and mud they jerked upright and pointed guns at us. It was a bladder-leaking moment. There was a crash of breaking glass, and Jill screamed loudly; a thump of metal hitting the floor told me she had dropped the iron.

Everything seemed to drop into slow motion as the first guy, his face all covered by his mask, reached us; he dropped Eric with a shoulder charge to his belly. Eric crumpled like a paper bag and went down with the guy kneeling on his chest. I saw the silvery glitter of handcuffs as the guy reached into his back pocket with one hand whilst pointing his gun at Eric's head with the other. The attacker stood up and rolled an unresisting Eric over into the mud. In a flash the handcuffs clicked onto his wrists, and he was a prisoner. The whole process had taken less than 20 seconds.

The second masked man who had targeted me couldn't knock me over as I was sat on the bike. He contented himself with shoving his gun into my chest and trying to pull my helmet off one handedly, but it was fastened by the chinstrap. I reached up to unfasten it and received a pistol slap across the back of my hands;

he snarled something to me and unfastened the strap. He pulled the helmet off roughly, nearly taking my ears off in the process and immediately rammed the pistol against my forehead saying something directly in my face. I felt the spray of his spittle.

He gestured with his free hand, and following his sign language I climbed slowly and carefully off the bike, all the time the pistol pressed closely to my head. As soon as I was off the bike he transferred the gun and thumped me hard on the shoulder pushing me face down on to the ground. I quickly dropped down and felt his knee dig into the small of my back as he reached for my arms. He pulled them down behind me, and I felt the click of handcuffs being fastened; he squeezed the ratchet and the cuffs bit tightly on my wrists. I was a prisoner now too.

I lifted my face from the gravel and mud and looked around. Eric was lying face down about six feet away sobbing quietly into the mud with a guy standing over him still pointing a gun at his back. Jill was still screaming, although the sound had now subsided to a sort of long, shuddering sobbing interspersed with an intermittent scream. There were loud crashes and bangs, and the sound of breaking furniture from inside the house. Barry was still in the garage behind the closed door. He obviously thought he would hide in there rather than take a chance outside.

I realized then we had been busted by a police squad. That was a relief! At first I thought we were being held up by another gang, but I quickly decided they wouldn't have a helicopter hovering overhead. The tinny noise of chattering police radios forced its way into my consciousness even above the deafening roar of the chopper. Bits of gravel, leaves and paper were blowing around in crazy circles, it was an incredible, unreal scene.

Amid the confusion, shouting and crying the police seemed to realize they were one man short. They ran up to the garage and pulled open the door pointing their guns into the gloomy interior. Barry shot out like a greyhound from a trap. He was either crazy or hadn't seen the guns, because these guys were pros. Barry reached as far as the edge of the field next to the drive when the two policemen who had given chase landed on him. He went down with a whooshing noise as the breath was knocked from his lungs. They sat on his back as they handcuffed his arms and legs, and he was trussed up like a chicken.

The helicopter moved away, and suddenly there seemed to be hundreds of police milling around the garden and roadway. The ones dressed in black pulled down Velcro patches on their jackets to reveal large police badges; on the back of their jackets the word POLICE was similarly exposed in bright orange lettering; others had donned plastic armbands.

We all lay on the ground whilst the search of the house continued noisily for about 15 minutes. A photographer walked up and started snapping away at everything in sight, including us on the floor, the vehicles and endless pictures of the van from every possible angle. Finally a tall middle-aged copper who seemed to be the one in charge walked over and stood in front of us.

On his command, as we lay looking up at him, we were picked up and taken, each of us between two coppers, to look at the cannabis lying on the floor of the garage. He started shouting at us in French, but I didn't have a clue what he was saying and could make out only the words, stupéfiants, cannabis and prison. He was ranting and shouting at the top of his lungs. Oh, shit, I thought this guy is really pissed with us. Barry looked across at me and winked, which drew him a sharp cuff across the face from a black-clothed copper. 'No contact,' he shouted.

The photographer came in and took a further series of snaps of each of us stood in front of the pile of cannabis. Then a few of the boss coppers posed there too, smiling in front of the gear. That's one for the family album, I thought. Incongruously it reminded me of an old sepia-tone American cowboy photograph, the sheriff standing over the body of the vanquished criminal. I smiled at the thought, a mistake not to be repeated, when a baton appeared from nowhere and hit me straight in the solar plexus. Fucking hell, that hurt! I doubled over and gasped, trying to get some air back into my body.

After the viewing the gear and photographing charade was over we were taken into the farm kitchen, which by this time had been thoroughly trashed. Cupboards and drawers were open, and all the contents thrown on to the floor: broken plates, cups and glasses were strewn everywhere. There was a constant sound of scrunching glass underfoot whenever anybody moved. Some of the kitchen windows were broken, and the curtains were blowing into the room. As Eric and Jill looked at the mess of their home, Jill set off crying again. At this a policeman snapped at her, presumably telling her to stop. Eric gave him a murderous look but wisely kept his mouth shut. The atmosphere was very tense and threatening. I saw Eric, Jill and Barry were by now really dejected and fed up. I suppose I looked the same way too.

After a few minutes a copper came in, plonked a large portable cassette recorder on the kitchen table and switched it on to record. He spoke clearly into the mike, presumably giving his name and basic details of the operation, then thrust it towards each of us in turn and in basic and hard to understand English demanded our names. We duly announced them to the machine.

A whoop and laughing outside signalled a new find. Two coppers came in with mud on their fatigues. Eric was dragged outside again, doubtless to view his attempts at growing marijuana in the coalshed. When he came back he was crying, tears streaming unchecked down his face. 'I'm fucked,' he said to no one in particular. 'Yes, you are fucked, mister,' said one of the coppers in a voice sounding remarkably like Peter Sellers' Inspector Clouseau. At least one of them could speak English, I thought.

The police left us in the kitchen with a couple of armed guards whilst they began to examine every piece of paper in the house; even old newspapers Jill had used to line shelves were inspected. We weren't allowed to talk to one another, although there was much glaring and shrugging of shoulders going on, it was a conversation by signals.

At the first opportunity I would inform the police of my undercover role in this smuggling operation. I wanted to let the police know who I was before the wheels of bureaucracy started turning. It was bad enough being arrested, but I didn't want to make any statements and be indicted by the French. I knew that once charges became more formal they would have to be processed, and then lawyers would be involved before my release on the intervention of the UK Customs. That would completely blow my cover, of course, and Kath and Natalie were sitting patiently in Spain, right in the middle of Benson's area, awaiting my return. Besides having guns pointed at my head wasn't covered by any agreement with Customs. Maybe it was a hazard that could be expected from the bad guys, but these were the good guys.

The coppers decided to hold initial interviews with us at the farm. We were all questioned together. Rather like a bizarre game show, it went like this:

'What is you name, smuggler?'

'John Lightfoot.'

'Is that your real name?'

'Yes, it's the name I was christened with.'

'Where are you from?'

'Great Britain and Spain.'

'Where are your guns?'

'I don't have any guns.'

'You must think we are fools, we know perfectly well all smugglers carry guns.'

'Maybe that's so, but I don't have a gun.'

'What is your name?'

'I've just told you, John Lightfoot.'

'And what is his name?' pointing towards Eric.

'Eric.'

'And his family name?'

'I don't know.'

'Salope! Do you think we are stupid? It will be hard for you if you do not cooperate with us.'

'I'm sorry, I don't know his full name, but if I'm under arrest I wish you to notify my embassy please.'

And so it went on for ages. All this was delivered by the copper in a stunning Inspector Clouseau accent, which obviously he did not realize sounded comical to our ears. Because of the language difficulties the whole interview had an aura of farce, which if it hadn't been so serious would have been funny. Eventually they gave up on questioning us and opted to move us to police headquarters. After a brief consultation they decided that Barry and I should be taken back to our hotel so that our rooms could be searched.

They put us in separate cars with three coppers in each, and we set off. They were obviously not familiar with the local topography, and I had to try and direct them. After nearly an hour of wrong turns and difficulties in communication we finally reached the town, and I directed them to the hotel. We all went in together, six coppers with guns surrounding Barry and me. The receptionist, a pretty girl of about 20, looked as if she might faint when we marched through the doorway. The senior copper explained in rapid-fire French what was going on and quickly obtained our room keys.

We went straight upstairs, where the police started a thorough search, looking under the beds in each room, even though they had obviously been cleaned, and between the sheets, despite the fact the bed had been made by the chambermaid. They checked my holdall containing clothes and washing kit very thoroughly. Eventually they knew they had drawn a blank, which they seemed pretty pissed about.

'Where are your guns, monsieur?' asked the senior copper for about the tenth time.

'We don't have any guns,' I repeated yet again, and we carried on this argument down the stairs back into the entrance lobby. More fast French to the receptionist and a bill was quickly made up and handed to the copper. He indicated to me to take some money from my wallet and pay it. Then leaving the hotel staff and clients standing agog in the open lounge area we climbed into the cars again and drove off.

By now it was pitch dark and raining heavily. The car windows were all steamed up, and there was the constant twitter of police radios. I was hungry, not having eaten all day, and had a raging headache. Worst of all was my desperate need for a cigarette, even a foul-smelling Gitanes that the coppers were chain-smoking would have been good at that moment.

'May I have a cigarette, please?' I asked. The guy sat at my side looked at me. 'Cigarette, tobacco, please?' I repeated. He grinned, one smoker to another and put his cigarette to my lips. I inhaled deeply and promptly coughed. God, that tobacco was awful, it tasted like old sweaty socks. He laughed and pulled the cigarette away.

During the nearly two-hour-long ride some of the tension leaked away, and their command of English gradually improved along with their more relaxed manner.

'Why do you smuggle narcotics?' one of them asked.

'I am not a smuggler,' I replied. 'I am an agent for British Customs & Excise, *Les Douanes*. When we reach your base I want to talk privately with a senior officer,' I added slowly, carefully enunciating my words. The effect of my remarks was as remarkable as if I had casually lobbed a hand grenade into the car.

There was a ten-second silence, and then they all began chattering at once. The boss copper in the front passenger seat picked up the radio handset and started talking earnestly to somebody. At last, I thought, now maybe I'll get a little sense out of them.

The one with the best English said to me, 'Why did you not confess you are a Customs agent at the farm?'

'Because I am an undercover agent. My role is confidential, it's a secret,' I said slowly, trying to make sure he understood. 'None of the others you have arrested knows I am an agent,' I added. The copper had turned round in his seat and was looking at me intently in the car's gloomy interior. I stared back into his eyes and nodded confirmation of my claims.

I was satisfied that when we reached the police station inquiries would be made, and my true role would soon be revealed. This was why I had been given a codename and had secret telephone numbers. As I sat there I drifted back to the conversations I'd had with Rob and Steve at our farm in England. It all seemed a long time ago, but I could recall our discussions vividly. I was sure the machinery would swing into action, and I would be 'released on a technicality'. Everything was going to be OK.

Once inside the police station we were all taken into the cells area at the rear of the building. Still handcuffed we were searched more thoroughly by uniformed police. They weren't just looking for knives or other weapons, they took all items from our pockets, including such things as paper tissues and small change. Jewellery, watches, belts and shoelaces were also taken from us, and everything inventoried on a big official list before being sealed into plastic bags.

Once we had been searched we were placed in

individual cells. It was a depressing experience. They were small with tiled walls and a slatted wooden bench fixed into the wall. There were no washing facilities, and the toilet was a concrete pad set in the floor with a hole in the middle emptying straight into the sewer beneath, the stench rising from it was vile. From the graffiti covering the walls I gathered that some enterprising souls had managed to sneak pens into the cell. It was interesting trying to decipher it.

Suddenly I could hear voices: Eric and Jill were shouting to each other between the cells. I joined in, and so did Barry. Eric had just yelled, 'Tell them nothing, they can't prove it's our gear,' which I thought was a particularly crass thing to say. A guard stomped down the outer corridor. 'Tais-toi,' he shouted nastily and banged on one or two steel doors for effect. I didn't understand him, but I gathered he wanted us to shut up.

After what seemed like a couple of hours of just sitting around thinking I began to get cold – the cells weren't heated, and I had no jacket. There weren't any blankets on the bench, so it looked like a cold night ahead for us. I lay for hours looking up at the wire caged lamp high up on the ceiling. There were no windows, and the whole place was damp and claustrophobic. Exhausted by the day's events I eventually drifted off into an uncomfortable sleep.

The next morning I was taken for questioning. The police had arranged a local high-school teacher as translator, and we got off to a good start. We went through a basic question-and-answer session; they wanted my home address, family names, mother's maiden name plus all the information that was in my passport, which they now held. Later in the morning one of the senior guys from the arresting team joined us.

'We have contacted the Customs in England, and they tell us that they don't know you,' he began.

I was dumbfounded. 'It's a mistake, you obviously didn't speak to the right person,' I said and gave them the full names of my Customs handlers. 'Call them on the number I gave you and tell them Benjy needs some help. Benjy is my codename with Customs and Excise.'

'We telephoned them, and they don't know you,' repeated the copper.

'Look, if they don't know me how come I have their private phone numbers and the names of their investigation officers?' I demanded. This was getting silly, and I thought he was trying to wind me up.

The police and the interpreter talked amongst themselves for a few minutes before the one who had been questioning me said, 'OK, why don't you tell us about your work with the Customs?'

I could see no harm in that, they were after all on the same side as the Customs, so for the next hour or so I told them of the names, operations and anything else that came to mind about the Customs and drug dealing. They listened avidly and took copious notes. During this time there was a distinct easing of the atmosphere. I was given coffee and cigarettes, and attitudes became more relaxed and friendly. It was a case of carrot and stick by the cops, as long as I was cooperating they would be nice to me. But although aware of their obvious show of basic psychology I wasn't bothered by it.

The information I was giving them wasn't secret, much of it had been ignored by the Customs, and I could be talking my way out of a tricky situation now that the Customs seemed to have abandoned me to my fate. I gave them all the details of the French operation, right from the beginning. When I got to the part about the van coming from England they were very interested and alert. They went into a huddle again and held a whispered conversation.

'John,' said the younger cop who spoke some English, 'we want you to cooperate with us and help us to catch the van from England. We will allow you to make some phone calls to arrange a rendezvous, and it will be good for you when we tell the judge.'

Ah, I thought, here is the trade-off, if I assist them then the 'technical hitch' ploy will be brought in, and I'll be released. 'OK,' I agreed, 'first off I will have to phone Benson in Spain.'

A tape recorder was produced and connected to a telephone. They locked the door so that no one could interrupt, and we quickly prepared a story to tell Benson. Two minutes later I dialled his number.

'Hi, Colin,' I said when he answered, 'we've had a bit of a problem here. Yesterday afternoon I came off the motorbike on a back lane and ended up in a local clinic. I got out this morning and went back to the farm. Everyone there was just about shitting themselves, but no van has turned up. What the fuck is going on?'

Benson was surprised to hear from me and even more surprised that I had fallen off the bike. But he didn't know what had happened to the van.

'Well, I'm not in the mood to hang around here much longer,' I said. 'I'm OK, just a bit bruised and sore, and the bike isn't damaged badly. But we're all getting really pissed off with your English mates, and we are leaving here one way or the other today.'

'OK,' he said, 'why don't you phone Tony direct in England and see what's happening?', and he gave me a mobile phone number.

'Great, I'll speak to you later,' I replied and quickly hung up. That was the last time I ever spoke with Benson.

Tension drained out of the room like air escaping from a balloon. 'Well done, John,' said the copper whose English was adequate enough to follow the conversation. He explained what had transpired to the others and then told me to phone Tony. But when I did so there was no answer. By now it was lunchtime, and the cops wanted to eat. One of them gave me a pack of cigarettes and a book of matches before I was handed back to a uniformed cop and returned to the cells.

Considering the circumstances things were going pretty well, and I could see me being released in the near future. I sat in the cell for a few more hours, and then the English-speaking copper appeared to take me off for further questioning. Later I made further calls to Tony in England and finally managed to arrange a meeting with the driver who was coming to collect the drugs consignment destined for England.

OCTRIS, a specialist drug squad operating from Paris throughout France, staked out the meeting spot and late that evening arrested a man driving a British-registered vehicle that matched the description furnished by Tony. Various bits of incriminating evidence were found on him, and he was charged with conspiracy to smuggle drugs across France. I never saw the guy and didn't even know he had been arrested until the following day. The cops were very pleased with my efforts and told me that I would get a greatly reduced sentence because of my help in nailing another gang member. But I wasn't after a reduced sentence, I was after a no-sentence scenario.

For now I was photographed, proper mug shots just like you see on TV, holding a card with my name printed on it in front of my chest. Then I was fingerprinted by a taciturn old man who stank of booze. Back in my cell I began to feel a bit worried. What was the point in photographing and fingerprinting me if they intended to release me?

Other than a guard bringing me a plastic cup of coffee and a sandwich nothing else happened until late in the evening. A senior uniformed policeman and a few juniors collected me from the cells and led me to a storage room across an open courtyard. It was great to be outside, even so briefly, and so what if it was raining. Inside the storage room all the goodies seized during the farm raid were displayed on the floor, everything marked with small orange identification tags.

The interpreter was in full swing. 'Mr Lightfoot, do you recognize this contraband seized at the time of your arrest?' he asked. I think he was feeling more nervous than me judging how his voice had gone up a couple of octaves. I suppose he wanted to make a good impression on the chief who would no doubt be paying him. I noticed the photographer hovering on the edge of the group.

'No, I've never seen this lot before,' I said loudly. That really threw them. The chief shouted, 'Imbécile! at me and started ranting at his mates before he turned and quick timed back into the main building, leaving me standing there grinning. Back again in my cell I felt a flash of pleasure. What an arrogant bunch of dickheads!

They had all the evidence they needed and plenty of statements to boot. All they had wanted with that little charade was the icing on the cake. What a great story it would have been for them.

Imagine the scene, an international drugs trafficker confronted with his misdeeds broke down and confessed to the chief of police and his band of arse lickers, all nicely recorded by camera, with the damning evidence forming a sinister backdrop. No doubt it had been timed to take place in the dark to increase the dramatic effect of the tableau. Well, bollocks to them. They could now work it out for themselves, I was going to look after number one for a change.

I got no food that evening and spent another cold night on the bench alone. As I lay there I could occasionally hear snatches of Barry singing 'Rule Britannia,' followed by a guard shouting at him. Barry responded with, 'Fuck off, you frogs. I want a cup of tea!'

A crazy feeling came over me as I realized there was nothing worse they could do to us. We were locked up, unwashed, unfed and without access to any lawyers. I joined in with Barry. We sang at the tops of our voices for a couple of hours to an accompaniment of French coppers shouting at us to be quiet, but they were powerless to stop us.

We pushed it as far as we could, encouraging each other to sing louder and louder. That night the French heard some wild renditions of 'Land of Hope and Glory', 'Rule Britannia', 'God Save the Queen' and so on; finally we moved on to some Queen songs before we petered out. It was a great demonstration of the good old British *Bridge on the River Kwai* spirit, and it boosted my morale tremendously, but now my voice was hoarse, and I was knackered out. I slept really well that night despite the cold and the stink of shit from the sewers.

* * *

The next morning everyone acted as if nothing had happened. I was given a coffee and questioned for several more hours. Repeated pettifogging questions and answers that became mind-numbingly boring as the hours ticked by.

After yet another bland, tasteless sandwich for lunch I was left alone and told that I was to see a lawyer appointed by the court. Shortly thereafter an important-looking middle-aged man walked into the office wearing a three-piece suit, floral bow tie and pince-nez glasses fastened to a cord around his neck. He was a sight, but he spoke perfect English.

He kicked off the short interview by saying, 'Good afternoon, Mr Lightfoot, I am your defence lawyer appointed by the court. During this period of the police investigation I cannot discuss the details of the case with you. I can check on your welfare and ensure that you are fed properly and allowed washing facilities. I can also check that a relative or your country's embassy is informed of your arrest and detention by the French police.' He smiled encouragingly as if he had just delivered some good news.

'Well, I can tell you that so far I've had a few cups of coffee, two sandwiches and not been allowed to wash. How does that fit in with the French rules for detaining prisoners?' I asked. 'Furthermore, I am an informant for the British Customs & Excise working on an operation to catch some drug smugglers. I have told the police officers who arrested me, but they claim the Customs don't know me. That is a ridiculous statement, and though I have cooperated in every way they still will not accept I am not a drug dealer, and that I am an informant for the Customs.'

Once I got into this area he started shaking his head and repeated, mantra-like, 'I am not allowed to discuss the criminal charges or their circumstances with you. You must take these matters up with the judge who you will see later when you are indicted.' In a wary tone of voice he finished, 'I will take up the matters of food and washing facilities with the police officer in charge of your detention, but that is all I can do. I am sorry for all the rest.'

He seemed more nervous than me. Perhaps he thought the conversation was being recorded, or he was expecting me, a desperado drug dealer, to jump at him. I don't know which, but he was definitely in a hurry to get out of the room. As legal advice went it was minimal. Within seconds the English-speaking copper had opened the door and reseated himself as the lawyer made a swift exit. The whole interview had taken less than ten minutes.

'Hell!' I said as the lawyer left, 'if that's all the law can do for me then I might as well represent myself.'

'You must understand the charges of international drug trafficking are very serious in France,' the young copper said. 'They are looked upon the same as terrorism. You will all face a maximum penalty of 30 years in prison when you are convicted, but you will be helped by your assistance in catching the other driver.' I just stared at him as he continued, 'It is in your interest to assist us to catch any other members of your gang, then your sentence will be reduced still further.'

'Just a minute,' I retorted finally, 'what about the small fact that you seem to forget that I am here with the permission of the UK Customs? This was a planned operation to catch the gang leaders in Britain, and it's not my fault you guys jumped in too early. You should be arresting Benson in Spain and Paul and Tony in England, they're the money men behind this operation.'

'We shall see. That is a matter for the judge,' he replied, in a similar vein to the lawyer. He then turned back to the prepared statements and starting asking the same set of questions over again.

As I answered him my mind was thinking, thirty years, bloody hell, I'm going to have to do something to make these jokers see sense, never mind a few years off for cooperation. But they had no intention of seeing sense. They were happy they had caught a gang of foreign drug smugglers with 300 kilos of cannabis. It was a major coup for them. I was merely an annoying side issue, a thread that needed tucking back into place so that they could present a nice clean picture of their efficiency to the judge. So they stitched me up properly.

Later that day they asked me to sign all the statements that had been taken. All together there were more than 20, each of which the translator went through with me. Although very detailed I noticed there wasn't a single reference to the UK Customs or my claims that I was an informant for them. I questioned them about this.

'We are trying to protect you, John,' said the young copper. 'All the other gang members and their lawyers will have access to these statements. If we put in that you are a Customs agent they will know, and you could be in great danger. We shall make a secret confidential report to the judge that will not be available to anyone else. We will tell the judge of your Customs connection in that document, but it is better that the statements are "clean'' and make no mention of the Customs.'

That seemed a reasonable deal to me. At that time I was in no hurry to have Barry or Eric and Jill know I was a Customs agent. If they knew it was only a matter of time before Benson found out, and Kath and Natalie were still down in Spain near to his vengeful hand. So I signed the prepared statements.

The next day, the fourth since our arrest, we were loaded into separate cars and each driven with a police escort to the criminal courts. There we were locked in individual holding cells under the main building. The cells were small, but at least they were warm. Before they handed us over one of the cops gave me another packet of cigarettes.

After an hour or so of kicking my heels in the cell I was handcuffed and led up a narrow staircase opening out into a public area. There was carpet on the floor and potted plants in a corner, which all looked very civilized. We then filed into an office filled with important-looking prosperous and overfed citizens. A man behind an impressively large desk introduced himself through a middle-aged female interpreter.

'Hello, Mr Lightfoot, I am examining magistrate Maurice Marlière. I am in charge of the criminal case and will be investigating the facts of this affair.' The translator spoke in a dry, schoolmarmish voice.

'Hello, judge, I would like to know why I have been held all this time without anyone formally acknowledging that I am an agent for HM Customs and Excise?' I started off hard, looking him straight in the eyes. From the surprise on the faces of the interpreter and the judge I could tell this was all news to them.

The senior OCTRIS guy immediately launched into a discourse with the judge telling him, I hoped, that I was an agent for the Customs. Whilst he was talking M Marlière was flicking through and reading various documents.

'Mr Lightfoot, if you are an agent for the Customs then why do you not say that in your statements?' he asked. The anger and frustration started to bite at me.

'This is ridiculous,' I said. 'There is no mention of my status because OCTRIS said it was better left out for my security. They also said they would report to you confidentially about my claims.' By now I was really indignant and nearly shouting. I could feel the policeman behind me twitching as he got ready to restrain me if my anger boiled over and I went for anyone.

The OCTRIS agent and the judge talked rapidly for a few more minutes before Marlière nodded his head in a satisfied manner.

'Well, Mr Lightfoot, it seems that OCTRIS have investigated your claim to be an informant and cannot get any confirmation from British Customs & Excise. They tell me you have cooperated well and assisted them to capture one other member of the gang. I will make my own inquiries into your position with the British authorities, and if what you say is true you should be released in the near future.'

'But now,' and he adopted a firm stentorian tone, 'you are charged with contravening several articles of the

French criminal code in that you as a member of a gang imported a substantial quantity of illegal drugs across the French border. You will be held in prison until I have completed my inquiries.'

And that was it. I didn't get the chance to reply before I was being led out the door. I don't know what forced me, but I had to have a last word.

'So this is French justice, is it?' by now I was shouting back into the room. 'The fucking Common Market, it's a load of bollocks. You just do your own thing. What happened to European cooperation, eh?'

It was too late, the decisions were already made before I had even entered the room. There was no way they were going to release me on a 'technicality'. I had been lied to, and now I was hung out to dry on my own. I could tell instinctively that things weren't going to be easy. I would have to prove to this judge that I really was working for UK Customs or else I was going to be in deep shit for a long long time.

Oh, well, I thought, that was pretty good. Within the space of five minutes I'd insulted and probably pissed off the one man who could help me get out of this mess. I would have to wait and see what the future held for me now.

10

Prison Strife

My induction into the French penal system took place one cold, wet night. Following my brief but fiery appearance in court I was hustled handcuffed past the stares of cleaning staff and outside. It was now very dark and raining in a steady, continuous downpour. I was dumped unceremoniously into the back of a closed van in the company of two large and armed gendarmes. They looked at me indifferently and talked quietly to one another.

Accompanied by a motorcycle escort lead squad with a back-up car behind I was driven through the quiet and near deserted town. After some slowing and jerking the van stopped, and I heard the driver talking and laughing with someone outside. We moved off again with another jerk for a few yards, then the van came to an abrupt halt. With my hands tied behind me and unable to hold myself upright during the irregular jolting motion I had rolled off the plastic bench seat and ended up lying on my side against the rear doors.

I was scrambling to sit up when the doors were suddenly thrown open. Unable to help myself I tumbled heavily out of the van and dropped on to a concrete floor at the feet of two prison guards. Disorientated and blinded by powerful arc lights I heard a grunted curse, and then my introduction proper started with a booted kick to my kidneys.

Not wanting another kick I quickly scrambled to my feet and tried to see where I was. The dazzle of the lights and a searing wind were debilitating, and I felt a wave of anxiety and exhaustion wash over me. Hot bile rushed into my mouth, and before I could clench my teeth shut stinking vomit erupted down my front, spattering on to a guard. He cursed again, and I heard the gendarmes behind me laugh crudely. A hefty push in the direction of the prison gates helped me empty the rest of my stomach contents on to the yard floor. I couldn't wipe my mouth, and the residue dribbled down my chin and burned the back of my throat. I felt a complete arsehole.

Tiredness, vomiting and the pain of the kidney kick combined to force tears of pain, anger and frustration to my eyes. Embarrassed by my show of weakness I shook my head and said as coolly and unemotionally as I could, 'OK, so that's a demonstration of the French sense of fair play. Well done.' They didn't understand the words, but another shove told me they had read my tone of voice. As I fell heavily on my left knee I screamed involuntarily and collapsed on the ground with a searing pain in my leg that radiated up my thigh from the knee.

To more curses and shouting I was roughly hauled to my feet and dragged through a small arched doorway. Squinting against the light I looked up and saw the inscription AD 1810 carved into the weathered rock. Snatching a brief look around me I saw we were in a large yard surrounded by high stone walls. Great, I thought, a bloody Napoleonic nick is all I need.

In a brightly lit reception area the prison guards accepted me from the gendarmes with the minimum of formalities. I was roughly searched, and my small bag of personal belongings was emptied on to a table and checked over again. My cash was counted and placed into a zip-lock plastic bag. My watch, wedding ring, St Christopher and chain were all placed into another zipped bag.

A guard shouted me over and after releasing the cuffs gestured to me to sign my name in an old-fashioned ledger that immediately brought to mind a Dickensian accounts book. The ordinary biro he was thrusting at me seemed inappropriate, and in my exhaustion I thought a quill pen would have been more fitting. This irrational unbidden thought brought a smile to my lips, but the touchy guards seemed to think I was laughing at them. This earned me a sharp, menacing reprimand from the guard. His fetid, beery breath overlaid with garlic rolled over me as he moved closer and glared into my eyes. Nauseous I looked away, and with a deep sigh I signed my name. And so I became a prisoner of the French penal system.

I was led down a flagstone corridor through a pale-blue painted steel grillage that incorporated a sliding steel gate, operated electrically by an unseen hand, and into a holding area behind the reception desk. The door slid shut behind me and clanged with that special sound that is so evocative of prisons the world over. There is a grim finality to that clang, over time you learn to recognize the differing tones of each door in the prison. Now I am a connoisseur of the clang.

I was dumped on a wooden bench whilst the guards and the gendarmes discussed me and the case in general. I heard my name and the word 'stupéfiants' a few times as they kept glancing across at me and laughing. I must have looked a mess. Without a wash or shave for nearly five days, wearing crumpled and torn clothes and smelling strongly of vomit, I looked more like a drunk raked up from a gutter than an international narcotics trafficker. I couldn't have been a pretty sight, but I seemed to amuse the guards all right.

After about half an hour of their chatting, during which I studied a notice board and started to doze, an older guard appeared. He was comical looking, sporting a large, droopy mustache and dressed in regulation navy-blue uniform with an incongruous pair of tattered tartan house slippers. He was smoking an evil-smelling briar pipe, which he pointed in my direction and gestured for me to follow him. As I did so the gendarmes and the reception guards bade me a mocking good night, and my new guard grinned, showing nicotine-stained teeth. But somehow his grin didn't seem as menacing as the others, and his manner was not overtly threatening.

I started to feel more at ease. Later I found out that he was just an old boy working his way towards his pension by doing the night shift, which, after the final lockup, is the quietest time in prison. Barring any problems in the cells the night guard's duties only stretched to watching TV and drinking coffee. My late-night arrival provided a small but interesting diversion for the old timer.

He unlocked a steel door and took me into another brightly lit room smelling of cheap disinfectant, which contained only a tatty wall cupboard, a metal-frame chair and a rather disconcerting steel eyebolt protruding from the wall at shoulder height. This room was painted the same institutional mustard yellow as the reception area and had the same well-used, drab and impersonal feel to it. There was an overall impression of depression and dejection — or was that just my overtired mind?

The guard started talking to me in a conversational tone, but as I didn't have a clue what he meant I just stared back at him and shrugged my shoulders. He left me for a moment and returned with my original tormentor, whom I had mentally nicknamed Garlic Breath. After locking the door behind him Garlic Breath began yelling at me. He obviously wanted me to do something but I didn't know what he wanted. Shouting didn't help me understand any more, and Garlic Breath was becoming increasingly frustrated when he realized he wasn't getting anywhere. Eventually, though, I got the picture: they wanted me to undress.

I quickly complied and stripped down to my boxers, which Garlic Breath signalled he wanted off too. No problem, I pulled them off and handed them over. He then pointed between my legs and said something to the old timer, laughing crudely. Unsurprisingly my dick didn't appear a good testament to British manhood at that moment, it had shrunk for protection and looked as if I had been in a cold swimming pool for a couple of hours. I felt my balls tighten in anticipation of worse to come. How right I was.

It was body-search time. My sprits plunged into free fall as Garlic Breath took a pair of rubber gloves from the cupboard and pulled them on. I stood naked in the centre of the room whilst he minutely examined every part of my body. Between my toes, my scrotum, armpits, ears, hair, all were thoroughly investigated. He used a wooden spatula to check out my mouth and teeth and his fingers for every other orifice. He felt my shrivelled balls in their scrotal sack and laughed lewdly. His squeezing wasn't sexual, it was simply to let me know that he literally had me by the balls.

Psychologists talk about the fight-or-flight syndrome, but all those chemicals being pumped into the bloodstream to fuel those primitive impulses don't count for anything when you're overtired, emotionally worn down, naked, and your enemy holds your balls in his hand. You just stay quiet and take the shit as it's doled out.

After the body search the older guard passed me a pair of cotton pyjamas to wear; this was the next episode in my humiliation. Those pyjamas would have been too small for me when I was 14 years old. Try as I might there was no way I could get into them, but it was obvious there would not be a larger pair forthcoming. In desperation I forced one leg into the bottoms and then pulled on the jacket as best I could.

The two guards were joined by more of their mates, and I was taken from the reception and administration area into the prison accommodation wing. Marched through more steel gates and up a flight of worn stone stairs I ended up on the ground floor of a large block. Stone built with high walls that disappeared from view in the darkness I could just make out three levels of cell doors, each reached by a painted metal staircase, and steel platforms running around the walls.

Catching nets strung below the landings and flagstone floors completed the living picture of an archetypal Victorian prison. Maybe it would have looked like home to Papillon, but it looked cold, stark and depressing to me. Illuminated only by low-wattage night-lights, it was grim and full of foreboding. The air smelt of damp, disinfectant and that dirty stale urine smell reminiscent of old council high-rise lifts.

The prison guards seemed to find it highly amusing to watch me hopping along barefoot in those ridiculous pyjamas, whilst holding on to a mattress and some sheets. Across the courtyard until we reached a cell door they catcalled and ribbed me just like a noisy gang of teenagers. As the guard opened the door to admit me I turned and said to the group, 'Goodnight, gentlemen, now bugger off like nice little frogs.' Instantly they became less amused, and I was roughly pushed across the threshold and into the cell. The door clanged shut behind me, and I listened for the first time as two shoot bolts were slammed home and a big lock squeaked as the tumblers turned. I was locked in. This was one of many occasions I would listen to that clanging and squeaking, and a great depression enveloped me like molten lead.

So here I was, many miles from home, lost to my loved ones for the foreseeable future. My heart weighed heavy in my chest, and I was filled with a soul-wrenching despair and loneliness. I had learnt a valuable first lesson that night as I lay in bed with a sore and bruised backside. The French sense of humour doesn't extend to laughing when the British poke fun at them. Deep down there is a well-hidden core of racism in the French psyche, much as there is in the British.

In the days to come I was to feel more lonely and isolated as well as having further lessons in racism, and I would discover what life could be like when you are in a minority of one on a playing field of hate and distrust. Eventually I fell into a troubled sleep.

I was awakened in the early morning by the sound of my cell door opening. A coalblack man whom I took to be a trustee prisoner, a longer-term, non-violent inmate working towards release, stood in the doorway, the smell of coffee wafting into the cell. I jumped out of bed on to the cold stone floor and limped over to him. He took one look at my pyjamas and burst out laughing, then he gestured towards a steaming bucket in his hand. I looked down and saw it was brimful of coffee. I didn't have any drinking utensils, and so I smiled and made a palms-out shoulder shrug towards him and said, 'Ah, coffee, oui, oui.'

The prisoner replied, 'English, eh? Manchester United? OK!' I was wondering how to advance further and get a coffee when a guard appeared who stopped our basic attempts at conversation by snarling something at the prisoner and without more ado swung the door shut. Obviously no coffee for me, a perfect start to the morning.

Dejected I sat on the bed and wondered what the day held for me. It was cold in my cell, and I wrapped myself in an old blanket to keep warm. It was still dark, and I had no watch, but I estimated the time to be about 6 am. I could hear the sounds of the prison coming to life: cell doors clanging, a hosepipe splashing nearby, the sweeping of brushes in the block area and the overall background noise of men coughing and hawking. I felt unbearably tired; my knee and back were stiff with bruising.

Some time later the door opened again, and a younger-looking, smartly turned-out guard appeared and gestured me outside. I followed him across the courtyard to another cell door. Looking around I saw there were various prison parties cleaning, and the sight of me set all these guys off laughing, pointing and whistling as I hopped along behind the guard still wearing my ridiculous pyjamas. All I could manage in return was a sickly grin.

I was shown into a musty black-and-white tile shower room. There were no individual cubicles or stalls, just a plastic-moulded bench along one wall and five shower heads with some old, rusty-looking pipework. Water flow was controlled by a small nipple-like button on each shower-head feeder pipe. I quickly stripped off and pressed the button. The spray of icy water was exquisitely painful. I've always preferred a hot shower to the masochistic pleasure of a heart-stopping cold one, but this cold water blasted the tiredness and cobwebs away.

I noticed the guard had left me alone, but he returned some minutes later to toss me a bar of carbolic-like soap. I thanked him and vigorously soaped myself all over. The water started getting hotter, and with the simple act of becoming clean I began to feel almost human again.

When I finished the guard nodded to get dressed again, and without any towel I did so whilst still dripping wet. There were again catcalls as I passed the workers, but feeling more alive now I turned to them, grinned and gave them the finger. On the floor inside my cell was a steaming glass bowl of coffee. What luxury! Maybe the day wouldn't be too bad after all.

After I had drunk the coffee the door opened, and a guard tossed me a plastic bag. Things were definitely on the up, the bag contained a personal hygiene kit including a toothbrush and toothpaste, soap, shampoo sachets, plastic comb, and most surprisingly, a tube of shaving gel and three disposable Bic razors. I immediately set to work and had a really good clean-up. Shaving was a bit tricky without a mirror, but what the hell! I wasn't about to enter a beauty competition. Anyway now I was in the best frame of mind since my arrest five days previously.

After about an hour the guard appeared again and passed in all my clothes and my own bag of gear. Cheered up no end, I dressed quickly, ignoring the sweaty smells from dirty clothing and socks. Now I was washed, shaved and dressed normally again, I felt remarkably human. It shows how a little deprivation and humiliation can depress even the most ebullient of us, but then give us back a little dignity, and our spirits soar and return to normal.

Later that morning I was taken to the infirmary to see the prison doctor. The infirmary was in a small white room that contained a stretcher trolley, a dentist's chair and a large glass-front cabinet housing a wide variety of shiny medical implements. A jovial old country-style doctor weighed me, measured me and looked in my ears, eyes and mouth. He then fitted a needle to a new plastic syringe and signed for me to make a fist. I shook my head, if anyone was going to take blood from me I wanted to know what it was for. The guard stood up and hitched his belt meaningfully. 'OK, OK,' I said. 'You can have the blood if that's what you want.' I smiled and offered my left arm, the guard relaxed, and the doctor tied a rubber strip around my upper arm and found a vein. He filled two syringes and offered me a small sticking plaster for my arm.

Sensing the perfunctory medical was nearly over I told him I suffered from high blood pressure and needed the tablets taken from me by the police. To an onlooker this pantomime explanation must have looked like a bizarre game of charades. Making pumping motions with my hands and miming taking tablets didn't help the doctor understand; it was obvious he hadn't got a clue. He dispatched a guard who returned with a small French—English dictionary and a large plastic bag containing my belt, boots and all the other forbidden items.

I quickly showed him blood and pressure in the dictionary. He got the message and produced an ancient-looking sphygomanometer from the cabinet. He took a bloodpressure reading and seemed surprised that it was 170 over 120. He made some tutting noises and carefully examined the box of tablets found by the guard in my bag. 'Ah, Tenormin,' he exclaimed and then berated the guard, presumably for withholding medication. The doctor pressed a tablet from its bubble cap and handed it to me; without the offer of water I dry swallowed it quickly. He made a few notes on a medical card, and that was it. It was interesting to note that French doctors write in the same illegible scribble as their British counterparts.

Back in my cell I lay down and took stock of my position. Rumbling in my belly reminded me that I hadn't eaten since the previous day, when I'd had a salami sandwich whilst waiting my turn to see the judge. That was nearly 24 hours ago, and now I was feeling ravenous. The effects of the coffee had long gone. Of course thinking of food set off a craving for nicotine. I would have killed for a meal and a cigarette.

Hunger forced me into action. I kicked on the cell door, which rash action chased away my boldness as I awaited a response with some trepidation. Minutes later the door opened, and the same guard looked at me questioningly. I said, 'Sandwich, please,' and pointed towards my stomach. The guard laughed and pointed across the block where I could see two trustees pushing a trolley laden with food containers towards the cells. A few minutes later I was served up a large piece of crusty bread and a stew that seemed to be made of celery ends, green beans and a few potatoes. It wasn't very tasty, but it was hot, and I ate it ravenously. Best of all I was given an orange, which I ate complete with the skin.

Later that day two guards came to the cell and indicated that I should collect my scanty belongings and follow them. They took me up the first flight of steel stairs and opened the door to cell 43. I entered to find a room not much larger than the first cell, but this one was occupied by four other prisoners.

All the others began complaining when they saw me and my bedroll, and I must say that I agreed with them. The room was smaller than a Barratt-style domestic garage and included a set of steel bunks fastened to the wall, a single bed, two wall cabinets, a small toilet enclosure and a caravan-size chipped porcelain sink. Unperturbed the guard shrugged his shoulders, introduced me as 'the Englishman' and banged the door shut behind him. Now there were five of us locked in a small room with only three beds, a brutal introduction to the French prison overcrowding problem.

'Hi, I'm John', I said, summoning a friendly smile, only to receive blank looks. OK, I thought, try again, and calling up my best schoolboy French, I said, 'Je suis John. Bonjour.' This time I got a smile from one of them. 'Salut, John. Je m'appelle Stefi. Tu es une personnalité.'

He pointed to a small portable TV mounted at high level on a shelf. They had seen the aftermath of the bust on the local TV channel news. They knew about the 300 kg of cannabis, and they seemed to look at me with a kind of grudging respect. Maybe they thought I was a kind of master criminal.

The tension broken, introductions were made all around. Soon I was sitting on one of the three stools smoking a roll-up cigarette and drinking a glass of strange-tasting black coffee. My cell mates were all French, two of them came from French territories, one from Algeria and one from the Seychelles. Two of them, Stefi and George, had been recently convicted and were awaiting transfer to a central jail in Rennes to complete their sentences, and two of them were remanded in custody awaiting trial.

Stefi was 32 years old and had been convicted of trafficking in cannabis for the second time. Caught with 1.5 kg in his possession he had been sentenced to four years. If I went to trial and was convicted and sentenced on the same ratio of weight of drug to sentence, I would go down for 800 years. Suddenly the 30-year maximum sentence bandied about by OCTRIS seemed reasonable. From the looks on the faces of my new cell mates I could see they thought I was in deep shit. This, I'm sure, prompted their sympathetic looks. It's always comforting when you have a problem to know that somebody else has a bigger problem than yourself.

George was a handsome, sun-tanned lad of 22 from the Seychelles. A crew member on an ocean-going tramp steamer, he had been involved in a fight with the local harbourmaster's son. A knife slash to the belly and a few grams of speed found in his pocket earned George a three-year sentence. He was a wild-looking lad who appeared as if he could handle himself in a situation. He was friendly enough, but there was a definite sense of reserve in his attitude to me.

Jacques was the oldest before I joined in. He was a 36-year-old lifelong felon who specialized in housebreaking. Getting somewhat ambitious he had been caught trying to rob the town's main post office in the early morning hours. As a recidivist he was expecting a sentence of about five years, his time spent on remand would be deducted from any sentence, so as he had a cushy job in the prison kitchen he wasn't in a hurry to go to trial and be transferred to a big central jail.

Yosef was a small weak-looking 18-year-old Algerian, accused of raping his young male cousin. I took an immediate dislike to this dangerous individual. He was treated with contempt by the other inmates, and I later discovered he rarely left the cell.

That first day passed fairly quickly and, tired by my experiences and the cumulative lack of sleep, shortly after the evening meal I made a bed of sorts and lay down under the table, the only space available. After bumming a last cigarette from Stef I had a contemplative smoke and soon drifted off to sleep.

I awoke once that night when one of them made his way to the toilet and trod on my outflung arm. Jumping up I hit the table overhead and knocked it over with a crash to the floor. Shouting curses I leapt to my feet rubbing my head. Everyone else woke up, and the light went on. I must have looked a strange sight stood in the middle of the room surrounded by broken glass and swearing like a madman. Nobody laughed. Later, when quiet was restored, and I was back on the mattress, I thought it was strange that no guard had come to investigate the shouting and noise of breaking glass.

'Bonjour, John,' said Stefi. I turned over and looked up at the battery-operated alarm clock; it showed 5.45 am.

'Shit,' I said, 'I'm going back to sleep.' I was dog tired and bad tempered, and in any case I'm pretty useless in the morning until I've had a cup of tea and a cigarette. The realization that I would get neither didn't please me any. Loneliness and depression came flooding back like a black tide. I groaned and rolled over again to bury my face in the pillow.

Soon the clanging of cell doors started. I could hear the guard coming inexorably along the passageway to our cell, opening doors along the way. Sure enough ours sprang open, admitting the bright light and a chilling draught.

'Bonjour, donnes-moi la poubelle,' the guard called cheerily. Not understanding, I just looked up at him from my prone position. 'Eh, rosbif, la poubelle maintenant!' he called. Clueless, I shook my head. He strode into the cell and picked up a plastic bag of rubbish from near the toilet door. He pointed to the bag and said, 'La poubelle, rosbif, comprends?' Cackling he backed out of the cell and slammed the door with a jovial bang. So ended my first French lesson: poubelle meant rubbish.

Now everyone was awake, and there was the usual cacophony of a group of men waking and getting up: hawking, coughing and farting. Everyone seemed to compete in making as much noise as possible whilst taking their first piss of the day. Five of us dressed to a concert of muffled curses as we constantly elbowed each other in the confined space between the beds and the table. What a carry on! Next on the agenda was the cigarette-rolling performance, and I bummed another from Stefi.

Just as the cigs were all ready the morning coffee arrived. We queued at the door for a ladleful of the steaming brew. I noticed everyone but me had glass tumblers or beakers, so I made do with a glass bowl. So there we sat at 6.15 am drinking coffee and smoking. Excellent.

After the morning ablutions the TV was switched on, and we all watched the morning news. There it was, the farmhouse looking deserted with open doors, broken windows and household debris scattered on the lawn. A couple of puffed-up gendarmes posed threateningly for the cameras. I think all the French have a keen sense of self-importance in front of a camera.

'Merde, t'as aucune chance, John,' said Stef sadly. This provoked a short conversation amongst my cell mates, and I noticed a few sad glances thrown in my direction. Suddenly their enthusiastic chatter drained away, and in the ensuing awkward silence I felt terribly distressed and isolated again.

Our reveries were broken by the guard opening the door and calling, 'Bon, messieurs, dehors.' Everyone jumped up and pulling on coats trailed outside. I had no coat to put on, but I followed anyway. All the cell doors on our side of the block were open, and many prisoners headed down the stairs. Crowding to a small exit after a cursory body search we passed through one at a time into an outside yard.

I tried to take my bearings, but there were no landmarks visible over the high stone walls. I followed the throng and started walking up and down the asphalt yard, which measured 54 paces lengthways and 41 paces across. A small oblong strip of muddy earth to one side was given over to prisoners playing boules. It immediately struck me as incongruous that in a prison full of dangerous inmates the authorities provided heavy steel balls for them to play with. Footballs I could understand, but steel balls, very strange.

During that first walk I was an object of scrutiny and curiosity. Some prisoners came up to me and thrust out a hand. Claude and Henri, Joel and Jacques and others all made their introductions that morning. A nod, a quick handshake, and they were gone back into the crowd. A big guy dressed in a grey shiny shell suit and Reeboks came up and stopped four square in front of me, blocking my path.

'Rosbif, je m'appelle Roget, le Chef,' he said and hawked a lump of phlegm on to the ground just in front of me. I put out my hand, which he ignored, and scowled at me. I was reminded of Paul Newman and Sylvester Stallone in all those prison films. I knew they would have kicked the shit out of him to take his place as the boss and hero of all the inmates. But that didn't seem on somehow. This guy was built like a brick shithouse and mean looking too, with a close-shaven head and an earring the size of a brass curtain ring in his ear, he would make mincemeat of me.

Discretion being the better part of valour I nodded to him and said, 'Bonjour, Monsieur le Chef,' with that I coolly walked on past him. Honour satisfied, he laughed and returned to his gang of mates in a far corner of the yard, where they held sway laughing and joking around.

Another, older guy sidled up to me. 'You are British, yes?' he asked in pretty good English. I looked at him amazed. These were the first friendly English words I had heard, other than the interpreter, since my arrest six days before. 'Yes, I'm English. My name is John. What's yours?'

We shook hands. 'My name is Jan. I'm from Holland,' he said grinning. 'You will not find many of the guards or prisoners here who speak any English, and those who do understand a little won't admit to it.'

Jan was a nice guy of about my age, on remand for a cheque scam. He had been travelling Europe using false chequebooks and identity papers. He told me that after serving his French sentence he expected to be sent to Germany to face similar charges there.

Having a common language we spent the next 15 minutes until the end of the exercise period talking intently about the prison and the rules. First on my list of priorities was the need to get my cash converted into francs and deposited in a prison account, to buy some essentials, such as cigarettes and toiletries, and to be able to contact my family. Jan explained to me that every request from remand prisoners had to be sent in writing via the prison director to the judge in charge of the case. All letters had to be written in French. He agreed to help me out in this regard.

Jan was fluent in four languages: Dutch, English, French and German. Why is it that many foreigners can speak so many languages, when most British people don't even have a rudimentary command of anything other than our mother tongue? Could it be our island mentality, or is it a hangover from the Empire period when English was the most important language in the world? Whatever the reason our language deficiencies affect our dealings with the rest of Europe.

When the exercise period was over we returned to the cell after a head count and further body search. Whilst we were out Yosef had completed the housework, tidied and swept out the cell. I noticed some clothes soaking in the sink, and after a while got through to Stef that I needed to wash my own clothes, which by now were pretty high, though, strangely, no one complained of the smell of stale sweat.

Stef lent me some washing powder, and I washed my jeans in a plastic bucket. There was only a cold-water tap in the cell, with no hot water at all for washing or laundry use. Prisoners in small French jails are almost exclusively local inhabitants, and they receive visits from family or friends nearly every day. During these visits they normally exchange a bag of dirty laundry for clean, but for prisoners like myself without family or visits there were no laundry facilities, so one had to wash clothes as best as possible in the cell.

Heating was provided by a length of three-inch steel hot-water pipe, which ran across the back wall of the cell at knee height. There was not enough surface area of pipework to give out sufficient heat, and during the day the winter temperature in the cell was cold. All the inmates wore jumpers or sweatshirts all day and in bed at night.

The heating pipe was the only place to dry wet clothing, and this caused a lot of condensation, giving rise to clammy walls and a streaming window. All books, newspapers, photographs tacked to the walls and bedding had a permanent damp feel; stored clothes developed spots of green mould. Because of the poor heating and ventilation arrangements my constant washing and drying of clothes made me unpopular, and many times I would find my clean but damp laundry thrown into a corner next to the toilet, where they lay stinking of piss.

Routine in the prison was fixed, and I soon fell in with the monotonous timetable. Reveille, rubbish and outgoing-mail collection at 6 am, followed by coffee delivery at 6.15 am. Morning exercise at 8 am for 30 to 40 minutes. Those lucky enough to have work went to the workshops from 9 to 11.30 am. Incoming mail was delivered at 11 am along with any prescribed medication. Lunch was served at noon, and, weather permitting, there was a second exercise period at 2.30 pm for 45 minutes. The evening meal was served at 5.30 pm, and after a final head count the cell doors were securely bolted for the night at 6 pm.

Twice each week we were allowed a ten-minute shower. Bed linen of dubious cleanliness was supplied on an exchange basis once a fortnight. Cell inspections were held at random intervals, and the integrity of the window bars was checked twice daily. The almost constant echoing clamour of a steel rod ringing on iron bars is a noise I will never forget. During the day the doors were kept locked closed at all times, and at night the shoot bolts were secured. There was no free movement or integration of prisoners, and you were only allowed out of the cell for a prescribed purpose.

Prisoners who didn't have any work were locked up for 22 hours each day, seven days a week. It isn't surprising that petty grievances and jealousies flared into brief but often spectacular fights between prisoners. Nerves were rubbed raw by the constant lack of privacy and noise. Many prisoners grouped together along ethnic lines and picked on minorities. As the only British prisoner I was subjected to a fair amount of anti-British feeling from inmates and guards alike, which on occasion flared into violence.

One wintry morning during the exercise period a guy I had never spoken with walked up to me and demanded a cigarette. This was a calculated threat on his part because tobacco was a form of prison currency, hoarded and only shared between cell mates or friends. I shook my head and explained as best I could that I only had a few left until my next ration. By now I had become an expert in reading body language and animal-like interpreting facial expressions, I often tried to express myself with a meaningful shrug, smile or grimace, but it was obvious from the guy's stance that he wanted a confrontation. In response to my refusal he gobbed a big lump of snot on to my shirt. Enough was enough, I was in a black mood that morning and not about to turn the other cheek.

I hit him, a good solid thump to his nose, which erupted into a great-looking nosebleed. Surprised and hurt he staggered back, and as if by magic a sharpened blade appeared in his fist. I kicked out at him, and my hard-soled prison boot connected with his hand and knocked the blade loose. At that moment I felt good; his attack had provided me an excuse to fight back, and all my frustrations against my arrest and the subsequent pettiness poured forth as blind rage. I remember roaring and going for him. His expression changed, and I saw a flash of fear in his eyes. Before I could continue and deliver a proper hammering two guards jumped on me, and a baton blow delivered with stunning force to my shoulder made me cry out in pain and finished the fight before it was properly under way. The show was over, but I bet matey was sore for a few days afterwards.

I didn't resist as they dragged me inside. Thrown into solitary I was back in the original cell where I'd spent my first night. Later that day the prison director reprimanded me and made notes in red ink in my prison file. I was kept in the solitary cell for a week without tobacco, books or personal kit. Nobody was interested that I hadn't started the fight or that my assailant had a blade, which, given the chance, he would have used. He was French, and I was a troublesome foreigner. I later discovered my new-found enemy was a real hard case, serving four years for grievous bodily harm after stabbing a nightclub bouncer.

When I was returned to my cell after a week my cigarettes, pens and postage stamps had disappeared, courtesy of Mr Nobody. On reflection maybe I should have given the bloke a cigarette, it would have been easier in the long run.

So life went on in the prison day after day with few breaks in the routine. With help from Dutch Jan I transferred my cash into a prison account and bought writing paper, envelopes and stamps. I used the interminable hours to write letter after letter to the judge, the police and my family. I spent time when I could in the library trying to discover the addresses of the British Embassy, the European Parliament and anybody else I could think of to whom to explain my plight.

I received my first letter in prison on 8 December 1994, 27 days after my arrest. It was from my wife, who, having learnt of my arrest and imprisonment, had left Spain and returned with our daughter to the UK. Getting no help from HM Customs she contacted the Foreign Office who had put her in touch with the London-based charity Prisoners Abroad.

They wrote to me and sent a batch of pamphlets containing all sorts of useful if depressing information for British prisoners in overseas jails. It made interesting reading, because, compared with the standards of jails in places like Thailand, Turkey and Egypt, it appeared I had it pretty easy. At least I was washed and fed on a regular basis. My heart went out to those British prisoners condemned to serve long sentences in cramped jails surrounded by intolerable cultural differences.

I felt a great outpouring of love and affection for my family, quickly followed by tremendous hate for the people who had condemned me to this private hell. I resolved there and then to get out of prison and make the guilty parties pay for their irresponsible and cavalier attitude with my liberty and life. I felt an overwhelming hatred for the people who were putting my family through such mental torture, and I planned all sorts of terrible vengeance against them.

On 12 December a guard called me out of the cell and took me for an unannounced visit. In a small side interview room a young woman of about 25 with a briefcase was waiting for me. She stood as I entered, and the guard locked the door behind me. I remember her watching me carefully as I entered the room. When she spoke it was in a neutral tone of voice.

'Good morning, Mr Lightfoot. I'm Madame Tardieu, Vice Consul with the British Embassy in Paris,' she introduced herself. 'I have come here at the invitation of the

French authorities to check upon your welfare.' Young and arrogant looking with dark hair pulled severely back into a bun she wore a smart business suit and an expression that matched her small tight voice. She proffered a tiny smile and a nod as if to encourage me to speak. She reminded me of an uptight Sunday school teacher, but there again we were hardly meeting under normal circumstances, and I suppose she felt a little bit tense. I know I did.

'Good morning,' I replied. 'What is it specifically you wish to know?' I was immediately cagey, maybe it was jailhouse paranoia kicking in, but I expected British Embassy staff to have English names. With her French name and slight accent I was suspicious of some trickery; by this time I would have believed anything could happen.

'I can tell you that your wife Kathleen, daughter Natalie and mother Dorothy will be coming to visit you within the next few weeks,' she said. 'We have assisted them in applying to the French authorities for visiting permits.' This was said to put me at ease.

'OK. How can I help you, and how can you help me?' I asked, somewhat mollified.

'Firstly you should know that we cannot interfere with the process of law in a foreign country, and we cannot intercede on your behalf in any trial or convictions. Our job is to ensure that you are treated in the same manner as other prisoners, especially as national prisoners of the host country, and that you have adequate medical, dental and religious facilities.

'We're a very busy department of the embassy, and though we will monitor your stay in France we cannot visit you more than once each year. Nor can we offer you any advice relating to the criminal charges against you or provide funds for you to buy goods or to obtain the services of a lawyer.' She parroted by rote. She sounded like an upper-class holiday tour rep, the sort of bird who would work for Kuoni.

'Just a minute,' I said, 'I'm not planning on staying here for more than a year, so this will be your only visit to see me. I hear what you're saying, but surely the government can intercede on my behalf when I'm locked in here because of the actions of the government's own civil servants. I'm not a drug dealer, lady, I'm a recognized undercover informant for HM Customs & Excise. When I was arrested I was working on an operation for them.' That got her attention; she sat down and opened her briefcase.

'If you wish you can explain to me the circumstances leading to your arrest. I will take notes of your claims and have a word with my superiors,' she said smoothly, though I could see that my outburst had rattled her. There was no warmth or emotion in her face or voice, she sounded as human as a speak-your-weight machine.

'OK, let's start at the beginning,' I suggested. Before your visit here today did you know I am an informer for the Customs & Excise?' I asked.

'Mr Lightfoot, you shouldn't assume that I know anything. I haven't seen or discussed your case with anyone. All we know is that you were arrested by OCTRIS on 11 November, and that subsequently you were charged with international trafficking in narcotics. This is a serious crime in France as it is in Great Britain, and our role in the Foreign and Commonwealth Service is to check upon your physical welfare. I am visiting several British prisoners in jails this week, and it so happens that you are on my route. There is nothing more than that,' she said tartly.

I felt the cool wind of bureaucratic indifference. 'Right,' I said, 'I was working as an undercover informer for the Customs & Excise Investigation Unit, based on the 4th floor of Aldine House in Manchester.' I gave her the names of my contacts there, plus the name of the Drug Liaison Officer (DLO) at her embassy in Paris, Chris Martin, who should have some information on me. Then I went on to fill her in on everything that had happened so far. As I got into my stride, Tardieu took copious notes.

'To date,' I concluded, 'absolutely fuck all has happened except that I have had a yard fight and all my personal gear nicked. You are the first representative of the British Government to turn up, and you tell me that all you can do is to check that I get to see a dentist when I need to.

'Well, it's nowhere near an acceptable situation, and if you people are not prepared to help me then I'll fight this myself, and heaven help you when I get out.' I finished, but by now I had lost it again and was starting to shout.

'I can see you are upset,' Tardieu responded, looking a little nervous. 'Obviously your claims will be investigated by the examining magistrate, and if they are true then I have no doubt you will be released from prison. We cannot interfere with the judge's enquiries, but I will make a full report of this matter when I return to Paris.'

There was little more to be said, and after some further general enquiries and wishing me an early Merry Christmas she left. I returned to my cell and brooded quietly.

11

'Perfidious Albion'

Just a few days before Christmas I received the promised visit from Kath, my mother and daughter Natalie. I had written to the prison director requesting extended visits on the grounds that I hadn't received any previously and that my family had travelled all the way from England to see me. I had received no response to my request.

Since arriving in prison I had started to grow a beard, and now with my hair long and shaggy I looked too much like a convict for comfort. I decided I needed a haircut. Getting one wasn't simple: I had to write a letter in French to the director to request it. Three times I wrote and still didn't get any response. Finally another prisoner cut my hair during an exercise period, for the cost of three cigarettes, and the result was not too bad.

The day of the visit eventually arrived. The guard had told me during the morning that it was imminent because a visit permit, complete with a passport-style photograph, had been authorized by the judge and a copy forwarded to the prison. It was a simple security device that enabled the prison to know exactly who to expect. I was allowed a shower that morning; afterwards I changed into my cleanest and least damp-smelling clothes and scrounged some aftershave from a cell mate.

At the appointed hour a guard took me downstairs, where I waited in line with the other prisoners. Most of them, lucky bastards, held plastic bags full of dirty linen, ready to exchange for nice clean clothes. The air was full of good-natured banter, and one or two of the prisoners I knew gave me a thumbs up; they seemed to realize it was my first visit.

We all filed one by one into a small, brightly lit anteroom. The guard told me to undress, a command with which I could now comply because by now I had learnt a basic French vocabulary, which was all I needed to get by from day to day. I hadn't thought about having to strip for the occasion, but what the hell! It seemed a small price to pay. I quickly dropped my clothes, and the guard searched me. At that time I couldn't imagine what anybody would want to smuggle out of prison; later I was to discover there was a thriving business in uncensored mail for onward posting.

After the search I was led into the visits room, a space with perhaps ten formica-top tables set out at various points around the perimeter of the room. At each table there were three plastic chairs. I picked a table at random and sat down facing the door through which the visitors would enter.

After about five minutes I could hear Natalie's voice echoing along a corridor. She came into the room shyly, and a few prisoners looked at her and said, 'Bonjour,' and smiled. Natalie stared back as if she was in a zoo, which I suppose she was really. I called her name, and she came over and jumped into my arms for a big bear hug from her dad. Mum and Kath followed her in, and we all had a hug, until a guard came over shook his head and wagged his finger at us. That was the sort of down-to-earth experience that set the tone of the initial meeting.

We all said our hellos and exchanged banter about how well we all looked considering the circumstances, until I pointed out that we only had 45 minutes, and that we should get down to business. There had been many things I didn't want to write in my letters to Kath, I could see no benefit in telling the judge all about my relationship with Customs, and what I intended to do about my predicament. After all he was the enemy, he was the reason I was still locked up.

Now I made up for lost time and quick fired questions to Kath whilst Natalie sat on her mum's knee watching me intently. I vividly remember stroking her hair whilst talking to Kath and my mum. From what we'd been told, we understood Customs were denying any responsibility for me being in prison and were claiming to Kath that the arrest was nothing to do with them. We'd heard that they had offered to assist the French, if they were asked formally to do so.

We decided that my current legal-aid French lawyer didn't appear to be doing as much as we thought he could to help me. We decided that the best way forward was to appoint someone else, and mum agreed to pay for a private lawyer to get the ball rolling a little faster.

I had made inquiries amongst the other prisoners, and the name Christian Traineau, a young, smart criminal defence lawyer, kept coming up as the best man to have on our side. I asked Kath and my mum to track him down and instruct him to start on the case immediately, which they promised to do that afternoon.

Then we talked of other events. It seemed that the

day after I was arrested the English police had raided our farm in the UK looking for drugs. They had apparently been understanding but claimed to be acting on an anonymous tip-off. Obviously the search had proved negative. I had never had any drugs at our farm, or anywhere else for that matter.

Kath told me that because I had been arrested in France I was not entitled to legal aid in England, so once again my mum stepped into the breach and said she and my dad would pay for an English lawyer to approach Customs direct to request that they acknowledge I was working for them. A contact in the police had recommended a supposedly good firm of criminal lawyers based in Sheffield, whom she would instruct on my behalf.

We'd been talking nonstop when suddenly I noticed the visiting period was over, and prisoners were saying their goodbyes to their families. I stood up and spoke to the guard, trying to explain that I was entitled to an extended visit. He shook his head and said something about see the director for permission. I was furious, but there was nothing I could do at that time: the guard had his instructions, it was pointless having a go at him.

Kath and my mum promised to visit the next day, and my mum told me she had brought some Christmas food: mince pies, Christmas cake, small pork pies and so on. From Kath there was a case full of paperback books, some clothes and a good English–French dictionary. I kissed them all goodbye, and off they went, looking very unhappy at leaving me behind.

I returned to the strip-search room and argued with the guard about the extended visit I was due; I might as well have talked to the wall for all the good it did me. I dropped my clothes on the deck ready for the search, and just to show me there were no hard feelings about our little argument the guard insisted on conducting an in-depth personal search. I wasn't into shoving cigarettes up my arse, that's a trick I'd rather leave to the French, but the guard felt he had to check anyway.

I made a complete pain of myself for the rest of the day, demanding to see the social assistant, the judge and the prison director. In the end they took me down to see the chief guard, who wasn't a bad stick really. We had no common language and spent half the time trying to understand each other. But I got my message across eventually by showing him copies of the letters I had sent to the director requesting extended visiting times.

The next day I was again called for a visit and went through the same procedure as before. This time the atmosphere among us all was a bit more relaxed, even so it was obvious we were all very much on edge, and we knew that if things didn't go right I could end up spending many, many years in a French prison.

If I was convicted of smuggling drugs over the French border then I would be in deep shit. So it was critical I got my liberty to allow me to clear my name before the trial. Afterwards would be too late because no one would believe me. It would just seem like the desperate claims of a convicted smuggler seeking a reduced sentence.

The best way forward seemed to be somehow to get Customs to confirm that I was working for them, or at least to acknowledge they knew that I was participating in the smuggling run from Spain to France and that I had taken part in it to assist them. This didn't seem at that time such a hard thing for them to concede, or so difficult for me to prove. Kath told me they had an appointment with the lawyer Traineau later that same afternoon, so I asked her to request that he visit me as soon as possible so that I could set him off on the right trail.

That day we got our extended visit and talked for nearly one and a half hours. Nevertheless the time seemed to fly by, and we were still deeply engrossed when the guard indicated time was up. The only jarring note had been when Natalie had offered me a toffee from a bag of sweets she had in her coat pocket. Without thinking I had taken the proffered toffee from her, unwrapped it and popped it into my mouth, just as the guard had turned around to see me do so.

I didn't know I couldn't accept a sweet from my own kid, but from all the fuss he made you'd have thought I was taking a speedball from her. He wasn't satisfied until I spat the offending remnant into a nearby wastebin. Natalie was upset by his intimidating mien and withdrew into her shell; she hardly spoke again during the entire visit.

That incident cast a shadow over our time together and broke the spell of hope that all this would soon be behind us. The guard's attitude demonstrated the lack of flexibility of the system. We all knew it was going to be an uphill battle, but it was one we knew that ultimately we could and must win, for if we failed then all our lives would change dramatically for ever, and that was something we couldn't countenance. We parted in a quiet and pensive mood, and I could sense that Kath and my mum were psyching themselves up for their important initial meeting with Christian Traineau later that day.

Christmas was for me a deadly dull and depressing event that year. There was no official acknowledgement that it was happening outside the grey concrete prison walls, and there was no break in the monotonous routine. It was a Christmas lived vicariously through glittery television shows and tinsel-laden adverts. We celebrated in our cold cell eating my mother's mince pies, a delicacy hitherto unknown to the palates of my cell mates.

I had received Christmas cards from immediate family and a handmade card from Natalie. They were little pools of light and cheer against the backdrop of the drab cell wall above my bed; I would lie on the bed looking up at them and transport myself away to other happier times.

On New Year's Eve we could hear the townspeople cheering in the main square not far away, the constant ringing of the church bells heralding the onset of another year. New Year's Day is not a happy time for any prisoner, they think about the time already served and then of the years left still on their sentence, waiting in line ahead of them, each one marked by yet another New Year's celebration.

If anything that miserable Christmas was a time of catharsis for me, and by the new year my resolve had hardened. I was still depressed by my day-to-day environment, but inside I was more sure it was going to be a transient stage. I knew I had the intelligence and the will to force a change in the tide of events surrounding me. Given a fair hearing and a little bit of luck I would be freed in the near future, and then I would be able to undo this great mistake and get on with my life. Buoyed up by this strong, welling rush of enthusiasm I turned with a will to kick-start my campaign for freedom.

The first meeting on a cold, rainy day in January with my new lawyer, Christian Traineau, set the format for our future relationship. We hit it off immediately and were soon chatting away like old pals. Traineau is well over six foot tall and heavily built with a swathe of jet-black shiny hair; he reminds me of a Russian dancing bear. His massive size and presence dominated the small private visiting room, and I could easily imagine him tearing a prosecutor limb from limb.

It soon became obvious that his size was matched by his formidable intelligence. He was married to a school teacher who taught English to teenagers in the local school. He too had a good command of English but had difficulty sometimes with his pronunciation. He spoke clearly, albeit with a strong French accent, which most women would call sexy, but which I thought sounded rather like John Cleese doing his French waiter act. But it was music to listen to him as he verbally destroyed the prosecution's case against me.

Throughout our relationship he was consistently truthful with me and laid out each position carefully and accurately. Not one to mince his words he would always tell me both good and bad news without any sugar coating. On this occasion, lighting yet another Philip Morris cigarette, he said, 'The first thing we have to do is to get you out of prison, and to achieve this we have to convince the judge that you really were working for HM Customs.'

The first thing I had to do was to write him a letter of authority appointing him as my defence lawyer so that he could go to the judge and buy a copy of the criminal file. In France they charge three francs a sheet for any part of the file required by the defence team. I was not allowed to have a copy of the file, or a translation, and I could only read it in the presence of my lawyer.

A week went by whilst Traineau got hold of the file and studied its contents. During that time I received a copy of a letter sent by Richard Crampton, my local Member of the European Parliament (MEP), to Valerie Strachan. I had never heard of her, but I soon enough learned that Strachan was the head honcho in HM Customs & Excise.

The MEP's letter was the opening shot in what was to become a series of misunderstandings between me and HM Customs. For whatever reason there was an alarming breakdown in communications. Perhaps I'd been misinformed myself, but it seemed they did not appear to be in possession of the full facts of my case; not one of them had actually met me since my arrest and heard my side of the story.

In France, Traineau was grappling with more down-to-earth problems. 'We need a letter of confirmation from Customs to say that you were working with their authority at the farm when you were arrested, John,' he said, spelling it out. 'Without such confirmation things are looking bad for you. This 300 kilos of cannabis is the biggest haul of drugs ever intercepted in the Vendée region of France, and all the protagonists are English, which inflames French feelings of sovereignty. It is a big news story and a high-profile case, and there will have to be a successful prosecution. I fear the sentences will be hard and result in many years in prison for you if we fail.'

Well, at least he was being honest with me, but I didn't

fancy spending years rotting in a French jail when I had done nothing wrong. HM Customs were surely aware of what I was doing at the farmhouse, and why I was doing it. It didn't make any sense. I told Traineau to contact my English lawyers and liaise with them to set up a meeting with Customs as soon as possible.

Life in the prison continued with boring regularity. I spent much of my time reading about French criminal law and their different methods of investigation and criminal trials' procedures. It was heavy, boring stuff, all in French. I would sit up for hours at night reading the law books, assisted by my French to English dictionary.

Light relief was provided by cell inspections, and opportunity the guards used to upset us thoroughly and tramp over our meagre possessions. They were supposed to be looking for contraband, but it was just a good opportunity for them to rummage through the cells. Searches rarely turned up anything for the prisoners were experts at camouflage and concealment. Smuggling illicit goodies into the prison was something at which the prisoners and their visitors were particularly adept. Alcohol, money, porn mags and drugs were all forbidden by the authorities and consequently much sought after by the majority of the inmates.

One ingenious method of smuggling alcohol into the prison was demonstrated by one inmate, whose wife visited weekly and brought the lucky bugger a constant stream of clean laundry. One night after lockup he pulled down a towel she had delivered earlier that day. He filled the sink with two inches or so of cold water and dumped in the towel; we all watched as the water turned a milky colour. Amongst much laughter and back slapping he filled a glass with this dubious-looking liquid and took a tentative sip, then he coughed and smiled and declared the drink OK. The glass was passed around and I had a tiny taste. The mixture was Pernod and water, with an a mixture of pine-smelling clothes softener, which left a strange but not-too-unpleasant aftertaste on the tongue.

The smuggling system worked thus. His wife would wash a towel and dry it normally, making sure all the washing powder was rinsed away. Then she would soak it in a bowl filled with Pernod or some other anise drink; the towel would then be dried again. Before it was taken back to the prison it would be lightly splashed with a *soupçon* of fabric softener to disguise the pungent smell of aniseed.

The towel was slipped into the middle of a batch of clean clothes and passed to a guard for checking. Generally the authorities were looking for knives and other metal objects. In any case I think most of them were too soaked in booze themselves to notice the smell of an alcohol-soaked towel, or at least if they did they turned a blind eye to this minor infraction of the strict rules of conduct.

Quite a few nights we sat watching TV, passing around glasses of Pernod and water. We had to ensure that all the anise and water mixture was drunk in the one session so that a snap inspection wouldn't discover our little enterprise, so the temptation was to use as little water as possible to release the dried-in booze.

I'm sure the fabric conditioner must have contributed to the terrible hangovers we all suffered, but it seemed to be worth it at the time. It's a wonder we didn't end up blind or with serious liver damage. Now I can't smell fabric softener without developing a headache, and the smell of Pernod always reminds me vividly of the nights sitting around getting pissed in prison.

Other prisoners went to great lengths to get hold of drugs. At night you could spot the cannabis smokers in the various cells. They puffed away with the windows open to help dispel the distinctive smell of burning hash and flicked the ash from their joints outside.

A couple of days after my birthday in late January 1995 I received another letter from my MEP enclosing a response he had received from Valerie Strachan. Although Strachan acknowledged they knew me, she claimed I had no authority for my actions. I considered its contents alarming to say the least, full of errors. She claimed, apparently, that one of her officers had visited me in December, and I had confessed my part in the failed smuggling attempt.

I hadn't had any visit from any British official, other than Mme Tardieu, the consular official from the British Embassy, so I could have hardly confessed my guilt to a nonexistent visitor. What worried me was that, though misinformed, the letter from the head of so powerful a British institution would automatically be given credence by anyone reading it.

All remand prisoners in French jails have each and every letter read by the judge in charge of their case. In my case Judge Maurice Marlière, the local examining magistrate, didn't understand much English, so all my mail, both incoming and outgoing, was translated into French by the official court translator. I could just imagine his eyes popping when he read Valerie Strachan's letter to the MEP claiming that I had confessed to smuggling. I had to get this sorted out as soon as I could.

Without access to telephones as soon as possible meant within a couple of weeks. The only way to get mail out without it being censored was to write to your lawyer, or use the risky method of a prisoner passing a letter to a visitor for onward posting. This method was fraught with risks and was expensive, each letter so smuggled out cost at least five cigarettes. If the circuitous postal attempt was discovered you were in deep shit with the prison director.

I decided to write directly to the judge in an attempt to clear up this mess. I sent him a lengthy missive telling him I had not received any visit; this he could easily check from a quick perusal of the visitor permits. He never did reply to my letter. Christian Traineau told me later that the Strachan letter carried a lot of weight with the judge, and, as you might expect, it militated against my early release. Traineau wrote to Customs, but it seems they were not prepared to discuss the matter with him.

By now I had been in prison for 12 weeks. It was then that I heard a meeting had been organized in Manchester between Customs and my English solicitors, who took along with them a barrister. The minutes of the meeting were handed over to the judge, who continued to keep his own counsel and wouldn't be drawn into comment one way or another.

Three weeks after the Manchester meeting the Customs indicated in a very short letter they were prepared to answer questions about my status to the right authorities. Christian Traineau buttonholed the judge in his office and coerced him into getting his translator to telephone Customs and arrange an urgent meeting. Bearing in mind Traineau's size I can easily imagine how he convinced the judge to authorize that call. The translator phoned Manchester, and a meeting was set for the next week. Two Customs officers were coming over to explain the situation to the judge.

They arrived the night before, flying into Nantes airport and lodging overnight at the translator's home. I was dressed in my suit and was ready from early morning for the call to go to the judge's office. They came for me in the early afternoon. I was escorted to the holding block under the main court building and locked in a tiny cell. Shortly thereafter Christian Traineau arrived and told me the two Customs men had been with the judge all morning; they had also lunched in his office.

When finally we went up to the judge's office we were initially asked to remain outside in the foyer. A secretary passed a lengthy statement to my lawyer, which was the official Customs stance on the matter of my arrest. Before we had time to read their document properly we were ushered into the meeting. Rob Williams was waiting in there, and he came over and shook hands with me; behind him was an older man who introduced himself as Alan Smith. I'd never seen or heard of him before, but it transpired he was Williams' boss.

The meeting didn't go too well. I was feeling very angry, and I wanted some explanations from Customs as to why, so I'd heard, they had denied I was their informant, and why Valerie Strachan had written that letter that didn't help my case at all.

In fact, in my presence that day Customs confirmed I had been a good agent and had helped them with seizures of drugs worth several million of pounds. But when we got on to the specifics of the French operation they became less forthcoming. They claimed in formal statements that I hadn't kept them informed of changes in the plan and that by allowing the use of my own van I had crossed the line, and they had heard I had become a smuggler myself. Smith said that they had received information from another source in Spain that I had gone beyond my agreed brief and they suspected that I had in effect changed sides.

He claimed that because I was out of touch for nine days after the last meeting they didn't know where I was or what had become of me, so they arranged for NCIS, the National Crime Intelligence Service, to send a fax to Chris Martin, the Drug Liaison Office (DLO) based in the British Embassy in Paris. Martin had then phoned OCTRIS and told them to expect a drug-smuggling attempt centred around Eric and Jill's farm. OCTRIS had staked out the farm and had watched Barry and me drive up and park the van in the driveway there. The next day they had observed all our comings and goings before they busted us late in the afternoon.

Smith produced the fax that had been sent by Howard Leather of NCIS to the DLO for the judge to read. The judge insisted that a copy of the fax be entered into the evidence file, which was a useful move on his part for it meant that I could study it later with my lawyer.

We went on to talk about the surveillance operation

at Hartshead services when at Customs' request, I had met with Paul and Tony to discuss the French operation. Rob Williams said that the photographs were not of a good enough quality for identification purposes; he also claimed that although they had identified the drug dealers' car they couldn't confirm that it belonged to either Paul or Tony.

This was becoming confusing. I was under the impression that the photos were acceptable. In any case what I did get Rob Williams to confirm was that it was agreed with him and Steve Brown that I wouldn't contact them again until I had the registration number of the van coming from England to collect the drugs.

By now it was past seven o'clock in the evening, and the judge started to wrap the meeting up. Christian Traineau submitted a typed bail application for me, after which the judge and I got into some good-natured wrangling about how much the bail sum should be. He wanted 100,000 francs, I offered 10,000. After five minutes or so we agreed, and bail was set at 50,000 francs.

Traineau used the telephone in the judge's office to telephone Kath at home in England and told her the judge had agreed to bail and that he needed 50,000 francs to get me released. If the money were received quickly I could be out within five days.

Everyone in the office was smiling, although there was a definite air of discomfort around the two Customs officers. I went back to jail contentedly that night and slept well. I was certain my problems would be quickly sorted out as soon as I was out of prison.

* * *

A couple of days later I had to visit the judge again for a confrontation with Eric and Jill. They were now claiming that I had inveigled and threatened them into accepting and storing the drugs. Naturally they wanted to be seen as victims rather than as active participants.

This didn't equate with the soaps of cannabis OCTRIS had discovered in their house or the marijuana plants growing in the garden, but the judge was obliged to investigate their claims. I was not too bothered by the story they were putting forward. I always believed the purpose of the operation was to snare the drug barons not the minions who carried out the jobs at the sharp end. Besides I didn't think the French courts would have too much of a problem getting to the bottom of their story.

After the interviews were over, and we had all restated our positions yet again, I noticed that the judge had the suspicion of a smile hovering around his mouth.

'I think, Mr Lightfoot, you are possibly suffering from what we French call Perfidious Albion.' I was taken aback, I didn't think he could speak any English, and here he was demonstrating his fluency admirably.

As the five days following my bail application sped by I started giving some of the prison things I had acquired during my stay to my cell mates. I collected some addresses and promised to write to various people and their families. I was cool, anxious and ready to get out of this stinking cesspit.

On the Saturday morning I was expecting to be released the guard opened the cell door and called me out. As he directed me to the visiting room, I felt the cold hand of dread grip me. Christian Traineau was sitting there quietly, brooding like a sleeping giant in the middle of the room. As ever he cut to the chase.

'John, I have just come from Judge Marlière's office, and I have to tell you he has refused the bail application,' he said.

I couldn't believe my ears. 'But, but,' I stuttered, 'he agreed last week. We even agreed the bail cash. There must be some mistake.' I was shattered.

'No, there has been a development in the case, and the judge thinks you should stay in jail until the matter is cleared up,' said Christian. 'He took a call from the Foreign Ministry in Paris, and they informed him that Benson has been arrested in Spain and is to be extradited to France as soon as possible. So the judge wants you available in jail to have a confrontation with Benson when he arrives.'

I slumped heavily into a chair. 'But extradition can take months or years. Surely he doesn't want to keep me here all that time?' I was alternating between deep despair and terrible rage. I was also developing the world's worst headache and feeling nauseous.

Christian was as upset as I was. We sat for ages in that little room, supposed to be talking about strategy and tactics for mounting an appeal to the High Court in Poitiers but in reality dealing with the shocking body blow the judge had delivered.

I told Christian I had given away all my bits and pieces, including chocolate and cigarettes; the next time the shop was open was five days away, and there was no way I could survive until then without nicotine. When he left Christian gave me a couple of packs of cigarettes to keep me going and promised he would visit the judge again to make him see reason. If all else failed, he said, he would appeal to the European Court of Human Rights to get my release. He meant well, and I could see that he was upset at the thought of having to telephone Kath and pass the bad news on to her.

What a pisser of a weekend I had! I felt unbelievably depressed by the whole situation. Life in prison is a series of emotional roller-coaster rides. Up and down, up and down, there is no end to the switchback of feelings, but that weekend I felt as if I had a season ticket on an emotional big dipper. It's not difficult to figure out why so many prisoners take the easy way out and top themselves in jail rather than continually face the boring certainty of life there.

During the ensuing weeks I rode that roller coaster many times, sometimes with Christian sitting at my side. I carried on writing daily letters to Kath and the family and received their responses in dribs and drabs as the judge saw fit. We mounted several appeals and further applications for provisional release, all to no avail.

Finally, on 3 April a guard called me out of the cell just before noon. Great, I thought, another cold lunch when I get back. As I walked along the platform towards the open staircase I could see Christian waiting at the bottom. He was grinning broadly at me and waving his car keys.

'Come quickly, John,' he called up to me, 'we are going out for a meal.' I almost fell down the bloody stairs. We went into the visits room for the last time, both grinning like idiots. 'It's true, John. The judge has just signed your release papers. His secretary will fax them to the director, and you will be released immediately,' he beamed at me, stupidly we shook hands. A guard knocked politely at the closed door and gestured towards Christian. 'There it is, the fax has arrived. Now go quickly and collect your belongings, we have to go to a party.'

I was truly in a daze. I had been expecting to be
released at some stage, but now it was suddenly a reality
I was having trouble taking it in. I floated upstairs and
back to my cell. Word was already out thanks to the
grapevine, and I was surrounded by cell mates wishing
me well. I grabbed my bag of clothes, files of documents
and letters, and I left the rest of my belongings for the
lads to share out and returned downstairs to the prison
office.

The formalities were quickly sorted, and within
minutes I was outside with Christian. Fucking hell! It felt
good. Before we drove off I turned and stared for a
moment at the façade of the prison. I had been in there
for 108 days of my life, and I had never seen the main
entrance in daylight. It looked rather like an old storage
warehouse, its grey, lifeless exterior belied the hundreds
of lives ticking away inside its grim walls. I turned and
climbed into Christian's old car; it was party time,
French style.

* * *

Driving across town Christian told me that to get bail
granted it is necessary that a prisoner has a registered
address in France where he lives and to where court
documents can be sent to him. Obviously I was lacking
this, so Christian had given the address of his sister,
who lived in a nearby town. The judge had accepted
Christian's proposal. He went on to explain that his
sister couldn't accommodate me because she had a
young family, but I was welcome to stay at his house in
the town.

This was the other side of French culture, not seen by

many foreigners. Here we had a prominent local lawyer giving shelter to a foreigner just bailed from prison, who was charged with international drug trafficking. For all he knew I could be an addict who would rob him blind, attack him or his wife and take off never to be seen again. I was amazed and couldn't think of the right words to thank him. He just laughed his great booming laugh and dismissed my attempts to do so.

'Everything will work out fine,' he said, driving and lighting a cigarette at the same time. This man was larger than life in every sense of the word.

Christian and his wife, Sylvie the teacher, lived in an old imposing townhouse a stone's throw from the Palais de Justice, the French court buildings and prosecutor's offices. When we arrived Sylvie was waiting inside, and Christian made the formal introductions in that typical French style. A sweet, petite woman, with high cheekbones and slim hips, Sylvie is like an immaculately dressed porcelain doll. She hangs on her husband's every word and willingly rushes to carry out every little task for him, like a butterfly hovering around a big almost bumbling bear.

That first day of my release was open house. First we had lunch with a journalist friend of theirs, Emanuel, a serious-looking individual. He reminded me of pictures of wartime French resistance agents, with flashing eyes and a stern demeanour. He is in a way a latter-day one for he writes some quite radical articles in the local newspapers. Throughout the afternoon and evening there was a constant stream of their friends and work colleagues, and I started to feel I had a type of celebrity status. With plenty of drink flowing, to combine with my soaring spirits, I felt as if I was floating on air.

I telephoned Kath and my parents in England, who were all overjoyed to hear me. Christian had tipped them off about my probable release, but he hadn't told me in case anything went wrong again. That was a downer he had correctly figured I could do without. I told Kath that I had to see the judge the next day, and he would set my bail conditions. My mum had sent Christian the bail money and an extra 2000 francs for me to pay my way.

Life felt great: I was free, amongst good company and had a wonderful, warm feeling of security in the happy household. Sylvie gave me a housekey and said I should come and go as I please, unbelievable charity from relative strangers. It would be easy for me to slag off the French as a race, as I suffered some degree of abuse during my time in prison with a lot of indignities heaped upon me simply because I was a foreigner. But here I was being offered a home, friendship and a tremendous amount of trust by two young people who only knew me through my criminal file and by way of professional prison visits. Without being aware of it, Christian and Sylvie went a long way to restoring my faith in human nature and showing me by their actions that there is good and bad in all nationalities.

The judge set some keen bail conditions for me to comply with, but he demonstrated he too had a human side. When I visited his office the day after my release his secretary gave me a cup of coffee and the judge passed over a couple of aspirins. I had a daddy of a hangover, and must have looked sorely in need of medication.

As well as paying the 50,000 franc bail money I had to sign in once a week at the local Gendarmerie. The judge held on to my passport, and I was restricted to movement within the Vendée region, unless I had his prior approval. That was no bother to me, there was nowhere I wanted to go except home.

I had to visit a panel of psychiatrists to be assessed as to my mental state, in other words to check if I understood the charges against me and if I could stand trial. They agreed I was sane. Bang went the idea of an insanity plea!

Life settled down into a pleasant rhythm for a while. I was allotted space in a file storage room in Christian's town-centre office. Kath sent me a word processor over, and I started collecting facts and figures, dates and receipts to justify my claims. By now I could read French pretty well fluently, and I spent many hours poring over the file, reading and cross-checking statements. I consulted Christian's law books at length, often burning the midnight oil in the office. We sat up into the early hours drinking our way through his excellent wine cellar, debating issues and strategies.

Christian introduced me to the world of politics and local ambitions as played out in the Palais de Justice, and it seemed that, as in Britain, justice in France is a fickle friend, depending largely on the whim or ambition of the local prosecutor or examining magistrate. I learnt that the judge in my case had a serious problem, unrelated to my case. Apparently he had been under suspicion of shoplifting in a local hypermarket. That really sealed his fate, and eventually other members of the bench refused to sit with him at trials. I don't know if he was guilty or not, but there was a lot of local unrest, and a couple of newspapers ran versions of the story. It all became too much to be ignored, and eventually he was transferred to the French dependency of Martinique, the Siberia of the French judiciary.

The weeks were quickly turning into months, and I was now chafing at what had become in my mind a sentence in an open prison. I was the proverbial canary in the gilded cage. It was a very nice one, but a cage nevertheless. Christian and I pushed the judge continually to allow me to return home. By now Eric and Jill had been released from prison on their own recognizance. Barry was still held in prison, and Benson was fighting extradition in Spain. The case was in a state of suspended animation, and there was little left to do to push forward any further. In a last desperate bid we made an application to the Appeal Court in Poitiers to have the travel restrictions against me lifted. On the day of the hearing we drove the couple of hours to Poitiers in Christian's Volvo.

It was a daunting experience, with three senior judges to hear the appeal. It was interesting to meet another court translator: she was thirtyish and looked like Farah Fawcett, a real doll. By this time my French was good enough to understand the proceedings, but I wasn't complaining when she sat down close beside me and whispered translations of the events taking place before us. It was quite a cosy meeting considering the circumstances.

The senior state prosecutor was there to argue against the appeal, but in fact he indirectly supported it by stating that never in all his experience of prosecuting drug trials had British officers ever turned up to give evidence on behalf of a defendant. The court's verdict was received three days later: the appeal court weren't able to interfere with the local judge's decision, but they suggested that I might wish to apply for acquittal against the charge on the grounds that I was working with 'legitimate authority' at the time of my arrest.

This was a ground-breaking decision in our favour. It meant that having looked at all the evidence in the file the three judges believed that I was working for Customs when we were busted. Despite any vagueness about the circumstances they were signalling that I would never be tried and convicted by them. This was great news, and me, Christian, Sylvie and all their pals held a big house party to celebrate. It was a pretty good bash, and I was surprised when another judge, a friend of Christian's, turned up to spend the evening socializing with us.

Armed with this strong decision we went back to Judge Marlière and asked for an acquittal. He replied that although he was sympathetic to my plea, he wasn't obliged to make a decision until the anniversary of the case being opened, which meant he would look at the issue in November. I was staggered. Nevertheless his refusal to act put the whole case in a new perspective for me. I was fed up now, the game had gone on too long, and I was stagnating. I was still charged with international drug trafficking and facing, if convicted, a very severe sentence.

The Customs continued to be less than helpful. I was now perceived as a dangerous, loose cannon to them. They had apparently closed the door and wouldn't respond to our letters or calls. It became obvious that I was impotent in France, and the judge wasn't at that time going to assist me.

the spanish connection

By now it was early June and getting hotter each day. We heard that the judge was leaving the town during the court's two-month summer recess. A new judge would be appointed in the autumn. I hadn't seen my family for more than half a year, and I was surviving on the largesse sent by my parents, who were also keeping Kath's body and soul together. They had dug deeply into their retirement savings and had ended up funding my adventuring into the drug world. I felt it was time to move on and repay the debt.

Privately I contacted Kath and laid out my plans. I knew that I had to make my move without implicating Christian and Sylvie in any way. If I escaped the French might well look hard for accomplices to victimize. Everything was set up between me and Kath by phone and fax. One Friday whilst Christian and Sylvie were at work I packed my bags and left. Christian and I had never discussed the possibility of my returning to England, and clever as he was I was afraid my abrupt departure would be a great shock to him. I fervently hoped that I was not about to ruin a great friendship by walking out and returning to my family. I hoped he would understand my need for proper justice.

I bought a one-way train ticket and set out on the long journey home. Overnighting in Nantes I walked around the old town centre for hours. My French was passable, and I stopped at various street cafés for a beer. I whiled away the evening contemplating the last year's events. My experiences in France, had been horrendous in some ways, but there had been good times too, both in prison and later with Christian and Sylvie. It was a shame that I was about to become an outcast from my new-found friends, but there was nothing else to be done: I had an overriding obligation to my family.

I reached the port of Cherbourg the next morning in time to watch the arrival of the ferry from England. It was full of tourists all heading south for the sun. A red car detached itself from the stream of traffic leaving the port gates and turned into the main terminal car park. I watched from a distance as Kath and my mum alighted and headed into the café and booking hall. Silently I sidled up behind them and put a hand on each of their shoulders. They were expecting me, but they still nearly jumped out of their skins.

'Hello, you two,' I said, smiling at them both, 'let's not make a scene here. We'll just go and grab a coffee over there.'

We walked to the hot drinks counter and then sat down to finalize the plan to smuggle me on to the ferry and into Britain without a passport. Kath had brought my birth and marriage certificate and electoral roll card. I had made enquiries and found out that a British citizen didn't require a passport to enter or leave Great Britain. All I had to prove was where I was born and show that I had a right of residence in the UK. Of course, if I were stopped by immigration officials in Britain it wouldn't be as easy as that, but once I was firmly stood on British soil they sure as hell couldn't deport me back to France.

By now the British newspapers had also picked up the story of my plight and had run articles questioning the Customs actions. If I were caught they were primed to create a big song and dance in the Sunday papers.

After a couple of calming coffees we ran through the escape plan one last time. Kath and my mum had bought two day-return tickets in England, and now Kath was to go to the ticket office and buy a single ticket as a foot passenger back to the UK. I was to drive the car with mum beside me as a passenger. I had no passport but held on to Kath's return ticket. I knew that there was only a passport check when buying a ticket and no police check when leaving France. It was all a bit tense. If the plan went wrong now I was going to be sent back to prison and held until the trial. There would be no second chance for me, not Christian or Perry Mason would get me bail a second time.

The plan in fact worked like a dream, and half an hour later I found myself standing in the queue to buy a duty-free drink at the ship's bar. We had made it so far; now it was just the British authorities I had to contend with. I took my drink and stood on the windy afterdeck watching the French coastline receding towards the horizon. I had the feeling I wouldn't be returning there for quite a while. I was ecstatic at the thought of returning home, but my elation was tinged with sadness at the friends I had deserted without so much as a goodbye. Still, I rationalized, you can't make an omelette without breaking eggs.

When we disembarked at Portsmouth we all did so together in the car and followed the line of traffic towards the Customs checkpoint. Immigration officers were passing down the row of parked cars checking passports. As a woman immigration official inspected the vehicle in front of us I tensed up: this was it, shit or bust.

Just then the line of cars lurched forward. I stuck ours close to the tail of the one immediately in front, and as the immigration officer approached my open window I waved at her and joked in a strong Manchester accent, 'It's OK, luv, we're all English. There's no hidden Pakis in here.' The woman laughed and waved us on towards the waiting Customs officials. As we drove up to the checkpoint we were all holding our breath. We must have looked rigid and as guilty as sin. Sure enough we were stopped.

'Where have you come from?' asked the Customs officer.

'We've been on a shopping trip to France,' I replied, 'but the prices were too high for us, so we just bought some wine.'

I jumped out of the car to open the boot, loaded up with a couple of cases of French wine and a few cartons of duty-free cigarettes. The Customs officer gave the contents and the inside of the car a cursory inspection.

'OK, sir, thank you. You can go now,' he said.

12

On the Run

Returning home safely was a tremendously uplifting experience and if I had been of a religious bent I would have kissed the ground and offered a prayer of thanksgiving. I am not religious, but I knew I was the happiest man in England at that moment, and I knew things were going to get better and better. But it wasn't the end of my nightmare adventures in the world of drug smuggling and bureaucratic indifference. Rather it was the start of another phase, a phase we are all still living through today.

One of the consequences of the campaign to force my release from prison was that I had been forced to adopt a high profile campaign, both in England and France. Now it was a racing certainty that many of the drug dealers in Spain and Britain knew about my role as a successful informant for the Customs.

After my return the media were interested in my adventures, and various articles soon appeared in national and local newspapers and magazines, and later I was featured in a Granada Television *World in Action* production.

I had cost the dealers at least £6 million in lost drug revenue as well as exposing their names and operating methods to the Customs. There was no doubt I was now a target, it was a question of when, rather than if, they would arrive to claim their payback.

The local police were sympathetic to our problems and installed a radio-controlled panic alarm system in our house. All we had to do was press the button, and a radio signal automatically triggered a priority alarm in the main police station. The flaw in this system was that our farm was in a remote rural location, exposed on every side. If a hit-team despatched by the drug barons came to visit us, they would probably come about three o'clock in the morning. They wouldn't hang around, it would be a quick in and out operation, the job would be over and done with in a couple of minutes. Far quicker than any police unit could respond to our call for help.

The police were aware of this unavoidable shortcoming, and after hours of consultations and family meetings we decided we would all be safer living at a different, more secure address. Yet again the knock-on effects of my volunteering to help the Customs was having a definite impact upon all my family. We moved into rented accommodation in a large town about a hundred miles away from our own home, which we put up for rent via an agent.

I spent many hours in meetings with lawyers and barristers. The general consensus of the legal experts was that my shabby treatment by the Customs was actionable at law. I gave the necessary instructions, and the legal machinery creaked into operation. It took 18 months to get all the requisite pieces in place, but eventually a High Court writ was issued against the Customs &

Excise, and that court case is still ongoing at the time of writing. The case seems destined to run the litigious process for at least another two years. Recently, applications from my lawyers to the French requesting copies of statements and interviews has fallen on deaf ears. Now it seems we must pursue the French judiciary in a battle through the European courts.

Through my lawyers, I made a formal complaint to HM Customs about my treatment, using their complaints procedure. After a brief, initial flurry of correspondence the complaints procedure ground to a halt. We are still waiting two years later for the first face-to-face meeting to be held.

Another consequence of the continued stress we had all suffered so long manifested itself in the weeks following my return home. I couldn't establish a normal sleeping pattern. Frequently waking with a start and then unable to drop off back to sleep I would wander around the house in the small hours fidgeting and mithering about trivialities. The constant lack of sleep made me irritable, and eventually I consulted a doctor. After listening to my story he referred me to a psychiatric specialist. I travelled to Northampton and had an initial three-hour meeting with the consultant.

His report concluded that I was suffering from moderate to severe post-traumatic stress disorder, an illness I knew little about. I thought firemen and policemen who attended catastrophes and major accidents were obvious contenders for it, I was shocked to be told that I was suffering exactly the same symptoms and worse, I was told that there was no specific cure, no magic pill that I could swallow to alleviate my condition.

For many months I lived in a twilight world of my own. I developed a habit of scouring newspapers and television news for stories of drug busts, and would find myself reliving the experiences I had undergone in Spain and France. For a while I truly feared I was becoming unhinged, but time and family love are great healers. Luckily for my sanity those terrible, vivid recollections are now mostly confined to my memory and no longer keep me awake night after night.

From time to time something would happen that would throw me back in time to my previous experiences. One day I was walking down a main shopping street with Kath and Natalie when a car engine backfired with a loud crack. Quick as a flash I hit the ground and rolled towards the protective shelter of a parked car. Kath and Natalie screamed, and Kath later told me she thought I had been shot. I realized what had happened: my brain had picked up the noise and categorized it as a gunshot. Without any conscious thought on my part my instinctive reactions had taken over.

I stood up and brushed off my clothes before we walked quickly away from the small crowd of shoppers who had gathered around us. Such events were totally beyond my ability to control, and it was as if somebody else was in control of my body and pulling the strings, not a pleasant experience.

Events like that and our almost obsessive need for security and safety caused us to cut ourselves off from our friends, and our social life died a quick death. Others who had heard the rumours about me, drugs and being imprisoned in France distanced themselves from us. We noticed that Natalie no longer received invitations to her school chums' parties, and it became obvious that something was going on when only two kids from an invitation list of more than ten turned up to her birthday party at our home. By now the local rumour machine was in full swing, fuelled by malicious gossip from people who couldn't possibly have known the truth of the story.

Such ostracization didn't bother me but was deeply upsetting for my wife and daughter. A few of the parents of the children had obviously heard all the rumours, but not one came forward to ask us about the matter directly, preferring quietly to withdraw their offspring from any connection with the tainted family. A prime example of good old British middle-class hypocrisy in action. Eventually I changed my name, and we moved again to a new town away from the gossips.

The rumour-mongers are a persistent bunch of buggers though. Anonymous phone calls were made to Natalie's new school, and an embarrassed head teacher called me in to discuss the problem. He had been told that I was a drug dealer and not a fit parent to have a child in the school. I was incensed at having to justify my position in such a manner, but the headteacher put a call in to my solicitor who set his mind at ease, and the matter faded away. Such callous handling by a society that I had been trying to assist left a very bitter aftertaste.

*　*　*

Meanwhile back in France a new judge was appointed in the town. Barry was released by the Appeal Court on bail and allowed to return to his address in England two weeks before Christmas 1995. I considered this a bit of a raw deal. I had been confined to live in France, but Barry, who had confessed his role in the smuggling, was allowed home. After he'd done so he contacted us, and after giving his proposal much thought I agreed to meet him. Feeling particularly cynical at that time I chose Hartshead services as the rendezvous spot, a location from which many of my unhappy experiences had begun.

Barry told me he was surprised when he had been taken to the Appeal Court in Poitiers and told that he would be released on bail. It had been decided it was unfair to hold him in prison on remand when Benson was still in Spain, and there was no date in sight when Benson would be extradited to France. No bail surety was required by the Appeal Court. Whilst I was not unhappy that Barry had been released it did seem iniquitous that he should get off with no bail money being deposited and be allowed to return to the UK. I didn't consider Barry a drug dealer, he was more of a down-on-his-luck opportunist who had grabbed the chance to make a few easy bob when the time was right.

He was pleased to see me, and we discussed French prison for a while. It was through him I learnt that Benson was still held in prison in Madrid. The extradition process was interminable, though it seemed it was temporarily stalled because Benson had been implicated in an international car theft ring. The extradition process would recommence when the outstanding Spanish investigations were completed. At least he was out of circulation for the time being, and we could all breathe a little easier because of that.

My lawyer Christian Traineau, who didn't hold any grudge that I had left without any warning, submitted another application that my bail conditions be relaxed. In an amazing *volte-face* the new judge claimed that because I had jumped bail I was obviously guilty of being a smuggler and promptly issued an International Arrest Warrant against me. This was an incredible step and flew in the face of the earlier Appeal Court verdict. The new judge, who had never met me, was obviously flexing his muscles and showing the Poitiers High Court that he would not brook any interference in the case he had inherited from Marlière.

This was a bad move and could have some serious implications for me. If implemented the International Warrant would be effective in Britain, and the French judiciary could reach out their arm and try to snatch me back to France. I would be arrested and taken before Bow St Magistrates Court in London for an extradition hearing. Christian told me that if I were extradited to France then I would be held in prison until the trial. Worse, he claimed I would almost certainly be convicted of international drug smuggling and condemned to a lengthy prison sentence.

We were told that it took about two or three months to execute an International Arrest Warrant. In a high state of nervous tension I spent the next few weeks appointing and meeting with specialist extradition lawyers and blowing new life into the old 'Get John Home' campaigners.

The sword of Damocles didn't fall as expected. In fact, even after Benson was eventually extradited to France and spat all sorts of lies about me to the judge I heard nothing from officialdom. We have tried to find out, both in France and England, what happened to the warrant, but everywhere our inquiries meet with a wall of bureaucratic silence. We know it was issued and have seen a copy of it. The extradition office at New Scotland Yard have my solicitor's details and have promised to call as soon as it reaches their in-tray. It never did resurface from the bog of European bureaucracy.

The strain of living with an arrest warrant floating around with your name on it is awful. For weeks I had a holdall packed and ready for my arrest and removal. I went everywhere with emergency contact numbers for all my team of lawyers and media plotters in my pocket. Plans for the future were impossible, we lived in a perpetual state of dread of strangers knocking on the front door.

I am more determined than ever that the whole truth of the matter should be revealed, now I know I am not alone with my problem. I have learnt there are others who have suffered similarly poor treatment after volunteering their services as informants.

A Customs drug investigation officer came forward following a newspaper article about me. He wanted to remain anonymous but met me in the company of a Granada TV producer and investigative journalist. He told us unbelievable stories of a powerful government-backed investigation unit running out of control. According to him, there were informants languishing in foreign jails too scared of repercussions from the drug barons to come forward, no help in the background for them from HM Customs.

Customs & Excise will have to stand up and explain what really happened just before the ill-fated drug run.

They cannot refuse to talk for ever; they must justify their actions. The general public and the courts are only too aware of the potential for error within Customs & Excise ranks. The Churchill Matrix affair demonstrated that they were capable of tampering with evidence and witnesses, and their interference with natural justice in that case was displayed to all. They have so far seen me imprisoned, supported damaging claims about me, refused to consider my demand for compensation and put my life and the lives of my family at risk. They admit I was a good informant who freely volunteered my services. Ultimately I assisted in stopping more than £6 million of drugs from hitting the streets of Great Britain, for which they paid me the princely sum of £500.

I believe they, more than the drug dealers, are partly responsible for the waking nightmare that both I and my family are constantly living.

On 1 December 1997 the trial was finally held in France, more than 3 years after we were arrested. Benson stood alone in the dock. Barry and Eric were absent because the summonses issued to them were incorrectly dated, so they can look forward to their trial some time in the future.

Jill was acquitted of the charges against her at the end of the Judge's investigation, based on her insistent denials and lack of physical evidence against her. But in another court, Eric was convicted of growing marijuana in his garden, he has still to face a trial for the importation of drugs.

My trial was held in the main court in the Palais de Justice. It was all over and done with in one day. Three judges presided, there was no jury and I was not entitled to a defence lawyer. Christian sat through the trial, impotent, unable to speak up in my defence as the Prosecutor and later Benson attacked me, my motives and my character. Of course I could not be there; Christian told me how it had gone that evening.

The Prosecutor demanded that I should be found guilty and condemned to eight years' incarceration. The judges conferred and pronounced sentence. I was found guilty of importing 300kg of cannabis into France as a member of an organised gang — a serious offence. I was sentenced to three years in prison, with two-and-a-half years of that term suspended. My previous jail term was all I would have to serve to complete my sentence, so if I had been in court, then I would have walked from the courtroom a free man. Additionally, I was banned from France for 10 years, but I managed to avoid any financial penalty.

For his part in masterminding the smuggling operation, Benson was condemned to eight years in prison, he was banned for life from French territory and fined FF1 million, with an additional two years' imprisonment if the fine is not paid.

The immediate result of the trial was that the international arrest warrant would be halted — now it would never arrive. But I was now a convicted drug dealer. Christian and I discussed the matter for hours; we had achieved a practical result which meant I would retain my liberty, but in his opinion, the guilty verdict flew in the face of the evidence. We decided to appeal against the verdict, and Christian began the formal process.

We weren't the only party unhappy with the verdict — the Prosecutor thought my sentence too lenient, and submitted an appeal as well. Both appeals will ultimately be heard by the same Appeal Court in Poitiers, which had already indicated that I should be acquitted.

The appeals procedure in France is a long and murky process. We expect a full court hearing some time during 1998, although we are unsure of the outcome; results can range from complete acquittal to an increase in sentence, along the lines of the Prosecutor's demands, or even greater. As Christian said, we have chosen to dance with the devil.

All bets are off once again, and the threat of an international arrest warrant is back to haunt us. Weary and tired of being harrassed, we have yet again been moved to a new location. We also knew that the drug barons in England would be able to locate our address from court records, and so, worried by the constant threat of their retribution, we thought another move might finally let us live in some kind of peace.

The story isn't yet finished. The civil proceedings against the Customs & Excise continue, my lawyers are now getting ready to travel to France to interview the senior OCTRIS officers in an attempt to discover just who was telling the truth about events leading up to my arrest. With the assistance of my lawyers and new-found friends in high places, we continue to unravel fiction from fact — those responsible for my untimely fall from grace should take this opportunity to rest easy while they can.

For them, the winged horsemen of the apocalypse can be heard approaching in the distance — they come for retribution.

COMING SOON FROM
BLAKE'S TRUE CRIME LIBRARY

November: ***DEADLY AFFAIR*** — the electrifying true story of a deadly love triangle
by Nicholas Davies

December: ***DOCTORS WHO KILL*** — terrifying true stories of the world's most sinister doctors
by Wensley Clarkson

January: ***VIGILANTE!*** — one man's war against major crime on Britain's streets
by Ron Farebrother

February: ***THE FEMALE OF THE SPECIES*** — true stories of women who kill
by Wensley Clarkson

March: ***RONNIE KNIGHT: MEMOIRS AND CONFESSIONS*** — the autobiography
by Ronnie Knight

April: ***WOMEN IN CHAINS*** — true stories of women trapped in lives of genuine slavery
by Wensley Clarkson

May: ***THE MURDER OF RACHEL NICKELL*** — the truth about the tragic murder on Wimbledon Common
by Mike Fielder

June: ***CAGED HEAT*** — what really goes on behind the bars of women's prisons
by Wensley Clarkson

The first twelve titles in Blake's True Crime Library series each contain a question relating to the book. Collect the numbered editions of Blake's True Crime Library, and when you have the answers to all the questions, fill in the form which you will find at the back of the twelfth book and send it to Blake Publishing to be entered into the prize draw.

HERE IS THE FOURTH QUESTION

What was Barry's job in the Army before he became a drugs courier?

The winner will receive the exclusive sleuth's silver dagger and five runners-up will receive three free copies of Blake's True Crime Library titles.

How to enter
Fill in the answer form contained in the twelfth book in the series and post it to us. If you have won, we will notify you. Whether you are a winner or not, you will still be eligible for a FREE True Crime Newsletter!

Competition rules
1. The 'How to Enter' instructions form part of the rules.
2. These competitions are not open to any members of Blake Publishing or their families, or Blake Publishing's advertising agents, printers or distributors.
3. The prizes will be awarded, in order of their value, to the senders of the first winning entries after the closing date.
4. Entries must be on the entry coupon supplied and will be not be accepted after the closing date.
5. No claim is necessary, winners will be notified.
6. In cases where a manufacturer discontinues a product which has been specified as a prize, Blake Publishing Ltd will substitute the nearest equivalent model of similar or higher value.
7. The Editor's decision is final, and no correspondence can be entered into.

BEAT THE RUSH!
ORDER YOUR COPIES OF FORTHCOMING
TRUE CRIME TITLES DIRECTLY.

Simply fill in the form below and we will send you your books as soon as they become available.

Name: ....

Address: ....

....

....

....

Daytime tel: ....

Card (please circle):   Visa   Access   Mastercard   Switch

Card number: ....

Expiry date: ....

For Switch cards only: issue date: .... issue number: ....

Please send me *(tick where appropriate)*

❑ *Deadly Affair* by Nicholas Davies (November)

❑ *Doctors Who Kill* by Wensley Clarkson (December)

❑ *Vigilante!* by Ron Farebrother (January)

❑ *The Female of the Species* by Wensley Clarkson (February)

❑ *Ronnie Knight: Memoirs and Confessions* (March)

❑ *Women in Chains* by Wensley Clarkson (April)

❑ *The Murder of Rachel Nickell* by Mike Fielder (May)

❑ *Caged Heat* by Wensley Clarkson (June)

All titles are £4.99. Postage and packing are free.

**No money will be deducted from your card
until the books become available.**